# Food Tourism

# A Practical Marketing Guide

# FOOD TOURISM
## A Practical Marketing Guide

**John Stanley and Linda Stanley**

www.cabi.org

**CABI is a trading name of CAB International**

| | |
|---|---|
| CABI Head Office | CABI |
| Nosworthy Way | 745 Atlantic Avenue |
| Wallingford | 8th Floor |
| Oxfordshire OX10 8DE | Boston, MA 02111 |
| UK | USA |
| | |
| Tel: +44 (0)1491 832111 | Tel: +1 617 682-9015 |
| Fax: +44 (0)1491 833508 | Email: cabi-nao@cabi.org |
| Email: cabi@cabi.org | |
| Web site: www.cabi.org | |

A catalogue record for this book is available from the British Library, London, UK

**Library of Congress Cataloging-in-Publication Data**

Stanley, John, 1948-
  Food tourism: "a practical marketing guide" / John and Linda Stanley.
    pages cm
  Includes bibliographical references and index.
  ISBN 978-1-78064-501-8 (hardback : alk. paper) – ISBN 978-1-78064-502-5 (pbk. : alk. paper) 1. Tourism and gastronomy.  2. Tourism and gastronomy –Marketing. I. Stanley, Linda, 1952-  II. Title
  TX631.S83 2015
  641.01'3—dc23

                                                             2014033213

ISBN-13: 978-1-78064-501-8 (hardback edition)
ISBN-13: 978-1-78064-502-5 (paperback edition)

First published 2015
Paperback edition reprinted 2015
Transferred to print on demand 2016

Commissioning editor: Claire Parfitt
Editorial assistant: Alexandra Lainsbury
Production editor: Shankari Wilford

Typeset by SPi, Pondicherry, India
Printed and bound in the UK by Marston Book Services Ltd, Didcot, Oxon.

# Contents

# About the Authors

John and Linda have been involved in the food industry sector for many years. Apart from owning a consultancy and conference speaking company they also own a sweet chestnut farm in Nannup in the south of Western Australia. This means that when they are not on the road working with clients they are managing 1100 sweet chestnut trees.

Linda has been involved in setting up Kalamunda Farmers Market and the Kalamunda Community Garden, which are located on the outskirts of Perth in Western Australia.

John has often worked with the farm associations around the world and is a regular speaker at farm-related conferences, especially where farmers are developing tourist operations.

Both John and Linda have written a number of books relating to retailing and especially perishable retailing.

# Contributors

**Mejer, Edwin**, Managing Director, Green Connect Ltd, Innovation Centre and Business Base, 110 Butterfield, Great Marlings, Luton, Bedfordshire LU2 8DL, UK. E-mail: edwin@gardenconnect.com

**Smith, Stephen**, School of Hospitality, Food, and Tourism Management, University of Guelph, Guelph, Ontario, Canada. E-mail: stesmith@uoguelph.ca

**Weaver, David**, Professor of Tourism, Department of Tourism, Sport and Hotel Management, Griffith Business School, Gold Coast Campus, Griffith University, Queensland, Australia. E-mail: d.weaver@griffith.edu.au

# Foreword

Food, as we all know, is essential for human life. It also is the basis for several major industries found in many countries around the world such as in agriculture, food processing, food retailing and food service. For millennia, the focus of those involved with food as a human and economic phenomenon was on its production, preservation, distribution, pricing and other utilitarian concerns. But in the late 18th century this began to change. Food became more than just a life necessity. Restaurants began to be developed, initially in France but eventually other nations, as a distinct institution offering people dining choices and table service, the opportunity for socialization and, over time, finer and finer ambience. The rise of restaurants eventually led to a class of diner who prided himself (they were usually men in the earliest years) on being arbiters of taste, food and cooking. Brillat Savarin is probably the best known of the 'culinary philosophers' or, in today's parlance, a 'foodie'. One of Savarin's better known aphorisms was, '[t]ell me what you eat, and I'll tell you who you are.'

The contemporary foodie is a global personality, as are food critics and commentators concerned with the quality, production and distribution of food as both a culinary experience and socio-political phenomenon. The Slow Food movement, which has emerged in the last couple of decades, is a well-known example of the latter. Today, there are thousands of books about food – not just cookbooks but books about food politics, food economics, food history and food customs. Food shows are one of the more popular genres on television. These include cooking shows, various culinary competitions, and explorations of food and travel, destinations and cultures. Food festivals are now among the most popular types of festivals in many nations. Festivals not devoted to food usually feature food as a significant attraction. Food is far more than just a source of nutrition for many people around the world. It is a source of entertainment, identity, family cohesion, cultural tradition, innovation and celebration.

This book is about food as a tourism product and an experience. It explores its nature, development, management, marketing and distribution as well as food tourists – their motivations and needs, uses of information, expectations and activities. Of the myriad tourism products and experiences in the contemporary tourism-scape, food is arguably unique. It can be an attraction in its own right – a primary motivation for a trip such as a tour of a wine region, a secondary activity such as lunch at a local pub while touring local sights, or an essential but uninspiring necessity as part of another tourism experience such as a box lunch served on a coach tour. It can also be a souvenir of a trip – a distinctive food product or beverage brought home to share with family and friends. The taste or aroma from a food product can conjure up memories and the desire to return to the place symbolized by the taste or aroma. Indeed, food is both a symbolic experience as well as a physical product. It is often co-opted by religions and political identities. For example, halal or kosher foods as well as the avoidance of certain foods are markers of faith. Hindus, Seventh Day Adventists, Sikhs and Buddhists also have food traditions that express belief, identity and cultural cohesion.

John and Linda Stanley provide, in this articulate book, informed, experience-based insights into the phenomenon of food tourism. They chose the term 'food tourism' over 'culinary tourism' for this book because it is more inclusive and less 'elitist'. Certainly the Stanleys are comfortable writing about upscale dining experiences, but they are equally at home stopping by a farm gate to pick up bread or eggs from a local farmer. Food tourism, as a concept, covers the gamut from shopping at a local farmers' market to dining at a three-starred Michelin restaurant.

Grounded in years of experience with food and culinary businesses, the authors will provide you with a rich understanding of the ins and outs of food tourism, from its definition, through its customers, to the development, management and marketing of a food tourism business. They conclude this fascinating book with predictions about the future of food tourism – again, based on their experience of working with food tourism operators, retailers and producers.

The authors understand both the demand and supply sides (customers and business) of food tourism as well as the many facets of food tourism. All these shape the contents of this instructive book. As a result, this book has something to offer not only the suppliers of food tourism products and experiences, but researchers and scholars as well.

The book opens by considering the nature of food tourism from both the consumers' and the farmers' perspectives. The authors then examine the potential benefits of food tourism as well as its challenges. They ask the questions anyone considering becoming involved in food tourism should ask: should they get involved in food tourism or what the implications are of inviting the public on to your farm. For example, there are many considerations covering health and safety of visitors, animal health, liability, the demands of marketing and operations of a food tourism business, and the formation of a business strategy and action plans.

A central concern for any tourism business is understanding and serving an increasingly diverse and informed market – one that seeks 'local' and 'authentic' flavours and experiences. The authors answer this by describing the contemporary food tourist and how she or he is changing. These changes include demographic and economic shifts as well as increases in education, travel, and a growing demand for what some others have called 'experience' as a feature of the so-called 'experience economy'. Tasting, preparing and learning about food in its myriad forms is quintessentially an 'experience' in this post-modern use of the term.

The Stanleys offer practical insights and advice based on their years of consulting. They will inform you about how food can be successfully marketed as a tourism or recreation commodity. Whether your focus is on the farm or off the farm operations, this book will provide you with advice about presenting, promoting and packaging food experiences and products. They take the reader on a breath-taking tour of myriad manifestations of food including food factories and museums, plantations and gardens, food and accommodations, food trucks and street markets. You will be guided though a wide variety of dining experiences from fine dining to airport restaurants. And they lead us through an informed discussion of food tourism marketing. Marketing strategies and platforms cover a potentially bewildering range of possibilities from roadside signs to the Internet. From marketing tactics to the use of culinary tourism as a destination positioning strategy, this book explores all.

So, sharpen your appetite and your curiosity. You are about to sit down to a banquet of ideas and information. *Bon appétit!*

**Stephen Smith**
School of Hospitality, Food, and Tourism Management
University of Guelph
Guelph, Ontario, Canada
March 2014

# Preface

Food tourism is one of the fastest growing sectors of the tourist market and covers many aspects of the food and tourism industry. Writing a book addressing the needs of that market is a challenge. There has never been a book that has tried to relate to tourism operators around the world providing the practical information they need to improve their business as well as trying to focus on the needs of academics and students.

That is the aim of this book. Do not read this expecting a theoretical book that looks at research in depth; the aim of this book is to address the needs of the practical tourism operator and to provide guidelines on how the industry can be developed at a macro and micro level. However, in doing that, we also hope that it will provide guidelines and motivation to students who are entering this growing and exciting industry.

Although we do come from an academic background, most of our work is directly with tourism operators helping them to develop their businesses. We therefore believe this book can provide a unique insight into this market.

We have tried not to be purists. Our goal is to look at the wide spectrum of tourists and their expectations and to help readers understand what they are looking for in food tourism.

Food tourism used to focus on farm markets, restaurants, food gardens and farmers' markets or shops. The expectation today is a lot wider as leading retailers now look on the food experience as a means to engage their customers. Tourism operators today realize that food tourism in fact covers many spectra. Some of the areas discussed in this book may not be considered as food tourism by some purists, but we believe they are areas that need to be discussed as the edges of food tourism become more blurred with every passing year.

Retail and tourist technology is changing faster now than it has ever done and readers of this book will need to read further as technology is advancing so rapidly. When you pick up this book there will have been technical advances that have taken place between when it was written and before you read it; that is part of the fun and opportunities that we are facing in the industry.

Our aim is to stimulate conversation and help the industry flourish, with this book being one of the essential parts of your tool kit to achieve that goal.

**John and Linda Stanley**
John Stanley Associates
PO Box 200, Nannup, WA 6275 Australia
john@johnstanley.com.au

# I Food Tourism and the Tourist

The world has become accustomed to tourism. According to the World Tourism Organization[1] a tourist is 'travelling to and staying in places outside their usual environment for not more than one consecutive year for leisure, business or other purposes.' In 2012 over 1 billion of us were tourists and as tourists we spent over US$1.03 trillion. In 2012 China became the biggest tourist spenders as a nation, spending US$102 billion on tourist activities.

According to Funk and Wagnall,[2] the difference between a tourist and a visitor is that a visitor is 'one who visits an area within their local area.'

'Food tourism' may be a new set of words on the tourist scene. Even though the first guide to food tourism was written in 1931, *Guida Gastronomica d'Italia*,[3] food tourism is still looked on as something new and trendy.

Food tourism in most regions of the world has been and needs to be integrated into traditional tourism activities, although in some regions, for example in France and Italy, it is becoming the main reason to visit the destination.

The wonderful thing about this type of tourism is that it is a 24/7, global and available 365 days of the year activity. The authors have been up at 3 am in Japan to join a line of tourists to visit the Tsukiji Market[4] in Tokyo (www.tsukiji-market.or.jp) and tolerated the snow of Vermont in New England, in the sugaring season in March to taste maple syrup (www.vermontmaple.org). At Christmas the Christmas markets of Prague (Czech Republic) and Germany are now major tourist attractions with a global market. Many business people may not even consider they are in food tourism. Ask the majority of tourists visiting the UK for the first time what they are going to do when they arrive and one common answer is to visit an English pub. This has become a real tourist experience, but how many publicans would classify themselves as working in tourism?

# 1 Introduction

## What is Food Tourism?

Tourism is experiencing rapid growth. According to Jane Chang of Chang Brothers Travel in Singapore, when she was interviewed in March 2014,[5] the growth in food tourism has been 30% a year for the last decade with food tours to China, South Korea, Taiwan, Hong Kong, Australia, New Zealand and Turkey being the most popular. In Singapore itself a one billion Singapore dollar fund was announced in 2012 to develop tourism, including food tourism, and Prime Minister Lee added part of the secret was 'High Touch' and 'High Tech' business development in the sector.[6]

Ten years ago the Food Tourism Association was formed, which now goes under the name of the World Food Travel Association (WFTA; www.worldfoodtravel.org). The WFTA is based in Portland, Oregon and its aim is to develop and promote food tourism internationally. Their definition of food tourism is where we should start our journey: 'The pursuit and enjoyment of unique and memorable food and drink experiences, both far and near.'

Food tourism has been gaining momentum over the last decade around the world for two main reasons. First, a desire for people to discover where their food comes from and second to discover new foods and food preparations.

The challenge is where does food tourism start and finish. How many of the existing activities carried out on the farm are tourism activities in the view of the traveller? A visit to a farmers' market is often cited as a tourist activity, whereas a visit to the supermarket in the past, to purchase the same product, was not classified as a tourist activity. Having said that we now have the 'Waitrose Effect'. This is where a specific food retailer, such as Waitrose in the UK, has such a highly desirable brand reputation that house prices around the store increase as it is such a desirable place to shop. This influence was reported by the BBC News in the UK.[7] Research by Savills, the estate agents (www.savills.co.uk), indicates that house prices in areas where there is a Waitrose store are typically 25% higher than the UK average. In London, there is a 50% premium in Waitrose postcodes.

The Daily Mail Online[8] newspaper in the UK reported: 'It's Christmas glee for Waitrose, but Sainsbury's suffer – shoppers flood to upmarket chain to buy Heston endorsed products.' The article went on to explain that TV celebrity chef Heston Blumenthal endorsed a range of products in store and sales in the lead up to Christmas 2013 increased by 4.1% against a Sainsbury's growth of 0.2%. This meant that 22,000 products a minute were sold by Waitrose on 23 December 2013, highlighting the influence celebrity chefs have on food retailing and food tourism in the UK.

In Austin, Texas, the Wholefoods store at The Domain fits into our definition of food tourism. It has an outdoor beer and bratwurst bar, is a venue for live music, has a Texas Ramen bar (sushi-style individual dishes), 11 different seating areas, an indoor oyster bar, a community meeting place and has local artists' paintings and artwork displayed around the store.

It is increasingly clear that the gap between tourism and retailing as we understood it is blending and that food tourism could now include the weekly food shop.

Farmers are also joining in on the new developments. In Chicago, Illinois, located next to Dunkin Donuts on North Clark Street, you will find the Farmer's Fridge: a vending machine developed by Luke Saunders selling healthy organic food from the farm in recyclable jars (www.farmers-fridge.com).

These developments are all based around food attracting visitors to a certain area. Whether they should be included in a book on food tourism we are sure will cause debate. The authors' approach has been to set the net wide

**Fig. 1.1.** 'Never Shop on an Empty Stomach' in Bath Spa, UK.

to ensure coverage of as many aspects that we can on the culinary tourist's journey, and hopefully inspire the reader to think outside of the box.

## Consumer Awareness of Food Tourism

In the 1970s the consumer became more aware of the different types of food available and the quality of food they were consuming. Prior to this most consumers relied on the local supermarket or grocery store, which in turn, in order to survive, evolved into out-of-town food halls. At the same time though, another movement started; the development of farmers' markets and farm retail experiences. This in turn was followed by a surge in food programmes on TV and the arrival of the celebrity chefs who today, in many countries, are as popular as rock stars.

In 1945 the Food and Agriculture Organization of the United Nations set up World Food Day[9] on 16 October each year. The original aim was to help develop further interest in food origins and bring attention to the food dilemma in third-world countries. Each year the event has a different theme and becomes more recognized as an important date in the calendar. Although originally focused on preventing starvation, over the years the day has developed to have a wider appeal and includes sustainability and the origins of food.

More and more consumers are now wanting to know not only where their food is coming from, they want to visit the source and experience new foods as they travel. Plus they want to experiment personally in new ways of adding value to food. As a result more small businesses are getting involved in food tourism. For example, in France there are over 246 varieties of cheese being produced and in the UK over 700 varieties of cheese.[10]

The Global Cheese Awards (www.globalcheeseawards.com) are held in Somerset in the UK. In 2013 they voted for a Canadian cheese as the best cheese in the world; this was a creamy-gouda style Lankaaster cheese from Ontario created by Margaret Peters.

In 2010 the International Culinary Tourism Association joined forces with the New Zealand-based International Culinary Tourism Development to produce the 'State of the Culinary Tourism Industry Report'.[11] This identified the most prepared regions of the world for culinary tourism. The top three in order of ranking were Scotland, Louisiana, and Ontario. The least prepared, but the one with the most potential, was South Africa. Peru had its own Facebook page to develop the market in that country, the only one to have done so (www.facebook.com/perumuchogusto).

## Key Drivers of Culinary Tourism – A Consumer Perspective

From a consumer's perspective the drivers are wide and varied, but can be summarized as follows.

## Increased awareness in improved nutrition

Many consumers are now more health conscious or want to be more health conscious and are therefore prepared to search for healthier food options, whether this be at a food store or farm.

Food deserts still exist in many cities, but this is also gaining more public attention and action is starting to take place to improve health standards. This serves to remind more affluent consumers about the importance of health foods. According to the Food Empowerment Project,[12] a food desert can be described as 'A geographic area where residents' access to affordable, healthy food options (especially fresh fruits and vegetables) is restricted or nonexistent due to the absence of grocery stores within convenient travelling distance'. A report prepared for the US Congress by the Economic Research Service of the US Department of Agriculture [13] estimated about 2.3 million people in the USA live more than 1 mile away from a supermarket and do not have access to healthy food.

Food publicity regarding food deserts has been promoted via urban farmers such as Ron Finley in Los Angeles, California, Will Allen from the US mid-west, who was voted one of the top *Time Magazine* 100 in 2010, and Robin Emmons, who is one of the CNN 2013 Heroes[14] (these are awarded yearly by the CNN TV network in the USA).

## An increasingly urbanized society

More and more people are moving to cities and the urbanization of the world's population is taking place rapidly. Many more affluent urban dwellers are

**Fig. 1.2.** Apple varieties for sale at a farm shop.

now looking for experiences outside of the city and want to reconnect with rural communities and local foods.

## Ageing population

Many western societies are ageing rapidly. Ageing Baby Boomers in western societies generally have large disposable incomes and are prepared to pay more for a quality food experience. They have furnished their homes, planted their gardens and now look to spend their cash in a different way. They are buying less per shopping expedition, but are going to food outlets more often and are therefore likely to be exposed to more interesting foods. This ageing population is looking for what the tourist industry calls 'soft' tourism. This is tourism where there is a learning experience such as in food or culinary tourism. They want activities that are safe, educational and with no physical risk as in bungee jumping for example.

Many Asian societies do not have this ageing Baby Boomer factor. Instead they have a large sector of affluent younger middle-class consumers who are now becoming global tourists and are looking for new experiences; in the future these will be important global culinary tourists.

## Dining out has increased in popularity

In Canada and the USA more than half of the average family food budget is now spent on dining out. This means that many people are being exposed to new foods and better quality foods. As a result, restaurants continue to open and expand, plus eating out encourages consumers to be more experimental and try more exotic foods.

## Farms as a fun family destination

Consumers look for 'weekday convenience' and 'weekend experiences' and a farm is a great place to go for such an experience. Many schools are now encouraging young people to visit farms as a learning experience to comprehend where their food comes from and have a fun experience in a natural environment. This in turn creates 'pester power', where children encourage their parents to take them to the farm and spend more time in the countryside.

## The Internet

The Internet has become the major source of information and has now been accepted by the wider community as the main search tool for discovering new information. Culinary tourists now plan their itinerary online and in the comfort of their own home.

# Key Drivers for Food Tourism – A Farmer Perspective

Before we look at development of food tourism from a farm perspective we should reflect back on the development of the farm.

## A brief history of the farm retail era

*Pre-1900: the Farm Era*
This was a period when farmers and growers grew crops. Consumers simply went to their own local market and obtained their produce. Nobody challenged the process; it was the way things were done. Take a visit to rural Spain or Italy and this system is still in place.

*1900–1950: the Production-Oriented Era*
During this period farmers and growers started realizing that they could both grow large-scale crops and try and influence the supply chain to buy what they grew. The sales era had started to arrive. The first supermarket was opened in 1916 in Memphis, Tennessee when Clarence Saunders opened his Piggly Wiggly store.

*1950–2000: the Market-Oriented Era*
Supermarkets evolved during this period into a market dominant position, being the 'top of mind' choice for grocery items. Companies started to do research on consumers and their needs and wants with the aim of satisfying consumers desires. New produce varieties started to be developed and the consumer was offered a wider choice of produce from around the world. This is the era when many consumers lost their understanding of seasonal foods.

*2000–2050: the Interactive Community*
We are now at the start of a new era when communications will be the key to success. The retailer and farmer can no longer dictate to the consumer. We now have consumers who feel empowered and who want to talk back. Customers are using an array of tools to communicate with growers and retailers and they expect industry to keep up with their lifestyle. In addition, they have changed their mind-set and are now looking at food in a different way and are prepared to search out new avenues for obtaining food.

In many countries in recent years farms near to urban areas, which are ideally situated for food tourism, have been squeezed out of existence due to urban pressure for building land. These farms are a valuable commodity to society. According to research by Professor Trevor Budge at La Trobe University in Australia, 25% of the dollar value of food produced for human consumption in Australia is grown on the edges of cities.[15] Farms near to cities not only have an opportunity to focus on the tourist potential, but also are needed for the essential food production.

Cities, such as Barcelona in Spain and Milan in Italy, have developed 'agricultural parks' to preserve the farmland around their cities and to create tourism opportunities. In 2015, between 1 May and 31 October, the Universal International Exposition in Milan focuses on 'Feeding the Planet, Energy for Life', and the agricultural park set up by Politecnico di Milano, Slow Food Italia and the Universita di Scienza Gastronomiche will be completed as part of the exposition. The agricultural park includes a farmers' market, local bread-making, a cooperative supermarket, pick your own and '0 Miles Tourism'.

Most farmers and farm organizations around the world have not reached this level of cooperation and are having to develop their own strategies. These include making decisions on whether the future should revolve around the 'long food chain' or the 'short food chain.'

Many farmers over the last few decades have relied on the 'long chain food network' to get their produce to the consumer. They have focused on raising or growing the 'raw' product and shipping it through the distribution network channels to a consumer who most likely will be many miles away or even overseas.

The 'long food chain' is still essential to the success of the world; according to the United Nations there are 193 countries in the world, with 26 of these countries producing 82% of the world's crops. The 'long food chain' is still a much needed supply system.

The 'long food chain network' has worked for many years. For example in the USA in 1980 the average farmer received 35 cents of the retail food dollar. But over the years, the supply chain has slowly squeezed farmers and in 2013 the average American farmer was getting 8 cents of the retail food dollar for the same commodity.

## Food miles

The other factor that has come into play is 'food miles'.

The definition of a food mile is 'a mile over which a food item is transported during the journey from producer to consumer, as a unit of measurement of the fuel used to transport it.' Excessive food miles are the fastest growing source of greenhouse gas emissions worldwide. Food is being transported across countries and continents in long-haul vehicles that often need a cooler to keep produce fresher. Plus produce is shipped from the northern hemisphere to the southern hemisphere and vice versa via long-haul air flights.

The average American potato in 2013 travelled over 2000 miles from grower to consumer and the average tomato 1569 miles.[16] This is not just happening in the USA, the average Swedish breakfast travels 24,901 miles[17] and the top 29 food items in an Australian supermarket shopping cart travel 43,994 miles or 70,803 km.[18]

To make matters more complicated farms, tourists and consumers have to consider the value of reducing 'food miles' along with its 'carbon footprint'. A carbon footprint is defined as 'the amount of carbon dioxide released into the atmosphere as a result of the activities of a particular individual, organization, or community'. It may be more sustainable not to grow or produce some food locally but to import it from another part of the country or from overseas. For example, is it more sustainable to produce tomatoes with a low 'food mile' in a glasshouse in the middle of the UK or to import field-grown tomatoes with a low carbon footprint from a Mediterranean country?

These are issues that producers need to be discussing with culinary tourists when they visit a farm. Many food tourists are confused by the values of food miles versus carbon footprints.

The 'short food chain network' became an alternative and this is where food tourism has a great attraction to the farmer. A shorter network where the farmer has more control over the produce, keeps more of the retail food dollar and engages with the consumer now appeals to many farmers and growers.

One of the global leaders in 'short food chain' thinking is Joel Salatin of Polyface Farm from Swoope in the Shenandoah Valley, Virginia (www. polyfacefarms.com). He and his family believe that the future is about symbiotic relationships on the farm and involving the community and visitors.[19] His farm thinking can be viewed on http://vimeo.com/81468461.

Tourism is one of the main drivers of the economies of many countries around the world. As the industry has matured it has segmented into different categories. Some areas of tourism have increased in popularity whereas other areas have found it more challenging to grow their market segment.

## Food Tourism Development

Food tourism is one the three key tourist drivers around the world and as a result is gaining more media exposure. It is difficult to pinpoint when food tourism developed.

Many experts believe the mainstream interest really started with wine tourism and has evolved into food in all its aspects. The wine producers of Australia, Canada, France, South Africa and the USA were considered the innovators of wine tourism. They saw the potential and diversified from just being vineyards into linking their facility to restaurants and general rural entertainment.

As a result of this growers and producers in the food production industry saw the opportunity for diversification and entered into the culinary tourism sector.

In the UK and the USA farmers have historically been more proactive in food retailing than in many other countries. Organizations such as the National Farm Retail and Marketing Association (FARMA) in the UK and The North American Farm Direct Marketing Association (NAFMA) in the USA are both 'peak' bodies for the retail sector of farming that have been established for many years.

Consumers are also now more concerned about food security and want to know where their food is coming from. The 2012/13 UK scare on horse meat being sold as beef meat helped to make more consumers more aware of food security.

Interested parties and organizations are now joining forces to help promote culinary tourism. For example in 2010 Ed Walker, the Chef Instructor at Thompson Rivers University, Kamloops, British Columbia, Canada was inspired to form Farm2Chefs (www.farm2chefs.com), which is based on Island Chefs Collaborative in Victoria, British Columbia. This not-for-profit organization has a mission to connect local farmers with local restaurants to help support local farmers and food security. Farm2Chefs now has over 70 farmers and chefs working together to promote local food and develop tourism in the region.

Food knowledge is now part of the school curriculum at many junior schools around the world and this is also helping a new generation to become more food aware.

The other two major tourist growth categories that are common to many countries are medical and rural tourism.

## Medical tourism

Tourists from many western countries are now travelling abroad for medical treatments and cures and this will increase as the population increases and ages. This activity will not be discussed in this book, but readers need to be aware of this growth as it may be an opportunity in the some regions of the world where herbal plants could be part of the remedy programmes. The authors have seen the growth of medical tourism in Hungary and the opportunities it provides to rural economies.

## Rural tourism

In the past it was the case that tourists were initially attracted to specific icon tourist locations, such as Paris, London or New York. Today's tourist is a lot more adventurous and wants to seek out rural and wild places; this has resulted in an increase in ecotourism.

Ecotourism covers a number of activities. The main objective is that the visitor leaves the area in the same or a better condition than when they arrived. Often they will become involved in preserving or enhancing the environment they are visiting (see box).

## Is it 'slow food' or 'food tourism'?

In 1986 Carlo Petrini, an Italian, started Slow Food International (www.slow-food.com). He started the movement because McDonald's, the American fast-food retailer, wanted to have a store at the Spanish Steps in Rome and it was evident that fast-food outlets were starting to penetrate the cities and creating 'food deserts' and, as a result, obesity and diabetes was on the increase. Carlo's aim was to build awareness of the wealth of traditional food that was at risk in order to stop the process as it was also destroying the ambience of key tourist locations.

---

**Box 1   Ecotourism – what is it?**

It is useful to place food tourism into the broader context of contemporary ideas about tourism development, and especially the concept of 'sustainable tourism'. Sustainable tourism became popular in the early 1990s as an off-shoot of 'sustainable development', an idea itself popularized in the late 1980s as development that meets the needs of present generations without compromising the ability of future generations to meet *their* own needs.[20] More operationally, and recognizing that there is no such thing as completely cost-free tourism, sustainable tourism can be regarded as tourism that is planned and managed in such a way as to minimize and maximize the associated costs and benefits, respectively, both locally and globally.[21] These costs and benefits are environmental and sociocultural as well as economic, leading to widespread support for 'triple bottom line' sustainability that takes all three dimensions into account at the same time.[22]

Food tourism, with its focus on delicious and distinctive food and drink, has obvious appeal to tourists, but is also increasingly seen as attractive by destination stakeholders interested in becoming more sustainable. The main association with the economic pillar of the triple bottom line is that many culinary tourists are high-spending and well-educated consumers who like to spend time in a favoured destination, are more likely to return, and are willing to say positive things about it to friends and family in person and on social media.[23] A more subtle connection is that this spending tends to strongly benefit the local economy, since culinary tourists are mainly interested in experiencing products and services that are *unique* to a particular destination. One hundred dollars spent at a local event such as the Manjimup Truffle Festival in Western Australia, therefore, is more likely to go directly into the pockets of local farmers, generating in the process strong revenue 'multiplier effects' within the local and regional economy.[24]

Positive environmental impacts arise from the same desire to consume special local products. In an era where consumers are barraged with media coverage of 'pink slime', genetically modified foodstuffs and rampant use of pesticides and antibiotics,[25] there is (at least among those who can afford it) a great desire to eat wholesome and healthy foods in the places where they are produced. The remoteness of Tasmania was long regarded as a tourism liability, but this same isolation is now being promoted as an asset that conveys an image of unadulterated, fresh and delicious food.[26] New Zealand has long recognized this connection in its wildly successful '100% Pure' marketing campaign. As such a 'clean and green' image becomes more important for attracting tourists, governments and other stakeholders have an enormous incentive to ensure that the image is accurate, which benefits local residents as well. Locally, this might be reflected in the establishment of organic farms, grass-fed cattle operations and sustainable seafood restaurants. From a global perspective, food tourism also helps in its own way to reduce the effects of global warming, generating a very low supply-side 'carbon footprint' because of local sourcing.

Higher local incomes and jobs from food tourism contribute significantly in their own right to a higher quality of life among residents, but powerful sociocultural benefits also result in the way that this sector promotes destination identity. 'Sense of place' is a term used by geographers to describe the unique combination of attractive characteristics that distinguish a particular destination from all other destinations, thus making it uniquely competitive.[27] It is very easy to cite Australian examples – King Island cheese, Barossa Valley wines, Buderim ginger – and to note how frequently the local sense of place is both developed and reflected in various food festivals. Such events generate and display a strong sense of community pride, and can be very valuable for building social capital, that is, connections and trust within the community.[28] These effects are not just confined to small rural communities, but also figure more and more prominently in the marketing of major metropolitan

*Continued*

---

**Box 1** Continued.

---

destinations. Thus, we are now seeing Sydney and Melbourne compete vigorously for the title of Australia's 'foodie capital', and Brisbane newspapers promoting the opening of a new gourmet restaurant as a major event on the local social calendar. Food and drink are also the main factors that have breathed new life into various 'Chinatown' and other ethnic neighbourhoods, further contributing to cultural legitimization, interaction and cosmopolitanism.[29]

Amidst this upbeat appraisal, we have to make sure that we recognize and address the potential negative impacts of food tourism. It is well known that some tourists will visit a destination for the thrill, cultural practice or perceived health benefit of consuming rare and endangered species.[30] Not illegal as such but just as concerning for the environment and for animal ethics are products such as shark's fin soup and foie gras, which are prominently featured in some food destinations. There are also health concerns, ironically, that arise from the incorrect production or storage of unpasteurised milk or cheese; associated disease outbreaks can have devastating consequences for a destination's marketing image, not to mention the victims. More unusually, the Heart Attack Grill in Las Vegas attracts tourists with its unapologetically unhealthy menu, which includes the quadruple-bypass burger and French fries cooked in pure lard. This is part of the dark or perverse side of food tourism, and one that the purists no doubt would prefer to ignore. Another perversity is that the carbon footprint of food tourism may actually be higher than for processed foods sourced from a distance, due to the carbon released by the automobiles of visiting tourists.[31]

Finally, we need to consider the association between elitism and some forms of food tourism (not a problem with the Heart Attack Grill!). Not everyone can feast on black truffles in Manjimup, and we have to consider the social consequences of fostering a tourism product that distinguishes the 'haves' from the 'have-nots'. It is also possible that demand from high-income tourists will drive up prices of desirable local products so that they are no longer affordable for most local residents. If we are truly interested in pursuing the path of sustainable tourism, then all such uncomfortable issues must be confronted – but the end result would well be worth the extra effort.

Contribution by Dr David Weaver, Professor of Tourism Research, Department of Tourism, Sport and Hotel Management, Griffith Business School, Gold Coast Campus, Griffith University, Queensland, Australia

---

The definition of slow food on their website states:

> Slow food stands at the crossroads of ecology and gastronomy, ethics and pleasure. It opposes the standardization of taste and culture, and the unrestrained power of the food industry multinationals and industrial agriculture. We believe everyone has a fundamental right to the pleasure of good food and consequently the responsibility to protect the heritage of food tradition and culture that makes this pleasure possible.

Carlo could be considered as one of the founding fathers of the culinary tourism movement. In 1989 the movement he started went international with a declaration in Paris and in 1990 they published the first directory, 'Osterie d'Italia'; a major move forward came in 1996 when the Salone del Gusto was established as a biennial event in Turin with the 'Ark of Taste'. This event is now a major event and food tourism attraction in the slow food movement where exhibitors from around the world now attend to promote their local foods.

**Fig. 1.3.** Mushrooms for sale at Modena market in Italy.

In 2008 the *Guardian* newspaper in the UK named Carlo Petrini one of the '50 people who could save the planet', and in 2013 Carlo was awarded the UN Environmental Award.

The Slow Food organization crystallized at the realization that 'eating is an agricultural act and producing is a gastronomic act.' The Slow Food organization is now established in 150 countries with over 100,000 members who are dedicated to promoting local food and the pleasure of slow eating and are opposed to the standardization of taste and culture.

## The key for producers is adding value

The challenge for many producers and farmers is to grow the produce and then add value to it to increase their profits whilst maintaining the authenticity of what they are doing with often limited financial and time resources. Most produce grown is of relatively low monetary value and as a result the producer often gets a low return. Adding value is where the producer provides something more valuable while adding little cost to the production to give them a competitive edge over their competition.

## Adding value to food tourism

Food tourism can be a tool to help producers add value whilst still being on the farm; there are four ways this can be achieved.

### Building a brand reputation for quality
This is where a producer can create a brand that consumers are prepared to travel to source. With online shopping, visitors will also pay a premium price for produce they have tasted and can have delivered to their home.

Branding in the food industry can become complicated.

A producer can, and in our opinion should, set out to establish their own brand and make that brand recognizable as a sign of quality. Around the world there are many examples of where the brand has become a household name. Chiquita, for example, the banana supplier in the USA, is still recognized as one of the top brands of all time.

Brand reputation can also be influenced by law.

The European Union has established three unique categories,[32] which is a form of branding, for specific food that should be mentioned here, as they add value to the produce and encourage culinary tourists to visit the designated regions.

- PDO: Protected Designation of Origin. This applies where the produce is a traditional produce and the whole process takes place within a designated area. Products within this group include cheeses such as Gorgonzola, Piave, Asiago, Camembert, Roquefort-sur-Soulzon and Parmigiano-Reggiano; pies such as Melton Mowbray pork pies; cider from Somerset and Champagne from the designated region.
- PGI: Protected Geographic Indication. The PGI is the name of an area, a specific place or, in exceptional cases, the name of a country, used as a description of an agricultural product or a foodstuff, which comes from such an area, place or country and has a specific quality attributed to its geographical region and whose production, processing or preparation takes place within the determined geographical area. An example is new season Comber Potatoes. Under the regulation only immature potatoes grown in a restricted geographical area surrounding the town of Comber in Northern Ireland and harvested between the start of May and the end of July can be marketed as Comber Earlies.
- TSG: Traditional Specialities Guaranteed. This applies to traditional food of a specific character but does not certify that the traditional food has a link to a specific region. To qualify for a TSG a food must be of 'specific character' and either its raw materials, production method or processing must be 'traditional'.

Although the regulations can be confusing to the layperson, they are mentioned here as a marketing opportunity where the produce has been given an added value status and a region, a food tourism opportunity.

### Adding value with customer service

Added value can be provided by businesses that deliver better customer service than anyone else who does what they do. This is a difficult challenge, as a business relies on people and all our perceptions as customers of customer service are different. Having said that, a well-trained team in customer service can soon build loyalty as well as increase the average sale to tourists.

### Adding value by providing benefits

Added value can be achieved by providing benefits that other producers do not provide. This may include processing the product to another level by adding a sauce or dressing or simply developing a different processing system that gives a visible point of difference to the visitor.

*Offering a more convenient product*
This can be as simple as providing meat in ready-to-eat packs or providing 'ready meals' using local produce that can be stored in the home fridge.

## Food Tourism Challenges

While food tourism is primarily a rural-based tourist attraction, we also need to discuss examples of urban food tourism. There is an increasingly popular move to urban-based food tourism, but rural tourism has created its own challenges.

Rural communities are often composed of three different residential groups.

**1.** The first group, the original rural residents, often have not been exposed to the consumer expectations of the visiting urban tourists and therefore sometimes fail to live up to the consumer's expectations. They may not have any idea of what is expected by the modern tourist and this can often cause misunderstanding. This can be as basic as not providing complimentary Wi-Fi access.
**2.** Urban-minded residents who have moved to a rural setting for a 'sea change' or 'tree change' with the aim of getting away from city folks now find that they need to generate an income. They have to develop a tourism package for the people they tried to escape from, they are often not passionate about what they are doing as a source of income and many of these businesses subsequently fail.
**3.** There are indigenous groups in countries such as in Africa, Australasia, the Americas and Europe who want to maintain their traditional culture and some may be sceptical of modern-day tourists and their desires. Yet indigenous groups have a lot to offer tourists, especially when it comes to local food knowledge. At the same time, culinary tourists are keen to engage with them and learn their crafts and skills.

The above is apart from the normal challenges all businesses face in a challenging economic climate. Those challenges include obtaining finance from banks that are often reluctant to invest in many projects, especially rural non-traditional farming ones and developing a marketing strategy that includes online and offline marketing techniques that seem to change by the day.

## Perception is Truth

One of the challenges of any business or individual is accepting that perception is truth. That is as true in food tourism as in any other industry.

Research carried out by Tourism Australia in 2012 and presented by Simon Burley, Tourism WA at the FACET Conference in Manjimup, Western Australia,[33] highlights how perception can influence the thinking process.

According to the global travellers the organization interviewed, those who had never been to Australia ranked the top five culinary tourism destinations as:

1. 54% France
2. 53% Italy
3. 31% Japan
4. 29% Thailand
5. 23% Australia

The global travellers interviewed who had been to Australia ranked their top five culinary tourism destinations as follows:

1. 62% France
2. 57% Italy
3. 53% Australia
4. 42% Japan
5. 42% Hong Kong

The overall observation is that France and Italy are the key global culinary destinations followed by Australia and Japan. Once a tourist has visited Australia their view of culinary tourism rises and improves significantly. This provides a marketing opportunity for individual businesses to develop unique marketing niches.

France has developed the 'gastronomic meal of the French'; this was awarded 'world heritage' status by UNESCO in 2010, to recognize the importance of their historic food culture. A number of other countries and regions have tried to develop the same model. Traditional Mexican cuisine and Peruvian cuisine have been listed as UNESCO heritage, and Catalonia in Spain is trying to gain UNESCO world heritage recognition. In Portugal, various elements of national and regional gastronomy have been enshrined as national heritage in Portuguese law. All these factors are helping to develop food tourism and the opportunities food tourism creates for individual tourist and culinary operators.

## Should a Business be in Food Tourism?

> When the rate of change outside of your business is quicker than the rate of change inside your business, you have a short-lived business
> Jack Welch, CEO, General Electric, USA

As food tourism is a growth sector of many economies around the world, should every rural food-based producer consider moving into the sector? The answer is a definite no.

Businesses in tourism have a different focus to those that are purely in production and the skills to develop a tourist-focused business are completely different.

A business should move into the tourism sector because it can see the opportunities, not out of desperation because what they are doing now is not working and they think more profits will be generated by simply changing the business model.

Often the decision depends on where the business is on the sigmoid curve. The sigmoid curve is a mathematical formula that applies to life cycles in businesses. Every business is situated somewhere on the sigmoid curve and an astute business knows where it is on the curve.

The sigmoid curve represents the lifespan of the business; it is not based on the number of years in business. In the beginning, a new business tends to start slowly through learning and experimenting. Once a business model has the correct formula it progresses and prospers and grows stronger. Moving up the sigmoid curve, at some point a business hits the high water mark or ceiling and then, unless it reinvents itself, it starts declining.

As mentioned, the lifespan of a business is not based on years; the time line alters with each business model.

Entrepreneurs develop businesses in the lower half of the upward swing of the curve, whilst many businesses that fail, leave it too late in the curve before they try to reinvent themselves. A business should venture into culinary tourism because the passion is there, not because the business is failing and an alternative has to be found.

Many growers and farmers have ventured into food tourism; some have prospered while others have failed.

Farming is an industry that relies on the seasons and it is also a 'non-people' profession. Farmers often work all day without seeing another person. In workshops we have held we have observed that farmers' motivational needs are often driven by 'achievement' rather than 'friendship'.

Food tourism is a 'now' industry in the sense that the consumer is in front of a business representative and wants instant gratification. Plus, our farming clients involved in tourism often tell us there is ongoing people pressure. If you do not like dealing with the public, then culinary tourism may not be the right business model for you.

The key to success is to work 'on' a business plan and not 'in' the business. Many businesses fail to work because the owner fails to plan. Food tourism is a fun sector to be in, but it is still business and a business plan is essential.

Before starting any business the following questions should be asked:

- Are you a self-starter?
- Can you start and follow through on what will be a long project?
- Can you accept responsibility?
- Are you prepared to work long hours, 7 days a week?
- Are you in sound health?
- Is there a replacement procedure if you are taken sick?
- Are you a natural leader?
- Are you an organizer?
- Are you a logical thinker?
- Can you easily work with others and the public?

- Can you compromise?
- Are you a good listener?
- Have you a background in food tourism?
- Can you cope in a crisis?
- Do you have the knowledge to start a business?

If the answer is no to any of the above questions you should seriously ask yourself if you want to venture into food tourism. Many businesses fail because of the management team's attitude rather than what they produce.

There are many books written on business planning and we recommend you read these and carry out the necessary research prior to developing a food tourism business. It is essential that a business plan be prepared before you venture into the business.

Questions that need to be asked include the following.

## Should the Public be Allowed on Your Farm?

For farmers considering getting into food tourism one of the biggest questions and challenges is 'should the public walk on to the farm?' and 'do you want the public on the premises when farm activities are taking place?' As in any business decision there are advantages and disadvantages and we will try to summarize these here.

### Advantages

1. It allows the farmer to supply fresh produce directly to the consumer.
2. The opportunity to get immediate payment for what you have sold.
3. Eliminates transport costs.
4. It allows the farmer to engage with the consumer and get instant feedback from consumers on the produce and what other offers the farmer can provide.
5. Prices are controlled by the farmer, not others in the 'supply chain'.
6. Niche products can be tested and established. All family members can be involved in developing the 'on-site' business.
7. Increases local awareness of what is grown locally and this message should spread through the community.
8. Improves the long-term security of the farm's survival.
9. It allows the farmer to experiment with marketing techniques.

### Disadvantages

1. Lack of time. Farming is about producing the crop and maintaining the farm, involvement with the public will take extra time.
2. The day will become extended as the farmer will also need to put in extra hours, especially over the weekend.
3. Diversification of product grown will be needed to provide the consumer with a range and to increase the income on the farm.

**4.** Customers are 'king'. You cannot afford to upset one, the message will soon spread.
**5.** Capital investment will be needed to build structures that are safe for public access.
**6.** Public safety and other regulations that involve dealing with the public will have to be adhered to.
**7.** The site may need to be modified to make sure public access is suitable and complies with legal requirements.
**8.** Do the neighbouring farmers approve of the venture?
**9.** Do you enjoy dealing with people?

## Developing a Culinary Tourism Strategy and Action Plan

Whether it is developing a regional concept or developing a concept on a site, success revolves around having a strategic and action plan. That plan may need to be shared with stakeholders including financial partners that may need to be engaged to make sure the development achieves its objectives in the timeframe proposed.

There are various ways to put a business plan together, but the owners of the venture need to define 'The Vision' and 'The Values' if they are expecting 'buy in' from outside parties.

According to the 'Ontario's Four-Year Culinary Tourism Strategy and Action Plan 2011–2015'[34] there are ten success criteria that have to be built into a strategic plan. Those criteria are:

**1.** Leadership.
**2.** Market-ready products and resources.
**3.** Integrated business strategy.
**4.** Partnership and community-based collaboration.
**5.** Financial support and performance measures.
**6.** Destinations with good access from key origin market.
**7.** Sufficient market intelligence.
**8.** Culinary tourism resources distinctive to the region.
**9.** Destination with multiple food tourism experiences.
**10.** An effective marketing organization.

This priority list could be used as the headings in developing the strategic and action plan for a business.

Our advice when developing a strategic and action plan is to approach it as follows.

### Step One
Carry out a SWOT (Strengths, Weaknesses, Opportunities and Threats) analysis.

What are the genuine strengths, weaknesses, opportunities and threats to the venture?

This needs honesty and a number of the team engaged in the project should be involved in the development of the plan.

### Step Two

List the strategies that need to be carried out; at this point do not prioritize them, but get the list out so that this can be shared with the working party. Once everyone has seen the list, then ask individuals to put them into order of priority and then obtain a consensus on the priority list.

### Step Three

Have a document that reads as follows, so it is easy for all parties to read and understand:

| Overall Objective | Strategic Plan | Action Plan | Timeframe | Person Responsible |
|---|---|---|---|---|
| | | | | |

### Step Four

Write your business plan, including the conclusion and summary, at the beginning of the report. The summary is the last thing that is written, but the first thing that is read by an outside party. Its aim is to draw the reader into the project.

The key to any business is to stand back, look at the opportunities, and be a realist. There are huge opportunities in food tourism, but businesses will still fail if they do not do their homework and plan to be successful.

Taking time at the start of the venture can save time later on in the project.

Successful businesses have a clear understanding of the consumer and what that consumer wants and more importantly what they do not want. The next chapter will focus on the culinary tourist and their changing needs and wants.

## References

[1] World Tourism Organization: www2.unwto.org (accessed 10 February 2014).
[2] Funk and Wagnall (1894) *A Standard Dictionary of the English Language*, 1st edn. Funk and Wagnell Publishing Company, USA.
[3] Touring Club of Italy (1931) *Guida Gastronomica d'Italia* [The Gastronomic Guide to Italy], 1st edn. Touring Club of Italy, Italy.
[4] Bestor, T.C. (2004) *Tsukiji, The Fish Market at the Center of the World*, 1st edn. University of California Press, Los Angeles, California.
[5] Jane Chang, Chang Brothers Travel, Singapore, interviewed for an article in *Go*, weekend supplement to *Sunday Times*, 2 March 2014.
[6] Prime Minister Lee, Singapore. Top Of The News, *The Straits Times*, Saturday 1 March 2014.
[7] Waitrose Effect. BBC News online. Available at: www.bbc.co.uk/news/magazine-24629300 (accessed 12 December 2013).
[8] Daily Mail Online. Available at: www.dailymail.co.uk/news/article-2536175/lt (accessed 11 January 2012).
[9] World Food Day Food and Agriculture Organization of the United Nations. Available at: www.worldfooddayusa.org (accessed 10 February 2014).
[10] British Cheese Board Cheese Varieties: www.britishcheese.com (accessed 10 January 2014).
[11] International Culinary Tourism Association and the New Zealand International Culinary Tourism Development (2010) State of the Culinary Tourism Industry Report. Available at: www.

great-taste.net/tidbits-kudos/tidbits/new-2010-state-of-the-culinary-tourism-industry-report-readiness-index-now-available-to-trade-2 (accessed 11 January 2014).

[12] Food Empowerment Project. Available at: www.foodispower.org/food-deserts (accessed 3 January 2014).

[13] Food deserts report by the USA Economic development. USA Government. Available at: http://apps.ams.usda.gov/fooddeserts/foodDeserts.aspx (accessed 20 February 2014).

[14] CNN Heroes. Available at: http://edition.cnn.com/SPECIALS/cnn.heroes/2013.heroes/robin.emmons.html (accessed 20 February 2014).

[15] Budge, T. (2013) Farm Squeeze [article quoting Prof Budge by Amadis Locheta]. *Green Magazine* 21, 19.

[16] Food Miles in America. Available at: www.foodmiles.com/food/potatoes (accessed 3 January 2014).

[17] Shillingburg, Darrol. Scandinavian Food Miles Web Article 'Your Food Mileage may Vary'. Available at: www.darrolshillingburg.com/GardenSite/NewsletterPDF/foodMiles.pdf (accessed 21 February 2014).

[18] Food Miles In Australia. Available at: www.choice.com.au/reviews-and-tests/food-and-health/labelling-and-advertising/sustainability/food-miles-aspx (accessed 9 November 2013).

[19] John and Linda Stanley: attending a workshop by Joel Salatin in Manjimup, Western Australia, 4 March 2014.

[20] WCED (1987) *Our Common Future*. World Commission on Economic Development, Washington, DC.

[21] Weaver, D. (2006) *Sustainable Tourism: Theory and Practice*. Butterworth Heinemann, London.

[22] Elkington, J. (1998) Partnerships from 'cannibals with forks': the triple bottom line of 21st-century business. *Environmental Quality Management* 3, 37–51.

[23] Harrington, R. and Ottenbacher, M. (2010) Food tourism – a case study of the gastronomic capital. *Journal of Culinary Science and Technology* 8, 14–32.

[24] Cela, A., Knowles-Lankford, J. and Lankford, S. (2007) Local food festivals in Northeast Iowa communities: a visitor and economic impact study. *Managing Leisure* 12, 171–186.

[25] Freidberg, S. (2004) *French Beans and Food Scares: Culture and Commerce in an Anxious Age*. Oxford University Press, Oxford, UK.

[26] Chang, H.-S. and Kristiansen, P. (2006) Selling Australia as 'clean and green'. *Australian Journal of Agricultural and Resource Economics* 50, 103–113.

[27] Weaver, D. and Lawton, L. (2014) *Tourism Management*, 4th edn. Wiley, Milton, Australia.

[28] Derrett, R. (2003) Making sense of how festivals demonstrate a community's sense of place. *Event Management* 8, 49–58.

[29] Santos, C., Belhassen, Y. and Caton, K. (2008) Reimagining Chinatown: an analysis of tourism discourse. *Tourism Management* 29, 1002–1012.

[30] Li, W. and Wang, H. (1999) Wildlife trade in Yunnan Province, China, at the border with Vietnam. *Traffic Bulletin* 18(1), 21–30.

[31] Coley, D., Howard, M. and Winter, M. (2009) Local food, food miles and carbon emissions: a comparison of farm shop and mass distribution approaches. *Food Policy* 23, 150–156.

[32] European Union food quality categories. Available at: http://ec.europa.eu/agriculture/quality/schemes/index_en.htm (accessed 5 October 2013).

[33] Presentation by Simon Burley, Executive Director, Tourism Western Australia at the FACET Conference on 3 September 2013 at Manjimup Town Hall, Manjimup, Western Australia.

[34] Ontario Four-Year Culinary Tourism Strategy and Action Plan 2011–2015. Available at: www.mtc.gov.on.ca/en/publications/Culinary_web.pdf (accessed 4 September 2013).

## Websites

Farmer's Fridge: www.farmersfridge.com (accessed 10 January 2014).

Farm2Chefs: www.farm2chefs.com (accessed 1 October 2013).

Global Cheese Awards: www.globalcheeseawards.com (accessed 11 November 2014).

Peru Travel Marketing programme: www.facebook.com/perumuchogusto (accessed 9 January 2014).

Polyface Farm, Swoope, Shenandoah Valley, Virginia: www.polyfacefarms.com (accessed 21 February 2014)

Savills, estate agents, UK: www.savills.co.uk

Slow Food International: www.slowfood.com (accessed 4 October 2013).

Tsukiji Market, Tokyo: www.tsukiji-market.or.jp

Vermont Maple Sugar Makers Association: www.vermontmaple.org (accessed 6 January 2014).

World Food Travel Association: www.worldfoodtravel.org (accessed 3 December 2013).

# 2 The Changing Tourist

Cultivators of the earth are the most valuable citizens.

Thomas Jefferson

## Introduction

Once there was a time when tourists would go to their travel agent, book a 'package' holiday and spend 2 weeks in the sun at a coastal resort. Those tourists looked for food that was familiar to them from what they ate back home. Over time, tourists have become more adventurous and now plan their own vacations on the Internet and have numerous 'mini' breaks through the year that may last a few days. This is ideal for the culinary tourism industry as it allows tourists to spend time in their own local farm-based tourist areas.

The modern tourist is more demanding, less predictable and more empowered than the tourist of the past. This is partially due to the power of social media.

The development of the 'package' holiday in the 1960s and 1970s was actually one of the early drivers of food tourism. Prior to the advent of the overseas vacation, consumers were only exposed to foods made available in their daily life, which came from the local supermarket and grocery store and occasionally, if they were lucky, a local food market. Populations in many countries were also less cosmopolitan than they are today and hence exposed to a lesser variety of foods in their lives. The retailers needed to provide produce they could sell quickly as 'turnover' of food was critical as shelf life, due to the lack of developed refrigeration, was short. As a result, the food offer provided was considered 'safe'. Exotic foods were rarely on offer as the customer simply did not understand how to prepare or cook them and often feared what they would taste like.

Once tourists started venturing overseas they were exposed to strange and exotic foods. Initially tourists wanted to take their familiar food with them and visitors can still see English 'fish and chip' shops across the Mediterranean beach resorts that serve traditional British travellers. Slowly tourists started to experiment with local dishes and as a result gained confidence in developing their own culinary adventures. Tourists are now travelling to more obscure places and eating more obscure foods, many of them local dishes they had never tried before.

This also meant consumers wanted to explore and discover more of what was in their own back yard and as a result local food tourism has grown dramatically over recent years.

Within most western societies, the majority of consumers today have become more removed from the farmer and from nature. This is a trend that is accelerating as urban living becomes more popular. There are many city people today who have no idea where their food comes from and assume that it is manufactured rather than grown or raised. At the same time there are an increasing number of urban dwellers who want to reconnect with the farm and the farmer and want to know more about the journey their food takes before it reaches them. They have become suspicious of the 'long food chain' and want to have more control over their own food journey.

The start of this century saw the rapid evolution of the culinary tourist. These culinary-minded tourists evolved because of a number of reasons:

- A curiosity to discover new foods due to their exposure to new and exotic foods and cooking techniques when on vacation or watching TV programmes.
- A more health-aware consumer due to a concern with what is happening to food production within the 'long food chain' and how that may affect their health. Many consumers have strong opinions on GM (genetically modified) food and the long-term effect it could potentially have on their health.
- An innate need to connect more closely with the rural community due to the increasing need to escape an urban environment that in many cities is getting more crowded and more polluted.
- The emergence of farmers' markets, farm shops and culinary tourist attractions as a new offer to tourists, mainly in rural areas close to the consumer's home.
- Awareness of 'big' retailers dominating the marketplace and controlling farming along with a clearer understanding of 'factory' farming practices and consumers questioning whether this is the right way forward for society.
- Food has become fashionable and trendy for all generations. A study of the local bookshop and the amount of space dedicated to food-related books will indicate the strength of this trend.
- The emergence of celebrity chefs on cooking programmes on television.

## Understanding Today's Consumer

We are all consumers and our needs and wants are constantly changing. Every year reports are produced on how consumers are changing and how business owners need to change to reflect those needs and wants.

The Trend Report[1] is a good indicator of the relevant consumer trends, and the 2014 report can be summarized as follows:

- Status seekers. Over the last 5 years it has not been acceptable to flaunt success in downturned economies, even though some of those economies may now be stronger. Frugality has changed and status seeking has changed to reflect those new values. This may not result in a consumer purchasing a new Porsche or expensive luxury items, but it will be reflected in consumers being prepared to pay more for premium culinary food offers.
- It is all about you. Of the consumers interviewed for the Trend Report, 47% mentioned that they were willing to share their location via a mobile device and to receive information via that device. This goes against the same research that indicated that 82% believe companies have too much information on us. It highlights that when there is a perceived benefit, consumers are willing to participate. It indicates that culinary tourist destinations can invite consumers to engage with them via their mobile devices.
- Local love. Businesses that champion local issues and promote local products will increase in their perceived importance in consumers' eyes. Of the consumers interviewed, 61% felt local companies should take a bigger role in local communities.
- Guilt-free consumption. Consumers, and especially culinary tourists, expect more ethical and sustainable consumerism. Of those surveyed, 93% want more of the products and services they purchase to support social or environmental causes. As a result we have seen McDonald's announce that it is joining forces with the Alliance for Healthier Generation and changing their food offer to include salads and fruit. Locals, an espresso coffee bar in Auckland, New Zealand, is a 'pop up' bar at weekends where consumers are asked to bring canned food for donation to the community and in return they get a free cup of coffee.

The challenge for many farmers, growers and tourism operators is to understand how these global trends can be translated to the new culinary tourist at a local level and to identify their needs and wants.

The term 'food tourism' is confusing in its own right and many people confuse this with 'gourmet tourism'.

According to the World Food Travel Association, gourmet tourism only makes up 8.1% of food tourism.

Gourmet tourists are looking for the true authentic experience and are often prepared to pay more for that experience. Food tourists are interested in food experiences; they lack the same amount of knowledge as gourmet tourists and are keen to learn more about food. Food tourists are prepared to learn.

The lesson for tourism operators is to make sure they know their target consumer. Talking down or up to the tourist will be offensive; the operator may be perceived as a food snob in the eyes of the food tourist and they may never come back to that business or region again.

According to the ICTA and ICTD 'State of the Culinary Tourism Industry Report'[2] there are 13 different types of culinary travellers. These tourists can be segmented as follows.

**1.** Adventure travellers; those travelling far and wide looking for food adventures.
**2.** Ambiance travellers; those looking for the experience rather than a specific food item.
**3.** Authentic travellers; they want the real thing.
**4.** Budget; money is a key issue.
**5.** Eclectic; those looking for a broad range of offers outside of the pure food offer.
**6.** Gourmet foodies; the top-end travellers.
**7.** Innovative travellers; those looking for new food ideas.
**8.** Localists; they want locally produced and prepared foods.
**9.** Novices; those new to food adventures.
**10.** Organic food consumers.
**11.** Social food travellers.
**12.** Trendy foodies.
**13.** Vegetarians.

The top five tourist types in ranking are localists, novices, eclectic, organic and authentic.

Tourists also include backpackers who may also work on the farm and Willing Workers On Organic Farms (WWOOFers) who will mostly be overseas young travellers who are working their way around a country. These 'tourists' may require accommodation and food, but are still part of the culinary tourist mix. They are in a particular location because they want to learn about organic food production and they can share ideas as well as time in developing a farm. They are often available at harvest time to help with a crop.

## What is Local?

One of the most common questions we are asked by our clients is for the definition of 'What is local?' The dictionary definition is 'somewhere near', which does not help when developing a culinary tourism package based on local food journeys. One major food retailer promotes that local food is food that is delivered to the store within 24 h. Experience Renewal Solutions Inc. in a report in 2009 titled 'On-Farm Marketing in Ontario –2009'[3] carried out a survey to try to define 'local'. Their survey of Canadian residents in the province of Ontario resulted as follows:

- 52% questioned on what is local, said food from the province of Ontario;
- 36% said from the county;
- 95% from Canada;
- 3% said from North America;
- 1% other.

The same survey revealed that 79% of the time-poor shoppers do not have the time to source local food; an example of the 'time poor society' in which most western societies live.

While discussing the concept of 'local', it is worth emphasizing that the current indicators based on observations carried out in tourism in Australia are that for every $1 spent locally by locals, $4 stays within the community. When a tourist from outside of the area spends money on local products, $7 stays in the community. Research carried out by Tourism WA[4] in Australia indicates that if a tourist stops in a town or small rural community they are likely to spend Aus$110 with local businesses during their stay in town. The concept of 'Shop Local' is about the financial aspects as well as the emotional aspects of the business.

Apart from the segmentation mentioned above, there are also two other groups of culinary tourists that are based on age that also need to be considered.

The first group are the 'Baby Boomers' and the 'Greying Tigers', those born in 1964 or before, who are now either facing retirement or who have already retired and are searching for rural experiences. Many of these tourists have paid off their mortgage and have a large disposable income. They are looking for quality experiences and this includes what and where they eat.

They are especially looking for a quality experience when they visit food tourism destinations although they may not define themselves as food connoisseurs. They are often eager to promote good eating habits both to their peers, children and grandchildren and can become strong advocates on where the younger generation should visit during their vacations.

The second group, in most western countries, and a key target for all retailers, is the 'Generation X' woman. The 35 year old Gen X woman has more spending power that any other age profile and is often health conscious and wants to understand more about what food she eats.

## What are Food Tourists Doing?

One of the challenges for all food tourism businesses is not only understanding the consumer, but also finding out what consumers are actually doing. Tourism businesses need to comprehend what consumers are doing before they become tourists, once they are tourists, and when these tourists arrive back home. It is important to remember that being a tourist is only a short-term mind-set change for a consumer.

Since culinary tourism activities include both food and ancillary shopping as an activity, it is valuable to find out where the target consumer shops before they become a tourist. A survey carried out by Rob Jankowski and Erinn Meloche in 2009[3] for the Ontario Government in Canada found the following answers:

- 43% only shop at grocery stores;
- 31% shop at farmers' markets;
- 22% shop at wholesale stores;
- 15% go to a butcher;
- 12% use superstores;
- 9% use the local farm shop;
- 9% use a bakery;
- 9% use a health food store;
- 14% other ways of obtaining food.

The results on shopping habits will differ with different regions, but this research shows the importance of the farmers' market in the shopping experience. It does not reflect the surge in online shopping for food nor the 'Amazon.com' effect with the introduction of Amazon Fresh in 2013 with 24 h delivery for online shoppers. This is especially important when you realize that 48% of consumers who go to a farm shop in Ontario would consider online shopping with the farm versus only 26% would do the same at a farmers' market.[3] One quote from this report is 'The farmers' market can steer people out of the grocery store... The farm is seen as a special outing.'

Once a business knows where their target market is shopping before they become tourists, then there is an opportunity to develop a strategy to attract them as food tourists to your business. The tourist shopping experience should add a new value to the tourists' lives compared with where they go for their weekly shop.

In 2006 the Travel Activity and Motivational Study (TAMS)[5] was carried out in Canada. This studied the travel habits of travelling Americans and Canadians. The results were as follows:

- 57.9% dine at restaurants that feature local foods;
- 40.9% go to local cafés;
- 20.9% dine at high-end restaurants;
- 19.9% dine at restaurants with an international reputation;
- 11.5% shop at gourmet/kitchen stores;
- 11.5% pay day visits to wineries;
- 6.9% attend food and drink festivals;
- 4.8% dine at a farm;
- 4.4% attend classes at a cooking or wine school.

This research indicates how important eating out is in the food tourism experience and many tourist attractions would not survive without providing a 'food offer', something we will discuss later in this book.

# Engage with Children – They Are Your Future

A key group that influences all consumer activity is often called 'pester power' or children. Traditionally, farmers have been wary of allowing children on to the farm for safety reasons, but the modern culinary tourist wants the farmer to engage with the whole family. Children are now an important group that need to be catered for. Children are the future. The more business operators can engage children in the food chain, the more secure is their future.

Food tourism must engage the younger population, if children are engaged and enjoying themselves then their parents are relaxed and enjoying themselves.

This means a number of different business strategies need to be considered.

## Make the business child-friendly

Before opening the door to the public, a business owner needs to ask a key question, 'Is the business child-friendly?'

The challenge here is that everyone's perception of child-friendly is different. For example, in a restaurant one family will perceive it to be friendly if the children are served a meal before the adults, whereas another family may believe it is a more inclusive environment if all the family are served at once. The key of course is for the wait staff to ask the preference for each family.

Remember, legally the business owner is responsible for the safety of all people on the premises. If the business has a children's play area, and it should have one, then loose toys, pencils and books can become a potential hazard.

The key is to make sure children are entertained. This can be by constructing a fully developed play area outdoors or supplying colouring-in books and pencils at a table. Or even more importantly getting children engaged in cooking using local foods. A pizza restaurant we visited in the outskirts of Johannesburg in South Africa has a pizza night for children on a Friday evening. Parents are encouraged to leave their children in a designated area where a team of young waiters and trainee young chefs make pizza with the children. They then serve those pizzas to their parents who have been seated next door enjoying a wine while they watch their children cook.

When developing your facility remember parents are well practised at scanning a facility to see if it is a child-safe facility before they decide to stay or leave. Uncovered electrical sockets, loose cables and slippery floors are quickly observed and all need to be avoided if you are a child-friendly business.

## Is the business engaged with a local school as a partner?

Part of the success of food tourism is engagement, both within the business and outside of the business. This is especially true when it comes to children and getting them engaged in farm activities.

Many children today have never been to a farm before, have no idea how food is produced and do not know how it is grown. In fact many children suffer from what Richard Louv called nature-deficit disorder. This was explained exceptionally well in his must-read book *Last Child in the Woods*.[6] In Richard Louv's book he explains that when he was a child he was encouraged and allowed to play outside and, for example, climb trees. Today's children are often told that being adventurous can be dangerous and they spend more of their leisure time in front of the computer screen rather than in the countryside. The result is a now recognized problem called 'nature-deficit disorder'.

Involving children with a farm business at a school level helps children understand the value of food production and will encourage them to talk to, and hopefully get their parents involved in food experimentation. There are a number of examples of how this works. One is 'Farmers in the Playground, Growing Gardeners and Healthy Eaters'. This is a Canadian development by the Common Roots Food Collective under the slogan: 'Dirt makes you grow!' Their Facebook page[7] provides an explanation of their activities. Local farmers setting up and supervising vegetable gardens in schools creates valuable connections between communities and farms.

## Develop a Kids Growing Magazine

It is impractical for many individual facilities to develop a children's magazine, but an association of growers could develop a culinary magazine and may want to work with a business or group of businesses to develop such a magazine.

This could include activities in which children can become involved, such as beet face painting, pumpkin carving or how to grow carrots. The Nursery and Garden Industry Association of New Zealand (www.nginz. co.nz) has produced an excellent children's magazine that engages with children and encourages them to grow their own food. In Australia in 2012 'Gardening 4 Kids' (www.gardening4kids.com.au) won the Best Kids Company award as part of *Green Lifestyle* magazine's inaugural Green Lifestyle Awards 2012.

## Allergies

Another major challenge when dealing with both children and many adults is the increasing awareness by people of allergies, especially when it comes to food. Culinary tour operators need to be aware of allergies and be prepared to alter recipes and meals to meet different people's requirements.

According to the Canadian Health Department,[8] the ten most common allergies to be aware of are the following.

**Fig. 2.1.** The Nursery and Garden Industry Association of New Zealand produces a magazine to engage children in garden- and food-related subjects. This is distributed to garden centres and schools across the country.

1. Peanuts.
2. Eggs.
3. Milk.
4. Tree nuts.
5. Wheat.
6. Soy.
7. Sesame seeds.
8. Seafood.
9. Sulphites.
10. Mustard.

Once a business has decided who is the target consumer, the next question is how will they get to your facility?

## Getting To and Around a Region and its Culinary Facilities

All culinary tourists have to travel to get to an area. Many will travel by car, although bus tours and other modes of transport are becoming more attractive as a means of travelling around an area.

### Car visitors

The car is still the most common means of transport for culinary tourists and all tourist attractions need to make sure they are car friendly. The size of the attraction and expected number of visitors will depend on how the parking on-site is arranged. There are a number of points to remember when thinking about visitors travelling by car.

**1.** The business will need a parking area for less-abled guests to park at the facility. This should be clearly marked and be near the main entrance to the facility. The width of a parking bay for these slots should be at least 3 m (12 ft).

**2.** In some parts of the world many car rental companies will not let their rental cars be driven 'off-road'. This means that dirt tracks to a facility may deter some potential guests. These guests are often international guests who could potentially be bigger spenders. If international visitors are important to the success of the venture, then it is well worth considering having a hard surface to get to the facility.

**3.** If possible have clearly marked car parking locations. Most tourist operators agree that visitors left to their own devices will park anywhere. Therefore to enable the facility to fit more cars in a parking lot there is a need for designated parking bays. A solid surface is most suitable, especially if you are expecting visitors in the autumn or spring when the soil could be soaked. Many urban drivers are not used to driving their vehicle off-road and can easily churn a field up and destroy a paddock.

**4.** According to the British Department of Transport,[9] the distance to a driveway at 48 km/h or 30 mph should be 22.8 m or 25 yards. This allows for 9.1 m or 10 yards of thinking time and 12 m or 15 yards of braking. If a vehicle is travelling at 96 km/h or 60 mph then you will require 68.5 m or 75 yards for thinking time and 50 m or 55 yards for braking.

**5.** An entrance should be 27.5 m or 30 ft wide at its entrance and narrowing down to 4.1 m or 14 ft across to provide easy access on and off a major road.

**6.** According to Louis Berninger in his book *Profitable Garden Center Management*,[10] you need 15 car park slots per 100 cars expected on an average day. This research was carried out studying garden centres, but acts as a valuable guide for culinary tourist operators as well, especially those with farm shops.

**7.** Electric cars are becoming a more common means of transport and an environmentally aware tourist operator may wish to consider putting in an electric charge location for consumer convenience.

## Coach tours

Most coaches are 60 seater and upwards. This means that a facility will need a special parking zone to park large vehicles. Most businesses need prior warning so they can book coaches into specific time slots. Coach travellers tend to spend less per head and also require good toilet facilities. Remember, the arrival of a coach means a rush of people at a specific time slot and a facility operator has to question whether they want and can cope with such an influx.

Most tourist facilities will gift something in for the coach driver and guide for bringing a group of visitors to their facility. This is often expected by the coach operator and should be costed into the financing of coach-party activities.

## Culinary walks

Not all culinary tourists want to drive or cycle to locations, some want to walk and 'smell' the flowers on the way. Walking tours are another way visitors may like to experience the culinary journey.

This may mean a walk as long as the 800 km 'Camino de Santiago de Compostela' ('Way of St James') in northern Spain that Linda Stanley took 2 months to walk, or it may be as short as a 30 min walk around the farm.

Walks can also be designed for different demographic groups and age profiles.

The main objective is that it provides the right amount of exercise with an educational and culinary experience. The depth of information provided can be targeted to the audience. For example, a survey of children in the UK in June 2013 indicated that 25% of children surveyed thought cheese came from plants. In other words, keep information basic for children. When working with professional groups, you had better know the Latin or botanical names of plants along the route.

An example of what can be achieved is the 'Urban Herbal Walk' of Grimsby in the UK. Grimsby is a fishing town located on the North Sea coast. An entrepreneurial group organized an herbal walk around the town to indicate to walkers what local plants were edible and to explain food sources of the past.

Forage walks are also organized in Epping Forest, Oxford and Brighton in the UK. In the USA there is Forage (http://foragesf.com/wild-food-walks), which organizes walks around San Francisco.

In Australia the town of Orange has F.O.O.D.[11] week and part of that week consists of organized forage walks around local farms and vineyards.

The same can be done in any country as every region has its local edible food plants that are often unknown to the modern urban dweller.

In Australia foraging has been taken to the next stage. Leviathan,[12] one food business, has introduced a Transient Degustation restaurant. The guests go foraging with the chef and then an eight-course meal is prepared by the 'foodie' with the chef. This must be the true bush culinary experience.

This is also an opportunity to work with local aboriginal communities in some countries.

When the authors were in Arizona we were fascinated to discover that the local tribes based their garden foraging on three plants grown in combination. Known as the 'Three Sisters', this growing method has been adapted by many aboriginal communities in the region. Beans were grown up the maize support and also provided nitrogen to the soil and squash shaded the ground around the plants and eliminated the weeds. Without going on a forage tour with a local, we would never have found this out.

The message is walkers may think that the natural plants around them are weeds or are common plants, but, to a 'foodie' walker it is a potential culinary experience.

## Touring by bicycle

Times change. John was raised in Birmingham in the UK and can remember the city promoting itself as a city designed for the car user and the future.

In our consultancy with retail and tourist businesses, in the past one of the key issues was, and still is, enabling efficient vehicle access to the business and the correct ratio of parking lots to retail space.

**Fig. 2.2.** Chicago in the USA is one of the cities that are promoting bikes as a means of transport.

Now cities such as Amsterdam and Copenhagen are promoted as bike-friendly cities. London, like many cities, now has a council-operated bike-sharing scheme where locals can pick up a bike from a set location and drop it off at the end of their journey at the nearest bike park.

In 2013, bike sales in Europe exceeded car sales in 26 out of 28 European countries. In 2013 19.7 million bikes were sold and sales are increasing.[13] In Australia, according to the Amy Gillett Foundation, bike sales have exceeded car sales for nearly a decade.[14]

The Tour de France is the most watched annual sports event in the world; farmers and local businesses know the power of the bike and sponsor it across Europe. In 2014 the race started in Yorkshire and was a huge benefit in the promotion of culinary tourism in that region.

The bike has re-emerged as an eco-friendly form of transport that also keeps tourists fit.

We now have promotions such as Bike Week, National Ride to Work Day, Car Free Days and Bike to School Days, all aimed at getting us more active on two wheels.

Bike trails are appearing around the world both in cities and as rural tracks. The longest bike trail in the world is the Munda Biddi Trail (www. mundabiddi.org.au) in south Western Australia.

### Being bike-friendly

The resurgence of bike riding provides new opportunities for businesses. For example, the Albany Bike Users Group in Albany, Western Australia, are promoting bike-accredited businesses. To become an accredited business the business has to provide free air, in case of a puncture or tyre needing to be pumped up, complimentary water to the cyclist, bike racks, and carbohydrates on the menu if a food outlet. Accreditation is a simple process, but could become a great marketing tool.

### Cycle-friendly accredited towns

The next logical progression is to develop cycle-friendly towns and cities and the Bike Users Group is helping to develop this concept. Towns and cities that want to develop this strategy need to establish a Cyclist Advisory Committee and a Bicycle Programme Manager.

Consideration needs to be given to the existing transport system and their attitude to carrying bikes. Buses, taxis, trains and rental car companies would all need to address their policy on bikes and develop bike-friendly policies.

Bike racks need to be strategically placed around the community, with guidelines on the correct ratio to bikes, and the rack would need to be to a national specification. Local authorities need to develop phone apps on bike routes to help cyclists plan routes around the town and to local attractions. One of the key strategies is to ensure bike tracks link in safely to allow the rider to travel around the territory and not have to negotiate heavy traffic and dangerous road junctions.

Transport will be an ongoing issue and new ways of transporting people to rural areas around the world will continue to evolve.

## References

[1] The Trend Report 2014, www.trendwatching.com, authors are subscribers to the book/report proceedings.

[2] ICTA/ICTD State of the Culinary Tourism Industry report 2010. Available at: www.great-taste.net/tidbits-kudos/tidbits/new-2010-state-of-the-culinary-tourism-industry-report-readiness-index-now-available-to-trade-2 (accessed 12 December 2010).

[3] Experience Renewal Solutions Inc. (2009) On-Farm Marketing in Ontario – 2009 Report. Available at: http://www.ontariofarmfresh.com/pdfs/newsletters/OnFarmMarketingInOntario2009.pdf (accessed 5 January 2014).

[4] Tourism WA Conference conversation at Wagin Workshop, Western Australia, December 2013.

[5] Ontario Ministry of Tourism, Culture and Sport. Travel Activity and Motivational Study 2006. Available at: www.mtc.gov.on.ca/en/tourism/research.shtml (accessed 10 December 2010).

[6] Louv, R. (2005) *Last Child in the Woods*, 1st edn. Algonquin Books, Chapel Hill, North Carolina.

[7] Farmers in the Playground, Growing Gardeners and Healthy Eaters. Available at: www.facebook.com/pages/Farmers-in-the-Playground-Growing-Gardeners-Healthy Eaters/ 371152483001433 (accessed 1 November 2013).

[8] Canadian Health Department allergy list. Available at: www.hc-sc.gc.ca/fn-an/securit/index-eng.php (accessed 4 December 2013).

[9] British Department of Transport. Vehicular Access to All-Purpose Trunk Roads. Available at: www.dft.gov.uk/ha/standards/dmrb/vol6/section2/td4195.pdf (accessed 5 January 2014).

[10] Berninger, L. (1978) *Profitable Garden Center Management*, 1st edn. Reston Publishing, Colorado.

[11] Orange F.O.O.D. Week. Available at: www.tasteorange.com.au/foodwk_home (accessed 21 February 2014).

[12] Leviathan Video. Available at: www.au.gwn7.yahoo.com/w2/news/a/-/local/19290393/ new-dining-craze-in-wa-video (accessed 21 February 2014).

[13] Bike Sales in Europe: article in *The West Australian* 5/12/13 on research by COLIBI and COLIPED. Available at: www.coliped.com/docs/29288.pdf (accessed 21 February 2014).

[14] Amy Gillett Foundation. Australian Study Blames Drivers For Bike Crashes. AlertDriving Magazine, December 2010. Available at: www.alertdriving.com/home/content/australian-study-blames-drivers-bike-crashes (accessed 21 February 2014).

## Websites

Forage walks in San Francisco, California: http://foragesf.com/wild-food-walks (accessed 14 January 2014).

Gardening 4 Kids. Available at: www.gardening4kids.com.au (accessed 13 February 2014).

Munda Biddi Trail: www.mundabiddi.org.au (accessed 21 February 2014).

The Nursery and Garden Industry Association of New Zealand: www.nginz.co.nz (accessed 21 February 2014).

# II  Farm Produce and Agritourism

The real challenge is defining from a consumer's perspective what food tourism is and what it is not. It used to be that the weekly shop was not classed as tourism and going away on a visit was classed as tourism. With more and more consumers now buying their food at a tourist-style location, the line between the two styles of activities is blurred and will continue to blend as the industry develops.

Traditionally farmers produced the product and then sold it at the local market. With the arrival of the supermarket, the 'long food chain' was developed and farmers became more and more removed from the end user. With the arrival of supermarkets, farm profits started to decline and in many cases seem to be continuing to decline. Many farmers started to ask if there was another way of developing the market and as a result the 'short food chain' is developing and evolving.

The 'short food chain' has taken a number of different routes and options. We now need to discuss how farmers and local food suppliers are growing the culinary food chain market around the world.

The real challenge has been for farmers to understand tourists' needs and wants and likewise for tourists to understand farmers' needs and wants. As consultants we have seen projects fail around the world due to a lack of understanding between both parties.

Farmer involvement in tourism has evolved in many ways. The primary developments can be classified as 'on-farm marketing' and 'off-farm marketing'; many farmers have often developed both concurrently.

The following chapters provide a range of ideas to develop food tourism both on the farm, off the farm and in rural and metropolitan areas.

# 3    On-Farm Marketing and Activities

## Introduction

As the name suggests, this is where marketing encourages the culinary tourist to visit the farm where retailing and leisure activities take place. Often the produce grown on the farm is sold either partially or completely direct to the consumer who visits the farm. This minimizes handling costs and eliminates the majority of shipping costs (some famers may also want to do a delivery service for loyal consumers).

In many regions farmers evolved their marketing to work as a group, and as groups of farmers have developed food trails and food cooperatives to the benefit of all the local members. Two of the most famous food trails are the beer route in the Czech Republic and the Malt Whisky Trail in Scotland.

We will discuss food trails in more depth later in the book.

## Farm Gate Sales/Roadside Stands

The early on-farm retailers and drivers of food tourism placed their surplus produce at the farm gate on a makeshift roadside stand often made of pallets with an honesty box and allowed the consumer to select product. One local farm near where we live still does that; the produce is placed in a roadside cool room and an honesty box is placed next to the cabinet. We suspect that the farmer does not think of himself as being in tourism or retailing, but every week we stop at the farm and buy produce. We have never met the farmer, but he is helping to build the tourism traffic in the area through word-of-mouth marketing as the produce is exceedingly fresh and one of the few sources of organic food in the region.

In our consultancy experience, farm gate sales are the way most farmers venture into retail tourism on the farm. Having experimented with this form of retailing and gained confidence, farmers have then ventured into bigger tourism ventures.

Farm gate sales are a low capital investment way of entering the marketplace. A box at the gate may be all that is needed to start the farm retail journey. Most consumers visiting a farm will be honest and an 'honesty' box saves the cost of employing sales labour. Farm gate sale is also an opportunity to engage 'face to face' with the consumer and to decide if dealing directly with consumers is the correct decision for business growth. Our experience has shown that successful roadside stands tend to evolve into roadside markets and eventually into farm shops.

## Pick Your Own/U Pick

In the 1970s in the UK Pick Your Own or PYO was a major activity on many farms. City folk would organize a day out to the farm and pick produce that was then eaten fresh or processed at home into jams and relishes. The same was happening in the USA and Canada, except there it was often called U Pick. It was such a popular activity that the original name of the UK retail farm association was 'The Pick Your Own and Farm Shop Association'.

Over the years PYO became less popular due to consumers demanding more convenience shopping and many PYO farmers either changed their business model or went out of business.

Today with consumers' desire to reconnect with nature and with the source of their food, we are witnessing a resurgence in PYO. However, there are some changes in the new PYO model, concerning consumer habits and free entry to the farm.

### Consumers have changed

The early PYO consumer picked fruit or vegetables in bulk and processed them at home. They had a reasonable knowledge of how to pick and process the produce. They came as a family unit and it was a major day out for the family, often associated with a picnic at the farm. They demanded very little in support structure from the farmer; they were happy to spend the day in the field.

The consumer of today has different needs and values: they have less product knowledge of how to pick and how to process food. They need more help on the farm. According to our clients, they are generally picking less than their forebears, they are picking for a specific meal, rather than harvesting for the season. They are often more of a 'gourmet' picker: they will pick less, but are prepared to pay more.

**Entry to the farm**

Entry to the farm used to be free: the farmer's income came from the amount of produce picked. There is now a debate in PYO circles that there should be a picking fee. Some farmers today charge consumers to enter the picking fields while others do not. The argument for charging is as follows:

- The farmer now has to construct more infrastructure for legal reasons and to appeal to the picker, these include toilets and facilities to entertain the children.
- Pickers have less knowledge and are more likely to damage the plants and these costs need to be taken into consideration.
- An entry fee deters people who are not really interested in the PYO enterprise but instead are just looking for free entertainment and a free meal.
- Pickers eat produce, even though farmers try to deter this, while they are picking and this eaten produce should be paid for.
- Fewer people picking fewer produce means that the old 'free' model is not viable.

**What to grow for PYO**

The answer to this is almost anything, the industry traditionally grew with strawberries as a core produce, but this has evolved.

In the vegetable category we know of farmers who are allowing consumers to pick lettuce, brassicas, onions, carrots and potatoes. In the fruit sector PYO is more established and PYO is being developed for soft fruit, top fruit and tomatoes. PYO is also being developed for cut flower and nut crops (our own farm has a PYO chestnut orchard and daffodil farm as part of the farm mix). As a family we go to a pick-your-own Christmas tree farm every year, tag our tree and then cut it down just before Christmas.

In general as long as the plant is robust and safe for the consumer to handle it can be developed as a PYO product. The only crops to avoid are the ones where consumer safety could be a concern, for example trees where consumers would need to climb ladders should be avoided.

**Get the structure right**

There are some basic rules to adhere to when planning a PYO site.

*Car parking*
In season a farm will get a quick rush of traffic for a short period of time. There are a few weekends in season where you will need ample parking. Luckily most crops mature in good weather and you can therefore convert a field to parking. It is often best to employ some students to direct vehicles. Experience

will soon tell you that give a motorist a field and let them park of their own accord and you will have a disorganized parking calamity on your hands.

### Toilets
Toilets are essential and a farmer will need to erect temporary toilets on the farm. There are numerous sources to rent temporary toilets, but they are essential.

### Signage
A PYO farm must have clear and large directional signage to guide people around the farm and to get them to go where the producer wants visitors to go. Some farmers use tractor trailers to take people to the picking grounds. A trailer with straw bales can be a fun experience for city folk.

### Entertainment
Children soon get bored, and for safety reasons a farmer does not want children running uncontrolled around the farm. Therefore children's entertainment is essential to allow parents to pick without concern. This entertainment could include a petting zoo, face painting, maize maze or other farm-related activity.

### Picking instructions
Most people have no idea how to pick fruit and vegetables and left to their own devices they will often pick unripe fruit and damage plants. A successfully operated PYO unit needs to provide the right advice if plants are to remain undamaged after the picking process. The best PYO instructions should be communicated with simple diagrams. These can be placed on leaflets and a phone app to help the picker.

In the USA, the main PYO crops and seasons are as follows,[1] although this will vary depending on the season and location and should be checked with the local State Association:

- March–April: asparagus;
- May–June: strawberries;
- June–July: cherries;
- June–August: blueberries, blackberries;
- July–September: peaches, figs, tomatoes, green beans;
- July–October: raspberries;
- August: figs, autumn raspberries start, early apples;
- September–October: apples and grapes;
- October: late apples, pumpkins;
- December: Christmas trees.

## Marketing online

Online communication is essential in the PYO industry. This is where the consumer goes for information on when, where and how.

Make sure you are listed in the tourist association directories that consumers would use as well as developing your own online presence. Facebook, Twitter and YouTube are also valuable communications tools for this sector. PYO is a very seasonal market with a small window of opportunity, therefore a farm retail business needs to 'yell' loudly to the marketplace when the crops are ready.

## Farm Shops or Farm Markets

**Fig. 3.1.** Richardson Farms, White Marsh, Maryland displaying locally grown apples in their store.

**Fig. 3.2.** The Home of Moo, Farmer Copleys, Pontefract, West Yorkshire, UK has developed an old barn into a major food tourism destination.

Farm shops are retail enterprises located on the farm. Over the years they have evolved into major retail operations for farmers and are now fully developed shopping experiences for consumers.

The most up-to-date research on this sector of the industry is the Experience Renewal Solutions Inc. report 'On-Farm Marketing in Ontario – 2009' for the Ontario Marketing Association (OFFMA).[2] This reveals that in Ontario, 36% of farm retailers reported sales of CAN$100,000 to $300,000 and 17% are achieving sales over CAN$1 million a year, a figure we concur with as we have seen similar results around the world with our clients. Of the farmers involved in the study, 60% stated that this is over 50% of their income. Over one-third of growers with a retail business served over 25,000 customers a season and 72% experienced their customer count increasing each year.

This survey allows benchmarking of the industry and allows comparisons with farm shops in other countries.

In the above report, 94% of farm retailers believe 'word of mouth' to be the most valuable marketing tool, which suggests a marketing opportunity, especially using social media marketing. Some 76% of consumers will travel less than 30 min to get to a farm retail operation, which highlights how important is the location to the market. It also reports that 68% of consumers spend on average $16 to over $100, whilst 32% spend less than the $16. Compared to many retail activities, this is a high average spend per customer and should result in a healthy gross profit. For example, in Australia, average couples without children spend around AUS$200 a week on food and drink.

The real value of farm shops or farmers' markets can be identified with:

- 97% customers saying farm shops exceed customer expectations;
- 95% will recommend the farm shop to a friend;
- 99% believe farm shops are value for money.

Not many business categories in the world get these high accolades.

Many pundits would argue that the tipping point in food tourism started with the development of professional farm shops, as they are called in the UK, or farm markets, the American term.

A farm shop is a professionally operated retail unit on the farm that sells home-grown and local produce. They can vary in size from small sheds to purpose designed and built out-of-town farm shopping experiences. We use the word 'professionally' on purpose as these are retail operations generating large sales per square foot or metre and designed by professional farm retail consultants.

The farm shop really took off in the UK in the early 1970s and has evolved over the years to be a major part of the British culinary food scene. Farm shops play a critical role in the viability of many farms around the first world and are now vital to the rural economy.

The route to success with a farm shop is as important as any other enterprise. Consumers look on a true farm shop as an opportunity to have direct contact with the farmer, purchase authentic fresh local produce, obtain more unusual niche local produce and provide a relaxed and pleasant 'back to nature' shopping experience. We say authentic fresh local produce, as many consumers in some countries have lost trust in supermarkets' honesty in their claims.

Before opening a farm shop a farmer needs to be able to answer five important questions.

## 1 Do I have the right location?

Is there a large residential population nearby and do they have easy access to the farm site? Is the farm in an attractive location to visit and can the consumer see the shop from the road?

There is a retail slogan: location, location, location. Farms are located in rural settings and are attracting urban consumers who tend not to wander too far from the beaten track. Therefore the location of the farm shop is critical. It needs to be easily accessed from a major road and be clearly visible from the highway.

## 2 Can the farm attract the right customers?

**Fig. 3.3.** It is easy to convert a farm building into a retail operation as can be seen by this farm in the UK.

Before setting up any type of business it is advisable to carry out a survey of the type of consumers in the catchment area. Who are they (age, sex, occupation, income and lifestyle interests)? Are the majority of the potential consumers going to be locals, day visitors or vacationing visitors?

When will they come, what will be the weekday versus weekend traffic and what would they most likely want to buy?

The more information you can find out about the potential consumer the more the store design can be planned to be attractive to them.

The closer to a large urban community the more sales per square metre or foot and larger the farm shop can be. Alas, it is difficult to obtain up-to-date research on demographics but in a survey in Ohio in 1994 and reported in HobbyFarms.com,[3] 20% of households with an income of less than US$25,000 would spend less than 15 min travelling to a farm shop. Of those with an income of US$25,000–35,000 53% would travel that distance. Of respondents with an income above $35,000 70% were willing to travel the 15 min. Although the salary brackets have changed since 1994, the overall thinking process has not changed; the more affluent the consumer the more likely they are to want to travel to a farm shop.

In Ontario, Canada the report by Experience Renewal Solutions Inc.[22] revealed that 66% of farm shop visitors are female and two-thirds of shoppers are between the ages of 25 and 49, which reflects the 'family appeal' of farm shops. Of these shoppers, 14% go on their own to the farm shop in Ontario, 11% with friends, 21% as a couple and 50% as a family unit. Although Ontario has a multicultural society, 89% of farm shoppers are Caucasian, the remainder being 5% Asian, 2% Hispanic, 2% East Indian, 1% African Canadian, 1% Arabic and 0.3% Aboriginal/Native. All the visitors travelled by car to get to the farm shop. Coach tourism seems not to have discovered farm shops in Canada although this is starting to be a factor in some UK farm-shop locations.

In retailing it is accepted that 35-year-old women are the biggest spenders and the ideal shopping unit is two 35-year-old women shopping together. In our experience this approach still works in farm-shop retailing.

The survey by Jankowski and Meloche[2] also revealed shopper frequency:

- 26% of shoppers return within 2 weeks;
- 14% of shoppers return within 1 month;
- 12% of shoppers come back later in the year;
- 40% of shoppers come back the next year;
- 0% never shop at the farm shop again;
- 8% of shoppers were unsure when they would return.

This is a high return rate and ensures that even though the industry is often seasonal this can be developed as an advantage and opportunity. Of the shoppers, 92% planned a purchase before they visited a farm shop. Out of the 8% who did not purchase on that visit 71% were planning just to browse and not purchase a product.

Today's retail shopper and hence farm-shop consumer can, according to Sue Allan of the Australian Retail Association,[4] be divided into one of four groups. Each of the groups must be communicated with appropriately.

The four groups are: Fast and Logical, Fast and Emotional, Slow and Logical and Emotional and Slow.

*Group One: Fast and Logical*
These are competitive consumers, they want to be:

- First to obtain an item when it comes in season;
- They want facts;
- Need a quick summary;
- Like cross selling.

*Group Two: Fast and Emotional*
These are spontaneous shoppers. They:

- Respond to limited offers;
- Want to understand how to cook and prepare it;
- Like reviews;
- Want to know how many others have purchased.

*Group Three: Slow and Logical*
These are methodical shoppers. They:

- Want to know the details;
- Want a good reason to buy;
- Like comparisons;
- Trust reviews;
- Communicate openly about your product;
- Sceptical of competitions.

*Group Four: Emotional and Slow*
The humanistic shoppers:

- Build loyal relationships;
- Care about what others have to say;
- Appreciate interaction;
- Communicate openly about your product;
- Each consumer that walks in the door has a different approach to how they want to engage with the business.

## 3  What type of farm shop is needed?

Farm shops fall into three distinctive types of business.

**1.** Local farm shops: these shops serve their community within a 5 mile or 7 km radius of the store. These stores sell local 'known' sourced produce and keep the merchandising and display strategy fairly simple.
**2.** Regional farm shop: these farm shops service a region and need to extend their facilities to provide entertainment for the children and often have a refreshment offer on site. They tend to be day-out venues and will provide produce from a larger catchment area.
**3.** Niche specialists: these are farm retailers that provide something unique in the food industry and consumers are prepared to travel longer distances

to reach them. An example of this is The Garlic Farm on the Isle of Wight in the UK and our own Chestnut Brae in Nannup in Western Australia which specializes in sweet chestnuts.

## 4   What competition is there to your retail offer?

Competition comes in a number of different forms and needs to be analysed. Do not look on competition as a reason not to open a store, but be aware of what competition is out there. It will include:

- Online retailers: whether that be Amazon Fresh or a local supermarket, consumers will buy food online and the trend is increasing to buy more food online.
- Supermarkets: consumers who shop at a farm shop will have to visit a supermarket occasionally to purchase other produce.
- Other farm shops: mystery-shop them and identify their strengths and weaknesses. Do not copy them, but try and complement them.
- Farmers' markets: these are competition, but also an opportunity for your farm shop to have a 'pop up' location at the market to promote the farm shop.

Find the gaps in the marketplace and aim to fill them with your unique offer.

## 5   What can and should the farm shop sell?

The golden rule of retailing is that 80% of sales comes from 20% of the product range. This is as true in farm retailing as any other type of retailing business. It is also true that at least 80% of the produce sold should be home or locally grown in a genuine farm shop. This is always a contentious issue. Some consumers expect a farm shop to be a purist and have 100% home-grown produce. Other consumers want to do their weekly shop at a farm shop without going to a supermarket for perishable produce and would expect, for example, bananas to be sold in many UK farm shops, knowing they have not been grown locally.

What do you have to sell and what can you add to the offer to increase customer count and sales? This will vary with location. Farmers have introduced butchers, fish counters, bakeries and coffee shops to add to the offer in the farm shop and ensure that they can attract the consumer they need.

Experience Renewal Solutions Inc.[2] asked farm retailers in Ontario what percentage of food retailed was from the farm; the results were:

- 11% of farm shops sold 100% farm-grown produce;
- 48% of farm shops sold 75–99% farm-grown produce;
- 23% of farm shops sold 50–74% of farm-grown produce;

- 11% of farm shops sold 25–49% of farm-grown produce;
- 7% of farm shops sold 1–24% of farm-grown produce.

We would suggest that the last group are general food retailers who happen to be on a farm and are not true farm shops.

The golden rule is **keep it local**.

## Do your SWOT analysis

Prior to developing a farm shop it is important to do an honest SWOT analysis of the business and identify the strengths, weaknesses, opportunities and threats. These will differ for every business and every location.

Experience Renewal Solutions Inc.[2] asked the consumers to participate in a SWOT analysis of farm markets and what they were looking for in a farm market. The following results may help the development of the farm retail sector.

Strengths:

1. 31% Freshness and quality.
2. 20% Great place for the children.
3. 15% The staff employed.
4. 14% The extra activities on the farm.
5. 13% Well organized.

Opportunities:

1. 10% Increase produce selection.
2. 6% Increase in activities.
3. 5% Signage improvement.
4. Parking improvement.
5. Better marketing.

Of the respondents, 62% said they would change nothing, but this is to be expected when doing a survey such as this.

Part of the threat is that nobody comes to a new venture. In the Experience Renewal Solutions Inc. report,[2] non-users were asked why they were non-users of farm shops, the response was:

- 55% Not located near me.
- 23% Not aware the farm retail venture exists.
- 19% I prefer a one-stop shop experience.
- 17% I do not have access to a vehicle.
- 17% I do not have the time.

We suggest the biggest threat is complacency. With farmers believing that 'word of mouth' is so high that they do not need to invest in marketing to a high degree and 23% of survey respondents saying they have not heard of the farm, there is marketing inertia that needs to be addressed.

When non-users are asked what is needed to encourage more on-farm shopping the responses include:

- A more convenient location. We have clients who have opened farm shops in retail urban environments, bringing the farm to the customer, but this does bring with it more challenges and takes the tourism element away from the farm. It is also questionable if this is a farm shop in the true sense.
- Consumers ask for more marketing information, including when the farm is open as well as more details on the web of what is for sale.
- Parking, city dwellers are not used to driving 'off-road' even if it is only for a few metres.
- Pricing. It needs to be fair in consumers' eyes.
- The lack of public transit availability is often a factor that deters some consumers.

## Developing a farm shop

Developing a farm shop that works takes time, and the more planning that you can do at the start of the business the more successful your business will be.

In our opinion there are three essential books you should read before you start developing a retail store. They are:

- *Why We Buy, the Science of Shopping.*[5] This book discusses consumer shopper psychology.
- *The Experience Economy.*[6] A book on developing the shopping experience for the consumer.
- *Just About Everything a Retail Manager Needs to Know.*[7] This is a practical 'how to' book on retailing.

Develop your thinking as a retailer when designing a farm shop. Take the following thought pattern to design the retail business.

### Access
The first impressions the culinary tourist makes when approaching the site are critically important. If the site does not have 'street appeal', the potential consumer is going to pass on by. The challenge is how to make an impressive first impression to stand out to the consumer, whilst still being safe for the traveller. It needs to be different, appealing and provide easy access. Less-abled visitor access, and secure and safe parking for vehicles once they have arrived on the property, should all be considered.

### The building
Ideally an iconic farm building of the right size in the right location makes life easy. Alas, it is rare to have the right building in the right location for successful farm retailing. Most farmers have to convert an existing building or start with

a new building. To be successful, it is wise to obtain professional advice from a farm retail expert as well as a building expert and keep within the local building regulations. As a guide you will need about two-thirds of the floor space of the building for retailing and one-third for storage and offices. The more square the retail space, the easier it will be to maximize sales per square foot or metre. The key is not to over-capitalize on the building. The building can be 'dressed up' using a facade to make it look attractive both inside and outside.

*Signage*

**Fig. 3.4.** Richardson Farms, Baltimore, USA signage is clearly visible from the main highway.

Signage can be like having another salesperson on the team or it may feel like it is a burden on the business. Signage is one of the best tools to grow a business when implemented in the right way. The key to signage is to keep it simple and memorable and ensure the signage also consistently reminds the consumer of the farm's brand. The signage strategy should be drawn up at an early stage in the development of the project. Signs to consider at this early stage in the project are the shop name and logo signs:

- Entrance sign needs to be easy to read and located 450 m either side of the entrance.
- Directional signs to the location: 'brown' tourist finger signs are the ideal sign if you can get them. These signs need to be developed with the local council.
- Category signage in store, e.g. Butcher, Dairy, Fruit, Vegetables. These should be clearly visible to the visitor when they enter the store. They remove confusion and help with customer flow.
- Hours of opening should be located near the entry door and on the webpage.

All these signs are going to help set the image for the business.

Produce signage should be used to promote the expertise of the business. It should mention the name of the produce, which farm it came from and three benefits of the product. If you provide more than three benefits you may give the impression the produce is too complicated to prepare and cook, less than three benefits suggests you do now know much about the produce. This is one area where a farm shop can really sell the benefits of buying local over other produce retailers.

Some easy guidelines for writing effective produce signs include:

- Be specific rather than general. Consumers do not like surprises, so make sure a ticket gives the size, weight or savings.
- Sell the 'sizzle' or the 'romance'.
- Write facts not fiction; this does not conflict with the above bullet point, sell the sizzle could be 'ideal', 'now is the season', or a sign we saw in Australia for local cherries, which started 'Australian cherries, only available for 100 days a year'.
- Explain what is not obvious; this may include a recipe using that produce.
- Help the customer make a decision.
- Do not state the obvious such as assorted sizes if this is clearly visible.

### Shop layout

The layout of the store is also critically important; get it wrong and it can reduce the average sale per customer considerably. Our own observational research in the USA suggests it can lower the average sale by as much as 20% per sale.

Supermarkets tend to be laid out on what is called the 'grid' system, that is aisle upon aisle of produce. The grid system enables supermarkets to maximize the amount of space for produce. The problem is that consumers find it boring and often rate supermarket shopping as a chore rather than a fun experience.

A farm shop should be a fun experience and have a 'boutique' store layout. The best example of boutique retailing is to look at high-end ladies fashion stores. In high-end fashion stores consumers are encouraged to browse shop, the theory is that once a consumer starts browsing she will spend more money.

Farm shops need to embrace the 'boutique' layout as it enhances the customer experience and increases the average sale per customer. As a guide, 60–70% of the floor space should be allocated to the consumer and 30–40% to produce. The variation is that space for shopping varies with culture. For example a French shopper needs less space for shopping than does an Australian shopper, as the French tend to stand closer together normally and find the close person less threatening than an Australian.

Consumer movement in the store is also important. In countries where they drive on the right-hand side of the road consumers prefer to walk counter-clockwise around the store. In countries where they drive on the left-hand side of the road, consumers tend to want to walk clockwise around the store. Therefore the location of the checkpoint is vital to successful retailing. Research by Paco Underhill[5] indicates that the wrong customer flow can cost a business as much as US$2 on the average sale per customer. Plus, if the customer flow and space ratio is correct, pilferage in the store will also reduce.

To maximize the customer flow around the store, the retailer allocates the purpose products in key locations, which are usually in quieter parts of the store. This is why the toilet paper and dog food are located where they are in a supermarket. The term is 'bounce' merchandising as the consumer is 'bounced' around the store to get most of the items on their shopping list. What are the key purpose products in the farm shop and where should they be located? A similar product to toilet paper in a supermarket could be potatoes in farm shops in some regions or rice in farm shops in other regions.

### The colour scheme

The colour scheme used is part of the brand strategy for the business. Having said that, there are colours to develop and use and colours to avoid. If we mention McDonald's most people can tell you the colour scheme McDonald's use, even if they have never been in an outlet – it is memorable. A farm retail store should have the same 'sticking power' without using hard colours such as red and yellow.

The aim is to enhance the rural atmosphere of the location and to convey the freshness of the produce on sale and therefore pastel rural colours are often used in farm retail locations.

White is an ideal background colour; it can make the store look bigger and can also lift and hide an ugly ceiling that may exist. Colours to be wary of include yellow, which can cheapen the look of the place, and red, which is a dramatic colour and does not create a relaxed atmosphere.

### Lighting

In our view the most under-thought through process is the lighting. Lighting is also a critical element of excellent retailing. Most commercial lighting suppliers have their own lighting consultant and it is well worth using these services at an early stage in the project.

Rely on natural light wherever it is possible. Old fashioned fluorescent lighting can be some of the worst lighting to use as it can often make produce look grey and unappealing to the consumer. A natural white light is ideal. Have a lighting plan: some lighting needs to highlight displays whereas other lighting needs to guide the consumer around the farm shop.

### Displays

Farm retailing is one of the best retail environments to build memorable displays. A farm should keep all its old farm equipment as it can be used as props for displays. There are a number of different types of displays that should be used in a farm shop to encourage sales.

- Power displays. The power display position is about four steps into the store from the front door. Research indicates that this location can increase sales by 540% compared to anywhere else in the store.[8] Ideally the power display theme should change at least once a month. The display should be seasonal, topical and circular, no more than 2 m wide and conical in shape (old tractor tyres make ideal bases for power displays). The product should be clearly signed and the stocking level should go from full to half full to full if sales are to be maintained.

**Fig. 3.5.** Chestnuts merchandised for display in a farm retail outlet in Modena, Italy.

- End cap displays or gondola ends. These are located at the end of merchandised linear displays. They should face the consumer and be changed at least once a month. The same research by The Russell R Mueller Retail Hardware Research Foundation[8] indicates that correctly merchandised end-cap sales should increase by 240% over anywhere else in the store. Ideally the shape of the display should be pyramidal and the building of the display should use the same principles as building a power display.
- Counter displays. We are all familiar with the counter display of confectionary at the supermarket or the petrol station counter. The reason for this is that the same Mueller research shows that correctly merchandised counter displays can increase sales by 40% compared to anywhere else in the store. There are some counter display rules that need to be applied. Take the average sale per customer, divide it by three, then the most expensive product at the counter should be no more than one-third of the average sale per customer if as a retailer you are to achieve the sales target. The product should also be a natural impulse buy for the consumer. New seasonal products are often ideal as farm retail counter display products.

One of the most important aims of display is to get the customer to stop and look at the display. This can achieved by placing the 'familiar with the unfamiliar'. This is where the old farm equipment can come in as a major 'prop' in building displays to make visitors stop and look.

Displays enable the retailer to embrace the season and create the theatre the culinary tourist is looking for. Successful farm retailers create the theatre in store to celebrate seasons and events.

The farm shop should change displays to embrace:

* Spring;
* Summer;
* Autumn;
* Winter; but also
* Valentine's Day;
* Mothers' Day;
* Halloween;
* Christmas;
* Pink October for cancer research;
* Movember – November for men's cancer research, started in Australia;
* Daffodil Day;
* Apple Day;
* and others that apply to your demographic target market or region.

## Merchandising

The rules of merchandising in any retail store are the same. Maximum sales are made in the sight and take position. The sight and take position is the space between the average height of a consumer's belly button and eyes. The farm shop retailer has some extra rules that apply to their merchandising strategy.

'Shelf life' is a term all retailers talk about. The shelf life is how long a product looks fresh on the shelf. The faster a retailer can 'stock turn' the product at a profit, in theory the more money can be made. Fruit and vegetables have one unique feature, ethylene gas. Ethylene gas is released as a natural gas during the ripening process and can shorten the life of other products located near to the high ethylene gas producer. High-level releasers of ethylene gas should be noted and displayed in strategic locations in store and products next to them need to be monitored carefully. The table below illustrates the level of ethylene release for a selection of fruits and vegetables.[9]

| High-level ethylene releasers | Medium releasers | Low releasers |
| --- | --- | --- |
| Apple | Banana | Cherry |
| Apricot | Fig | Citrus fruit |
| Avocado | Honeydew melon | Leafy vegetables |
| Peach | Tomato | Cut flowers |
| Kiwi fruit | | Potato |
| Nectarine | | |
| Cucumber | | |
| Pear | | |
| Pineapple | | |
| Plum | | |
| Passion fruit | | |

To add to the complexity of merchandising, colours need to be split to maximize sales; the location of the colour red is critical to success. Red can be used to draw the eye to certain locations. The positioning of, for example, red apples, red capsicum and tomatoes can affect sales across the whole category. The key is to use red as a draw card to attract customers' attention. We recommend placing red produce in the middle of displays rather than at the end of a display as this will help even out sales across the display: the customers' eyes will focus on the end of the display and then the middle of the display.

### Keep within the law

As mentioned at the start of this section, farm shops are becoming more popular and a major driver in food tourism. They are a form of retailing and must comply with the local retail regulations in the area. They will need planning permission and the local authority can help with advice in this area. Planning permission will include access from roads, building regulations, road signage, advertising and fire regulations.

The Food and Safety regulations also apply to the farm retail store. This will cover food labelling, food and personnel hygiene, animal and meat products, food additives and packaging materials and those regulations will change from region to region.

### Price perception

When we talk to farmers about food tourism, price is often a subject that is discussed. How much is a visitor prepared to pay?

Price is about perception and large successful retailers have done an excellent job when it comes to price perception. Within Australia and the USA, retailers promoting by-lines like 'everyday low prices' or 'low prices are just the beginning' have successfully presented an image to the public of being the lowest priced retailer in the category. Research has consistently shown, however, that more often than not they are not the price leader, but are in actual fact the price 'perception' leader. Consistently these large retailers have produced the highest gross profit margins, making them daunting competitors to smaller on-farm retailers who feel the need to follow and compete.

Promotions conveying the message that if a customer can find an identical product for a cheaper price at another outlet it will result in a price match or bonus discount have further supported low price perception that these large retailers are the source of the cheapest product.

Price perception is the single biggest driver to consumers considering a shopping category. It would be fair to say this is reflected in the real world with these price perception retailers managing to expand at rapid rates and return high levels of profitability.

### So how do you match a price-perception retailer?

You certainly do not mark all your merchandise down. The art of perception is about visual impressions. This is how you create the visual price competitive impression. Select five high-profile consumable products and position them in the highest profile positions within the store and mark them at the most competitive retail price in your 10 km radius.

Positioning signage that states the farm provides the best value in the region will help build that perception. Statements like 'compare our value' will attract the discerning bargain hunter's eye and help build perception.

Use those five items as the base plate to any advertisement to underpin your position as a price leader.

Many farm retailers are afraid to address this issue for fear of losing profitability. There is a reality attached to this strategy. Sales of the low priced items will explode, usually in the scale of 250–700% on what they would have previously. In the scheme of the total merchandise mix within the store they will create an imbalance that will need to be addressed and this is simply managed by an increase of the remainder of the merchandise's gross profit margins of just 1–2%. This will, in actual fact, increase the total store's gross profit dollars dramatically whilst building both customer traffic and the business's price competitive perception.

There is another reality attached to this strategy. Dynamic retail competitors will match or better the prices within weeks. The main aim of this strategy is to create price leadership and a monthly rotation of the items featured will help a farm business remain in front of the competition. A 12 month price perception strategy has the potential to transform a business if consumers feel you are not already a price competitive retailer in the category and it will actually improve business gross profit value from merchandise.

### Perception pricing

This is a technique that has proved to work in the restaurant industry and we are sure will work for other culinary tourist operations as well. We came across it in a blog by Roger Dooley entitled 'Neuro-Menus and Restaurant Psychology'.[10]

The principle is that you price an inferior product at a close price point to a genuine great quality product with the aim of boosting sales of the higher priced product. The two products need to be located near to each other to enable the consumer to price compare and they both need to be heavily signed. This system could work where a retailer offers a small and large version of the same product. Put the price up of the smaller product to make the larger product look more attractive to the consumer.

### Romance the sale or selling the sizzle

This is a technique used by the perfume industry, food retailers and plant sellers. It is a simple technique where the retailer literally romances the product in the words used to promote the product. If you are not sure how the system works, pick up a women's magazine and look at the words used to promote products in the adverts. As we write this section of the book we have a magazine next to us and the words in the adverts include:

This season the rules are being rewritten with a trend…

What a great way to sell a new product, in this case it was lipstick.

Feel, Imagine, Enjoy

to sell a perfume, and

Splash out on Timeless Treats

to sell blouses.

The key is to develop in-store romance promotions using emotional selling.

### Priceless pricing

Priceless pricing is an example from the hospitality industry that has been used many times. Research at Cornell University Hotel School[11] indicates that if the '$' sign is removed on a menu's price signage the average sale goes up. If the hotel or restaurant prices a meal at $14.55 it will sell less than if it was priced at 14.55, that removal of the $ or £ or € sign can make a significant difference to the bottom line.

We recommend each business should take a fresh look at its pricing strategy and consider how to manipulate it to increase sales. Often customers will not notice the change. We worked with one client in the garden industry where we changed the price based on whether a plant was in flower or not. The consumer expects to pay more when the plant is in flower and it is the job of the retailer not to disappoint them.

### What customers expect is 34%

In 2011, research was carried out in Australia and reported on the ABC News on 24 May[12] on how much profit consumers felt retailers should make on products sold. The average response came out at 34%. This is how much mark-up consumers feel retailers should put on products. We are not suggesting you do this, we are proposing that is a consumer perception of how much mark-up consumers expect retailers should be making.

Price is an important driver. Research carried out by retail researchers around the world consistently reveal that price is a major driver. To be successful you need a price driver in your business. It is important that you provide a positive retail experience for shoppers, but you have to get the consumer into the farm shop in the first place. Having the right product at the right price will remain a key traffic driver in the future.

### The free 72 ounce steak

Yes, it does exist in a restaurant, and this is a key tourist attraction in Texas. Visit the Big Texan owned by Bob Lee and you can have a free 72 ounce steak, all you have to do is eat it all. If you leave anything on the plate you have to pay US$72. Most people cannot eat all of it, so Bob wins. But this is an example of 'non-linear pricing' that could be adapted in your store. You could offer a very large product at an expensive price point to help sell the smaller products. Prada do it with handbags. Why not try it with apples?

### Benchmark your store

Farm shops are retail ventures and as such have the opportunity to benchmark with other farm stores in the country and around the world.

The critical figures to monitor are:

- Average sale per customer;
- Sales per square foot or metre;
- Labour as a percentage of sales; and
- Gross profit.

By monitoring the above figures, a retailer can measure how successful the business is and take appropriate action immediately. Failure to not take action often results in stock sitting on the shelf from reducing sales. Retailing is a 'now' industry and action to remedy faults needs to be immediate.

Many countries have a well-developed farm shop retail network, especially in Canada, the USA and the UK. Any farmer thinking of entering this tourism sector should take a close look at what is happening in those regions. The above countries each have annual conferences organized by the farm retail association for this sector of the market. The annual conference is a great opportunity to network with existing farm retailers and pick up new ideas.

*Suggested benchmarking guidelines for farm markets/shops*
Although each farm shop or farmers' market has a different marketing mix, a farm retail business needs a guideline to measure the business against.

The following, by Nigel Chandler, farm manager at Garson Farm in the UK,[13] is meant as a guideline to measure farm retail business performance:

| | |
|---|---|
| Average labour bill | 15% of turnover. Note: 20–25% if a production kitchen is part of the mix |
| Marketing | 2% of turnover |
| Bakery department | |
|     Overall gross profit | 35% |
|     Cakes | 65% mark up |
|     Frozen bake off bread | 100% mark up |
|     Fresh bread delivered | 45% mark up |
|     Wastage | 3% |
| Frozen | |
|     Ice cream tubs | 70% mark up |
|     Frozen meals | 37% gross profit |
|     Loose frozen fruit and vegetables | 100% gross profit |
|     Wastage | 2% |
| Butchers | |
|     Based on the butcher having own business | 15% gross profit or a fixed rent |
|     Deli | 42% gross profit |
|     Grocery | 40% gross profit |
|     Chilled foods | 65% mark up |
|     Cut cheese and cooked meats | 90–100% mark up |
|     Olives | 150% mark up |
|     Fruit and vegetables | 40% gross profit |
|     Wastage | 7.5% |
|     Grocery wastage | 1% |
|     Average store gross profit | 40% |

## Grow the Unusual

Culinary tourists are often searching for the unusual, especially the local unusual. They are searching out specific food items and meals that they cannot eat or buy at home; it is part of the fascination of the travelling experience.

When we arrived in northern Italy in November we found the markets to be full of Treviso Radicchio. There were a number of varieties of Radicchio, each variety named after a town in the Veneto region of Italy where they were originally grown. This is an example of discovering the unusual and is what makes food tourism an interesting adventure. Not every region has its unique products although often there are some gems hidden away. Growers can often seek out unusual varieties to create a new market niche, for example heirloom fruit and vegetables.

## What is an heirloom fruit or vegetable and how does it fit into food tourism?

One of the key market drivers is 'nostalgia' tourism, visitors want to escape the hectic modern world they live in, they want to spend a few days enjoying things from the past, and this is particularly true of the culinary tourist.

A culinary heirloom fruit or vegetable fits into this search for nostalgia. It is difficult to get a definition of an heirloom that fits everyone's understanding of a product. The most common definition is that it is a food product that was developed before the early 1950s and therefore before hybrid fruit and vegetables entered the food chain.

According to the University of Florida IFAS Extension,[14] to be an heirloom variety a plant must meet three criteria: the variety must grow 'true to type' from seed saved from each fruit; seed must have been available for more than 50 years; and the variety must have a history or folklore of its own. The time restriction of '50 years ago' was before the mechanization of agriculture and the growth in plant breeding to focus on uniformity of the produce and maximizing yield. Many argue the heirloom varieties taste better, but that is a case for individual palettes to decide.

Because of the pressure from supermarkets for uniformity and efficiency in modern-day farming, heirloom varieties became scarce. However, there is now a resurgence in interest in 'old varieties' of fruit and vegetables.

Many pundits will argue that heirloom fruit and vegetables taste better than the same fruit or vegetable available in the supermarket. In Australia in 2013, The Diggers Club (www.diggers.com), a supplier of heirloom varieties, carried out a tomato taste test with 16 chefs, garden and media experts.[15] In their opinion the top 18 tomato varieties tasted out of 27 fruit in the taste test were heirloom varieties. Their top five in order of taste were Hungarian Heart and Jaune Flamme as joint winners, followed by Tommy Toes, Black Cherry and Wild Sweeties.

There are clearly two sides to the changes taking place in farming and it is not our aim here to take sides. It is worth noting that in 1950 in the USA one farmer grew enough food to supply 15.5 people using 'old varieties'. In 1990 each farmer was growing enough food using modern hybrids to supply 100 people. At the same time farmland in the USA had decreased by 200 million acres. There clearly is a role for both heirloom and modern hybrids in the agricultural scene.[16]

## The tourism opportunity

Heirloom varieties are a tourism opportunity to expose the public to more unusual varieties and cultivars.

When John was on Vancouver Island in Canada he saw this excellent sign outside an agricultural tourism business:

Did You Know. … that if you ate a different variety of apple every day, it would take 20 years before you ran out of choice.

With over 7500 known apple varieties to choose from consumers could easily have an 'apple experience'.

Plus every apple has a story and telling consumers the story not only helps to provide the education they seek, it can provide nostalgia and an opportunity for theatre.

For example, in the late 1800s an Iowa Quaker farmer was growing Hawkeye apples in an orchard, a seedling emerged and he tried to destroy it on two occasions. On the third emergence of the seedling he decided that the Lord had decided it should live. He grew the tree on for 10 years and then picked a fruit. He ate it and commented that it was 'Delicious'. The rest is history.

Today's culinary tourist can visit heirloom farms such as Cashmere Cider Mill in the Cascade Mountains of Washington State. They can also attend Heirloom Apple Butter workshops at the same farm.

Heirloom variety tourist attractions around the world include:

- Kelowna Farmers' and Crafters' Market, British Columbia, Canada;
- Monterey Bay Certified Farmers Market, California;
- The Huckleberry Festival, Montana: www.huckleberryfestival.com
- National Heirloom Exposition, California: www.theheirloomexpo.com
- The Sun Valley Harvest Festival, USA: www.sunvalleyharvestfestival.com
- The Hood River County Fruit Loop Heirloom Apple Celebration: www.hoodriverfruitloop.com

# Rare Breeds

The pedigree breeder is the custodian of one of our national heritages.
'A Brief History and Description of the Lincolnshire Red Shorthorn Cattle', written in 1943.

Preserving old varieties and cultivars is not exclusive to the fruit and vegetable sector of the farm.

Stand in the middle of a herd of White Park Cattle in the UK, a breed from medieval times, and you can be taken into a time warp into another era.

Of the documented livestock breeds, 22% are at risk; 1881 of the 8262 breeds around the world could be lost forever in the next few years.[17]

It is not only the larger animals, such as sheep, pigs and cattle that are at risk. A 2004 survey by ALBC (American Livestock Breeds Conservancy, now

**Fig. 3.6.** Lincolnshire Curly Pig at the Pink Pig Farm, Scunthorpe, North Lincolnshire, UK.

renamed The Livestock Conservancy: www.livestockconservancy.org) in the USA found that out of the 70 breeds of chickens in the USA, 35 were classified as endangered and within that group 20 were classified as practically extinct.

Preserving rare animals is not only saving a great genetic pool but is also a food tourism opportunity.

Rare breeds should not be kept just for the sake of keeping them for nostalgic reasons, they should be raised for commercial usage, even if that is on a limited scale. Luckily culinary tourists want to know what they are eating and knowing the species of the animal is a marketing opportunity for the farmer and the chef.

The Mangalica are made up of three breeds of Hungarian pig that were on the verge of extinction. Some local farmers in Hungary started breeding the species and it is now making a comeback. There is a restaurant in Budapest called Mangalica & Társai Húspatika that only serves Mangalica. We have had a three-course meal there where Mangalica was served with every course.

Mangalica breeds are closely linked to the Lincolnshire Curly pig that became extinct in UK in the 1970s and is currently being reintroduced by Rectory Reserve into the UK from Hungarian breeding stock. Their webpage (www.lincolnshirecurlycoat.co.uk) highlights why rare breeds need to be preserved and are an important part of the new culinary journey:

> The vision of Rectory Reserve is to develop a sustainable future for the Curly Coat pig in Lincolnshire. This encompasses breeding and selling the pigs whilst also developing a market for their products. Their meat is as distinctive as the animal itself: marked by an unmistakeable nutty flavour. It is ideal for smoking and curing, lending itself equally to 'Parma' style ham and piquant 'chorizo' type sausages and to more traditional 'English' sausages and flavoursome bacon. The lard is pure white and slow to carbonise which means that it can be cooled, stored in the refrigerator and re-used. Additionally, research has shown it to be low in cholesterol and high in Omega 3 which is particularly appealing to the health-conscious consumer.

Rare breeds add value to the culinary experience.

---

**Case Study: Southampton Homestead, Southampton, Western Australia**

---

Jeff Pow, the owner of the farm, breeds heritage chickens and ducks.

The chickens, which include Australorp, Frizzle, Rhode Island Red and Plymouth Rock, produce different coloured eggs and Jeff sells these as 'Rainbow Eggs' to connoisseur food outlets. To add that extra touch each egg carton contains a feather from one of the birds. This is a low cost, high value way of adding value to an unique product to make it memorable.

Farms such as Norwood Farm in Somerset in the UK have turned rare breeds into a tourist attraction. They are rearing rare breeds of cattle, sheep, pigs, goats and poultry and have installed a café and farm shop to provide an entertaining experience for tourists.

Food tourism is one way that the conservation of minority breeds can be encouraged and help with genetic conservation for the future.

Rare breeds can also include exotic animals to a region. We are aware of farms that raise alpaca, camels, buffalo, bison, ostrich and other exotic game as a culinary offer and tourist opportunity.

## Rare breed associations

The aim of rare breed associations is to preserve rare farm animals. Some associations have member farms that are open to the public as tourist attractions.

### Australia

- Rare Breeds Trust of Australia.

### France

- FERME (Fédération pour promouvoir l'Elevage des Races domestiques Menacées; Association for the Promotion of Endangered Domestic Breeds).

### International

- Rare Breeds International (RBI) – the mission of RBI is to prevent the loss of diversity in global farm animal genetic resources (AGR).

### The Netherlands

- Dutch Rare Breeds Survival Foundation.

### New Zealand

- Rare Breeds Conservation Society of New Zealand.

### UK

- The Rare Breeds Centre is owned and operated by The Canterbury Oast Trust, a charity dedicated to the care and occupational development of adults with physical and learning difficulties. All income from each visit goes directly towards helping fund their vital work. In addition, the centre is helping to preserve many historic breeds of British farm animals, which are in danger of dying out.

- Rare Breeds Survival Trust (RBST) was founded in 1973 to conserve Britain's native livestock heritage.

## USA

- American Livestock Breeds Conservancy is a non-profit membership organization working to protect nearly 100 breeds of cattle, goats, horses, asses, sheep, swine and poultry from extinction.

# Fish Farms

When most people think of food tourism they think of fruit, vegetables and meats. But it is often the more unusual products that catch the visitor's imagination.

The major pastime in the UK, the fifth most popular hobby in the USA and the main pastime in Australia is fishing and fish farms can be a major visitor draw to a region.

It is more difficult to develop a culinary attraction around sea fish, but relatively easy to do it around freshwater fish, such as trout or freshwater crustaceans such as marron in Western Australia.

Fish farming attractions can be built into a one-day attraction. For example, Bibury Trout Farm (www.biburytroutfarm.co.uk) in the Cotswolds in what William Morris called the most beautiful village in England has become a key tourist destination in the village. They have built a restaurant and gift shop to encourage visitors to linger longer at this beautiful location.

If you are thinking about developing a fish farm attraction you need to consider:

- Children will be attracted to this type of attraction and it must be made child safe. Remember a toddler can drown in 5 cm of water.
- Provide fish food for the visitors to enable children and adults to engage with the fish.
- With fishing being a major hobby, you can get visitors to linger longer by encouraging them to fish for their meal.
- Have ready caught and cleaned fish available for sale.
- Provide information boards on the fish farming process; your visitors will have little knowledge of the procedure.

In Western Australia in the south west, the local marron is farmed and a few entrepreneurs have developed culinary attractions around this freshwater crayfish.

Fish farms can add to the local culinary mix and become a major tourist attraction with a point of difference.

For those located near the sea, there are other opportunities. Darts Farm (www.dartsfarm.co.uk), a culinary centre near Exeter in Devon in the UK, has developed a 'Catch and Cook Food Safari', which is held every Father's Day.

The farm networks with the local fishmonger. On Father's Day, for a set fee to the public, the farm provides breakfast and then the guests go 'line' fishing off the local wrecks on a boat. They are provided with lunch on board. Back at the farm they have afternoon tea followed by fish preparation of the caught fish and a cooking demonstration from the fisherman chef. The day finishes with a three-course fish meal and wine.

## The Farm as a Classroom

What could be a better classroom than the farm. More and more schools are linking with local farmers to develop an outdoor classroom where children can be taught firsthand about food, geography, language development, maths and other subjects.

Erica Croce and Giovanni Perri in their book *Food and Wine Tourism*[18] recommend that gastronomic activities for children need to be developed remembering that children have a short attention span. They suggest:

- Manual activities, such as painting a pumpkin or making a cake;
- Ask the children questions to get them engaged;
- Keep the language you use at the level of the child;
- Use measuring devices, such as spoons, that children can use;
- Provide a simple map of the farm;
- Have paper and crayons at the ready as they are always useful;
- Use all the child's senses whenever possible;
- Keep the facility safe;
- Make sure they have a take-home gift and praise the children.

Always work closely with the relevant school teacher when developing the classroom on the farm. The big opportunity is to take the children out into the fields and let them experience an outdoor classroom as well as an indoor facility.

Polyface Farms in Swoope, Virginia (www.polyfacefarms.com) have linked with schools and developed 'Grass Stain' school tours. They now have over 60 school tours a year to the farm.

## Cooking or Culinary Schools on the Farm

One of the biggest drivers to gain loyalty is consumer engagement and one of the best ways of engaging the culinary tourist must be with cooking schools.

Cooking schools and classes as a vacation are a growing tourist trend. It may be a cooking school in Italy to make pasta, to Japan to make sushi, on a cruise liner with a celebrity chef or at a local farm.

There is a lot of confusion around what the name should be for this type of activity; publicity promotes Culinary Schools, Cooking School and Cooking Classes.

A culinary school tends to provide more education associated with the food and is often extended over a week, months or even a year. A cooking school provides a more basic approach and again may take place over a period of time, whilst a cooking class is just that, a session where consumers learn to cook during a day or a few hours on the farm.

Most people love to cook and the kitchen is becoming more of a focal point in the home than it has been in the recent past. Cooking classes are therefore something that is an integral part of food tourism. The key to success is 'Make and Take'. The food tourist wants to be able to make a meal and take it away with them.

Cooking classes we believe will become more popular on the farm in the future, but it is not only the farm where cooking schools are taking place. Consumers are now engaging in 'community cooking centres' where shoppers can collaborate and learn from each other in the supermarket. These social events, according to Phil Lempert,[19] are the ideal venue for the aging millennial population. They are a group that likes to cook, but do not necessarily have the skills to make elaborate meals at home. This is also another example of where the mainstream retailer can take advantage of the trend in food tourism and blend retailing and tourism.

The key to success is to ensure that the cooking school or class is established, plus, it needs to be different from other cooking schools on offer in the catchment area.

Consider the following ideas to make it a point of difference:

- Introduce special offers during the workshop. This could include a basket of food harvested from the farm. Make sure the visitor takes home something authentic from the premises. When we attended a cooking school recently in Italy we were presented with a cook book written by the demonstrator and a unique apron that has become a conversation piece when we cook at home for guests.
- Provide local dishes, especially those that are unique to the area.
- At the start of the lesson find out what allergies exist in the group and address those in the demonstration, plus explain the nutritional value of the products being used in the cooking school demonstration.
- Provide interesting information that will make the experience memorable. This is where the stories about the food and the farm can make a huge difference to the experience.

For marketing the cooking school or class:

- Leaflets are an essential tool even in this connected world. Get the leaflets distributed into local tourist information kiosks and hotels.
- Invite local organizations to a cooking class; this will help build 'word of mouth' and 'word of click' marketing.
- Hand out leaflets at local shows and schools and again offer special events.

Consider the following when you are demonstrating:

- Gather all the ingredients and cooking utensils together in advance and double-check all the equipment is at hand, working and clean. Some culinary schools actually go into the field or to the local farmers' market to gather the produce and then take it back with the students for preparation. The more that this experience can be made a 'Plough to Plate' experience, the more the delegates will enjoy the experience. Some schools are now developing a programme that starts with harvesting the produce, then shows how to prepare and cook the meal and finishes with showing how to compost the leftover food; a complete cycle.

- Prepare recipes and place them on a blackboard in the cooking area as well as on a leaflet for the students.
- Cooking is a form of entertainment and should be approached that way. The demonstrator needs to be proficient, efficient and entertaining.

One of the most advanced culinary schools we are aware of is 'The Welbeck Project' (www.welbeck.co.uk/work-live/work/welbeck-project), which was started in 2007 in heritage buildings at Welbeck House in Sherwood Forest, Nottinghamshire in the UK. The school and facility are divided up into different areas:

**Fig. 3.7.** The Welbeck Estate in Nottinghamshire, UK has developed The School of Artisan Food.

- The Welbeck Abbey Brewery specializes in teaching how to produce old local ales and they now export to over 70 countries.
- The Wellbeck Bakehouse provides classes on handcrafted organic breads.
- The School of Artisan Food opened in 2009 to provide classes on baking, butchery and cheese making. Attendees can take a short weekend course or a year-long diploma (www.welbeckbakehouse.co.uk).

## Long Table Dining on the Farm

The family tradition in many countries, and especially in Mediterranean countries, is for the whole family to get together and to eat at a long table. This tradition has disappeared for many families and the nostalgic idea of a long table meal has now become a popular culinary tourist attraction.

In 1998, Jim Denevan was sitting at Gabriella Cafe in Santa Cruz, California, thinking of a business idea. His idea evolved in 1999 into 'Outstanding in the Field', a roving culinary adventure based on setting up long table meals in unusual situations using local chefs. His long table meals at iconic venues across the country include being on mountain tops, farmers' fields, beaches and gardens and have helped build interest in the long table as part of the culinary adventure. Many organizations now develop long table events and often link them to charities.

Long table meals need planning and an alternative plan needs to be in place in case the weather goes against the plans, but they can be a lucrative venture for the organiser.

## Vineyards

Mention food tourism to many people and they will instantly think of vineyards. Their mind will wander to vineyards in Bordeaux in France, the Rhine Valley in Germany, Napa Valley in California, Margaret River in Western Australia or another wine-growing region of the world.

Vineyard owners have definitely shown what can be achieved with food tourism. They have made a wine tour a major holiday destination. This has been achieved by getting to understand the needs of the consumer. Their core business is growing grapevines, but when it comes to tourism they have really engaged the consumer. Wine tasting in its own right is an engagement. Consumers like to feel, taste, smell and generally become involved with a product.

A tasting station is the ideal venue for this engagement. In the retail food sector 70% of consumers will sample food and 30% of the tasters will purchase. Tasting stations have created the ideal buying environment. According to research carried out in 2009 in the wine industry, 66% of wine sales take place as direct sales in the tasting room, up from 59% in 2008.[20]

Tasting rooms or cellar doors are a key part of the food tourism experience and can get very busy in season over weekends. Crowd control may need to be considered on certain busy weekends.

One of the big debates is whether a vineyard should charge for wine tasting. This seems to be a cultural issue. In Australia the tendency is not to charge for wine sampling whereas in the USA, for example, a charge is often the norm. Some companies give the consumer a free glass for sampling and let the guest keep it as a souvenir, while others wash them and recycle them.

Whatever the country there are two key issues. One is that tourists come as families and the children will need to be entertained whilst their parents are sampling the wine. Second, customer service and product knowledge provided by the server is vitally important. They do not need to have the knowledge of a sommelier, but they have to gauge the knowledge of the consumer to ensure they do not talk down or up to them.

Most guests come via car and it is the responsibility of the server to ensure that the driver does not get over-enthusiastic with sampling wine.

Many vineyards have added restaurants providing local food with their wine. This allows the guest to experience which wine goes with which food, and the ideal culinary day out has been achieved.

We have also been to concerts and seen Leonard Cohen, Tom Jones and Lionel Ritchie and other star performers at concerts at vineyards. These vineyard events have evolved into major entertainment facilities.

## Bakeries

Many farm shops have a bakery as a way of adding value. Bakeries are more popular on farms in the USA and Canada than in Australia or Europe. The best bakeries we have seen are located on apple orchards in the Americas. The apple pie is a much loved bakery product in the USA and hence the bakery is an essential part of the mix on an apple farm.

One major value of a bakery is the aroma. Very few people can resist the aroma that comes from the bakery.

There are two styles of bakery to consider:

**1.** Scratch bakery. This is where the baking is started literally from scratch. It means the organization will need a qualified baker and the capital installation cost will be higher. On the positive side it means more ingredients can be used from the farm and from local suppliers. Many of our clients believe that it is less profitable than a 'par' bakery. The truth depends on the skill of the baker.

**2.** Par or 'bake off' bakery. As the name suggests, this is where an outside bakery partially prepares the baking off site. The farm purchases readymade pies, bread etc., and these are partially cooked or 'baked off' on the farm. Premixed powders and ingredients come from the food service industry often as frozen units to the farm. Less skill is required and many farmers prefer this option as it removes some of the cooking risks. However, some customers feel less trusting of a bakery that does this.

## Butchers

The family butcher used to be a familiar scene in many local towns and villages, but in many communities the butcher has slowly been replaced by the supermarket butcher.

**Fig. 3.8.** The Butchery at Gonalston Farm Shop and Deli, Gonalston, Nottinghamshire, UK.

We are now seeing a revival of butcher shops, with many butchers appearing as a major feature in farm shops, especially in the UK. Most butchers operate their own business set up on the farm to assist sales in the farm shop. They are often the anchor tenant to the enterprise and pay a rent for space.

The majority of butchers keep to the standard red meats of beef, pork and lamb plus poultry. Extra income can be obtained by developing a range of added value products such as sausages, ready meals, pork pies and sauces and chutneys.

In most countries the rules that apply to selling fresh meat are different to those that apply if the meat has been value-added and these need to be checked out. Before opening a butchers' shop there are a number of pieces of legislation that need to be considered, these include:

- hygiene;
- waste disposal;
- food labelling;
- weights and measures;
- prices;
- meat product compositional regulations;
- transportation;

- temperature control;
- health and safety;
- employment of staff;
- planning;
- company law; and
- insurance.

Butchers are now diversifying into more unusual and exotic meats. On our travels we have dined on crocodile, camel, emu and kangaroo in Australia: donkey and wild boar in Italy; alligator and buffalo in the USA; and even culled elephant in Africa.

Butchers have also developed mobile butchers' shops and provide home delivery services to boost sales and develop a loyal following.

## Farm Delis

Delis complement the other offers in a farm retail situation. A deli is where cheese, cold meats, prepared salads, pickles and the like are on offer. Deli items are often some of the most profitable real estate in the retail section of the farm.

Deli management should be carried out by a skilled operator in this area. Cooked products should be separated from uncooked products using sanitation dividers, whilst the produce still has to be laid out in a logical way for consumers.

A typical layout that works would include fresh fish next to chicken and chicken pieces, next to uncooked meats and then cooked meats and small goods, salads, cheeses and finally olives and gherkins. A deli in a supermarket operates on around 38% gross profit and a farm-based deli should be achieving around the same profit if not more.

The principles of merchandising are important in all areas of produce retailing, but are particularly important in the deli section. Consumers want to see 'fresh', well-presented food, the cabinet should have a seasonal feel to it and look full and inviting. Keeping the glass sparkling clean is vital as is good signage. Glass cleaning should be a daily procedure; dirty glass can quickly reduce the average sale.

Products should be well lit. Normal light yellows the product, whilst blue light enhances the colours. Pink is only suitable over red meat. This is one area where a lighting consultant who understands how light works over food should be employed.

Hygiene in a deli is an area that is particularly important. The key issues are:

- Monitor and maintain temperature regimes.
- Use tongs when handling food and have them colour coded so that no food contamination takes place. Tongs for uncooked food should not be used for cooked food.
- Have a rotation system to keep produce fresh.
- Always wear gloves when handling food at the deli.

## Cheese

Cheese is one product that can develop its own tourist niche. Cheese advocates, like wine advocates, have their own clubs to discover more about cheese and are prepared to travel to discover new and exciting cheeses.

Cheese clubs include:

• The Smelly Cheese Club: www.smellycheeseclub.com.au

Phone apps have also been designed purely for cheese connoisseurs:

• Ask the cheesemonger
• Cheese'wich
• Cheeseman

There are festivals exclusive to cheese:

• Cheese Fest is held in South Australia every year and attracts 15,000 cheese lovers;
• The Festival of Cheese, American Cheese Society: featuring over 1500 cheese entries in more than 100 categories;
• California Artisan Cheese Festival: the California Artisan Cheese Festival is held annually in March in Petaluma;
• Vermont Cheesemaker's Festival: Vermont is America's top cheese-making state per capita;
• Oregon Cheese Festival: the festival is held at Rogue Creamery in southern Oregon;
• Great British Cheese Festival: over 400 cheeses made from cow, goat, sheep and water buffalo milk. The event is held in late September, and locations vary;
• Bra Cheese Festival: the biennial Bra Cheese Festival attracts cheese lovers and professionals from all over the world. Held every other September outside Turin in Piedmont, Italy;
• Great Wisconsin Cheese Festival: on the first weekend of June, cheese fans travel to the town of Little Chute;
• The Great Canadian Cheese Festival: first held in 2010, this June celebration is held in Prince Edward County, Ontario;
• Seattle Cheese Festival: every May, held at Seattle's world famous Pike Place Market;
• Amish Country Cheese Festival: this Illinois festival takes place on the American Labor Day weekend.

There are even lists for the top ten most awful smelling cheeses in the world.

On-farm classes are available showing guests how to make cheese and serve cheese, for example how to put the perfect cheese board together. The experts[21] tell us the perfect cheese board includes:

• Holy Goat, La Luma;
• Le Conquerant, Camembert;
• Pont l'Eveque;
• Roy des Vallees;
• Bleu de Basque.

## The Labour Challenge – it Could be WWOOFers

Much of food tourism is seasonal and one of the biggest challenges is getting labour, especially the right labour. One source for organic farmers is the WWOOF organization, Willing Workers on Organic Farms (www.wwoof. com.au). This is an organization that connects mostly overseas backpackers and travellers with relevant farms. This is a labour pool of young people who could help develop food tourism activities during busy periods. The farm should provide 4–6 h work and provide meals and accommodation for the workers. Other schemes for non-organic farms such as HelpX (www.helpx. net), Backpacker Job Board (www.backpackerjobboard.com.au), The Job Shop (www.thejobshop.com.au), Backpackerboard (www.backpackerboard. com), Nomads World (http://nomadsworld.com) and Workstay (www. workstay.com.au) are available around the world and should be researched for suitability.

## References

[1] Pick Your Own: www.pickyourown.org (accessed 12 February 2014).
[2] Experience Renewal Solutions Inc. (2009) On-Farm Marketing in Ontario – 2009 Report. Available at: http://www.ontariofarmfresh.com/pdfs/newsletters/OnFarmMarketingInOntario2009.pdf (accessed 5 January 2014).
[3] Selling on the Roadside. HobbyFarms.com. Available at: www.hobbyfarms.com/farm-marketing-and-management/selling-on-roadside-15048.aspx (accessed 22 February 2014).
[4] Allen, Sue. Australian Retailers Association, Conference Presentation to Lottery West, Western Australia.
[5] Underhill, P. (1999) *Why We Buy, The Science of Shopping*. Simon and Schuster, New York, USA.
[6] Pine, B.J. and Gilmore, J.H. (1998) *The Experience Economy*. Harvard Business School Press, Boston, Massachusetts.
[7] Stanley, J. (2003) *Just About Everything a Retail Manager Needs To Know*. Lizard Publishing, Australia.
[8] Mueller, R. (1998) *Merchandising to Maximise Sales Productivity: A Product Movement Study Tracking the Effects of Various Merchandising Techniques*. The Russel R Mueller Retail Hardware Research Foundation, USA.
[9] Ministry of Agriculture (1999) *A Guide to Retailing*. Ministry of Agriculture, London.
[10] Roger Dooley. Neuro-Menus and Restaurant Psychology. Blog. Available at: www.neuro-sciencemarketing.com/blog/articles/neuro-menus-and-restaurant-psychology.htm (accessed 22 February 2014).
[11] Yang, Kimes, Sessarego. Priceless Pricing. Cornell University. Available at: www.hotelschool. cornell.edu/research/chr/pubs/reports/abstract-15048.html (accessed 14 November 2013).
[12] ABC Midday News Report, 24 May 2011. Price Perception report.
[13] Chandler, Nigel. Manager, Garson Farm, Surrey, UK (email: retail.detail@gmx.com). FARMA Conference presentation at Brighton, UK, February 2012, updated 15 April 2014.
[14] Heirloom Definition, University of Florida IFAS Extension. Available at: http://okeechobee. ifas.ufl.edu/News%20columns/Heirloom.Vegetables.htm (accessed 18 November 2013).
[15] Diggers Club. Tomato taste test. Available at: www.gustoso.com.au/blog/tag/diggers (accessed 23 February 2014).
[16] Report of the Food and Agriculture Organisation of the United Nations. Available at: www. fao.org/publications/sofi/2013/en (accessed 10 October 2013).

[17] USDA Agriculture in the Classroom Program. Available at: www.nifa.usda.gov/nea/education/in_focus/education_if_aitc.html (accessed 23 February 2014).

[18] Croce, E. and Perri, G. (2010) *Food and Wine Tourism.* [A tourism text from Italy on food tourism.] CAB International, Wallingford, UK.

[19] Lempert, Phil, The Supermarket Guru. *The Parade Newsletter* Nov 2013. Available at: www.supermarketguru.com/newsletters.html (accessed 21 November 2013).

[20] Tasting Research. Available at: www.winebusiness.com/news/?go=getArticle&dataid=73501 (accessed 3 January 2014).

[21] Naddia di Cele, Cheesemonger at Richmond Hill Cafe and Larder, Australia: www.rhcl.com.au (accessed 12 January 2013).

## Websites

Australian Pick Your Own. Pick your own online directory: http://pickit.com.au (accessed 24 February 2014).

Backpacker Job Board: www.backpackerjobboard.com.au (accessed 22 February 2014).

Backpackerboard: www.backpackerboard.com (accessed 22 February 2014).

Bibury Trout Farm: www.biburytroutfarm.co.uk (accessed 11 September 2013).

Californian Pick Your Own Directory: www.pickyourown.org/CA.htm (accessed 10 February 2014).

HelpX: www.helpx.net (accessed 22 February 2014).

Lincolnshire Curly Coat Conservation: www.lincolnshirecurlycoat.co.uk (accessed 15 November 2013).

National Heirloom Exposition, California: www.theheirloomexpo.com

Nomads World: http://nomadsworld.com (accessed 22 February 2014).

Polyface Farms in Swoope, Virginia: www.polyfacefarms.com

Rare Breeds Survival Trust (RBST): www.rbst.org.uk

Rare Breeds Conservation Society of New Zealand: www.rarebreeds.co.nz

Rare Breeds Trust of Australia: www.rbta.org

The Diggers Club: www.diggers.com

The Hood River County Fruit Loop Heirloom Apple Celebration: www.hoodriverfruitloop.com

The Huckleberry Festival Montana: www.huckleberryfestival.com

The Job Shop: www.thejobshop.com.au (accessed 22 February 2014).

The Livestock Conservancy: www.livestockconservancy.org (accessed 16 November 2013).

The Smelly Cheese Club: www.smellycheeseclub.com.au

The Sun Valley Harvest Festival, USA: www.sunvalleyharvestfestival.com

The Wellbeck Bakehouse: www.welbeckbakehouse.co.uk

The Welbeck Project: www.welbeck.co.uk/work-live/work/welbeck-project

Workstay: www.workstay.com.au (accessed 22 February 2014).

WWOOFers: www.wwoof.com.au (accessed 22 February 2014).

# 4    Off-Farm Marketing and Retailing

## Introduction

Not all food tourism developed by farmers and growers needs to be farm based. Many farmers may prefer that the public do not go on their premises due to family, business, safety and hygiene reasons. Or the farm is in the wrong location to attract tourists. In this case off-farm marketing and retailing is the best approach.

Off-farm food tourism can be split into two distinctive activity areas.

**1.** Where the farmer establishes an offsite activity where the culinary tourist has to travel a distance to the venue.
**2.** Where there is food tourism activity taking place in the local community, often within walking distance of the tourist's home.

The more local the better for many consumers, this is not just a convenience factor, The Local Food Movement is an increasing force and one that will influence food tourism in the future.

## Pop Up Everywhere and Anywhere

Walk down many streets around the world and you will see boarded up shops. This does not mean that retailing is in decline, it means that retailing is changing. Today's time-poor consumer now wants an alternative retail offer.

In the old model of retailing the consumer came to the retailer. Now the time-poor consumer often does not have time to drive to the store, park the car and then walk to the store and bring items back to their car. In many communities the retailer has to go to the consumer and provide them with a convenience offer.

**Fig. 4.1.** A 'pop up' grocery in Padua, Italy.

Today's world is about weekday convenience and weekend experiences. Food tourism fits into the weekend experience, but this does not mean that the weekday convenience consumer needs to be ignored, it is the same person.

The most popular method of connecting with the 'convenience' consumer has been online retailing. Online retailing has seen significant growth in recent years and continues to develop. The challenge with this style of business is that the consumer becomes more price aware as they have no other aspects of the experience to build into their mental picture.

The other growth area is 'Pop Up' businesses. This is where the food tourism entrepreneur can combine convenience with the experience and an opportunity for the retail-minded farmer. The aim of the food tourism entrepreneur is to 'pop up' when and where the consumer either wants them to pop up or to ambush them and 'pop up' when they least expect it.

### 'Pop up' when consumers want or need you to

Street food retailers realize that they need to 'pop up' at lunchtime or in the city for the evening crowd if they are to generate sales. Florists often 'pop up' at railway stations during peak times, especially of an evening rush hour. These have been standard retail practices for many years.

Farmers' markets 'pop up' towards the weekend to allow consumers to obtain their weekly fruit, vegetables and meat from local growers.

For some entrepreneurs, they need to pop up seasonally. This means in the busy seasonal period operators may have a number of 'pop up' stores that supply the 'must have' products and then use this as an opportunity to drive consumers to the main store or tourist attraction.

### 'Pop up' when consumers least expect it

Traditional thinkers may find it difficult to grow their business whilst entrepreneurs who think outside of the box are developing new style business models.

### Food tourism operators can be at the forefront of 'pop up' business ideas

To establish a 'pop up' facility you need transport for you and your product and the ability to build and dismantle a small shop or booth quickly.

Many pop up retailers will rely on their vehicle to also be their store. It is then a simple process of driving to where the consumer wants you to be, setting up your stall and start trading. Make sure you check with the local council before you set up shop as you must still abide by the local business regulations.

## Box Schemes

The popularity of 'box' schemes varies from country to country. A box scheme is where consumers receive a box, or other suitable handling unit of produce at their door or an agreed collection point from a farmer or group of farmers. It is a home delivery scheme for fresh food.

In days gone by, the milkman, the baker and other fresh produce suppliers provided home delivery. Then as transport and labour costs increased it became too expensive to provide such a personal service.

Today, home delivery is back in vogue with leading supermarkets delivering groceries to the consumers' door, often within 24 h of them ordering the produce.

The main advantage of a farm box scheme is that the supplier controls the whole supply chain and therefore their own destiny. The disadvantage is that the produce mix is seasonal and many consumers are still not aware of the seasonal variations and cannot understand why a box does not provide a consistent mix of produce.

The farm box scheme has become particularly popular with organic growers, but any farmer could develop such a scheme. Whereas around the world organic growers have generally seen a decline in overall sales, organic box schemes have seen enormous growth. But, one word of warning for consumers: they should check that the box scheme is from a farmer or group of producers. Supermarkets have started branded box schemes in certain parts of the world that look like they have come from the farmer when in fact they are coming from a large corporate business.

A successful farm box scheme is based on a weekly delivery of in-season produce using returnable boxes. The consumer is provided with a limited choice, based on what is available at the farm or in the region.

In our view the main challenge is marketing. The message must get across to individual home owners. One of the most cost effective ways of getting the message across is to use the local farmers' markets or farm markets as they are called in the USA, as a marketing platform. Put up a stall and sell produce, but make sure every consumer is made aware of your box scheme delivery service.

Some producers use a delivery agent to supply the product, which puts a critical part of the process in the hands of an agent and this can be risky once a third party is involved in the supply chain.

When developing a farm box scheme, put on your customers' shoes and think like a customer, ask yourself the following questions:

- Does the box size suit the average family needs? You will need at least two box sizes for different family units and you may opt for three.
- Can they specify the produce they want to purchase or is that under your control?
- Is it clear on the box that the product is local and are your details on the box to enable the consumer to easily contact you? Is it clear the scheme is locally owned and operated?
- Is the information about the produce you sell available to the consumer on your online webpage?
- Is the packaging kept to a minimum and reused plus does the customer know how to return the box to you?
- Do you produce a newsletter covering topical issues e.g. GM?
- Are you encouraging the consumer to visit you on the farm and have farm walks or open days at your convenience?

The Salatin family at Polyface Farms Inc in Swoope, Virginia (www.polyfacefarms.com), have taken the box scheme to another level and developed a Buyer's Club. This club started with 30 members and now has over 5000 members and these members purchase 40% of what the farm grows. The buyers have to be within a 4 mile radius of the farm and they get a delivery to a local representative's house every 5 weeks. This means the group get together on a regular basis and are now engaged with the farm. Plus it means food tourism is now focused on Polyface Farms.

## Consumer Cooperatives

Agricultural cooperatives have been a traditional food distribution chain for many years in France and Japan. In Japan for example, 60% of food is distributed via cooperatives. A cooperative is where a group of farmers set up an organization as equal partners to sell their produce to consumers. Consumers who are concerned about food quality around the world have also set up similar partnerships to source local fresh food. With the development of social media marketing we believe there will be increased interest in consumer partnerships in food purchasing. This will take the 'box' scheme to another level as well as give a group of farmers and producers the opportunity to work together to develop food tourism.

## Farmers' Markets/Farm Markets

**Fig. 4.2.** A farmers' market sign at the Swindon Farmers' Market, Swindon, Wiltshire, UK.

Think food tourism and farmers' markets/farm markets must be one of the most important retail strategies that you would find in the food tourism mix.

Farmers' markets have been around since people started trading in Mesopotamia (in what is now Iraq). Local farmers would bring their produce and animals to the town market and trading would commence. This style of trading carried on through the centuries with the village or town square being used for the weekly farmers' market.

It is believed the first American farm market was developed by Governor John Winthrop in 1634 in Boston; this was followed by Market Street in Philadelphia in 1693. In France and other European countries there are street markets, as well as covered marketplaces, where farmers and purveyors still sell their produce. In 1997 the first new-style farmers' market in the UK was developed in Bath, Somerset. These markets focused on local food with a small amount of added value food products. Retail skills were often limited, but the passion of the owners made sure that the majority of those markets prospered over the next two decades. Since then the number of markets in the UK has grown to over 550 nationwide.

**Box 4.1.** Farmers' Market Associations

Australia
Peak body:
Australian Farmers' Markets Association: www.farmersmarkets.org.au
Associations:
Victorian Farmers' Markets Association: www.vicfarmersmarkets.org.au

Canada
Peak body:
Farmers' Markets Canada: www.farmersmarketscanada.ca
Associations:
Alberta Farmers' Market Association: www.albertamarkets.com
British Columbia Association of Farmers' Markets: www.bcfarmersmarket.org
Farmers' Markets Ontario: www.farmersmarketontario.com
Farmers' Markets Association of Manitoba: http://fmam.ca

Ireland
Peak body:
Good Food Ireland: www.goodfoodireland.ie

New Zealand
Farmers' Markets New Zealand Inc: www.farmersmarkets.org.nz

UK
Peak bodies:
National Farmers' Retail & Marketing Associations (FARMA): www.farma.org.uk
Farmers' Markets in Wales: www.fmiw.co.uk
Scottish Association of Farmers' Markets: www.scottishfarmersmarkets.co.uk
Association:
Kent Farmers' Markets Association: www.kfma.org.uk

USA
Peak bodies:
North American Farmers' Direct Marketing Association NAFDMA: www.nafdma.com
National Association of Farmers' Market Nutrition Programs: www.nafmnp.org
Associations:
California Farmers' Markets Association: www.cafarmersmkts.com
Colorado Farmers Market Association: www.coloradofarmers.org
Farmers' Market Federation of New York: www.nyfarmersmarket.com
Wisconsin Farmers Market Association: www.wifarmersmarkets.org
Mass Farmers Markets (Federation of Massachusetts Farmers Markets): www.massfarmersmarkets.org
Minnesota Farmers' Market Association: www.mfma.org
New Hampshire Farmer's Market Association: www.nhfma.org
Oregon Farmers' Markets Association: www.oregonfarmersmarkets.org
Pacific Coast Farmers' Market Association: www.pcfma.com
Vermont Farmers Market Association: www.vtfma.org
West Virginia Farmers Market Association: www.wvfarmers.org

## King Cullen

The drive to develop the modern farmers' market can be traced back to the 1930s. In 1930 Michael Cullen opened what many believe was one of the first supermarkets.

King Cullen opened in Queens, New York, and changed the face of food retailing for ever. In the same year a company called Birds Eye introduced the first frozen foods into the American market. This revolution meant that in 1933 the National Association of Food Chains was formed and in 1934 inexpensive low temperature food display units were developed for retailers. The Supermarket Institute in the USA was formed in 1937 and from there on, mass retailing of food developed rapidly.

As a result of this evolution, farmers lost contact with consumers and became part of what is now called 'the long supply chain'. In other words they became a supplier to a retailer who developed their own marketing strategies. Farmers did what the retailer asked. For many years this reduced the stress on farming communities as farmers did what they did well and left the marketing to other experts. But, profit margins started to slowly be squeezed and as a result, farmers started ask how they could short circuit the supply chain to the consumer.

Consumers also started questioning the supply process. In the old days food was grown locally and the consumer knew the farmer. Under the long supply chain 'globalization' became the buzz word. Initially, consumers were impressed that they could, for example, buy strawberries all the year around from all corners of the world. But today, many consumers have started to ask if this was a good strategy for their health and the planet in the future.

The existing shift started in the early 1970s when farmers' associations started to emerge to encourage farmers to sell direct to the consumer. The early days saw the emergence of Pick Your Own retailing and farm shops on the farm.

The key to success today is to take the product direct to the consumer once more. As a result the wheel has gone full circle and the farmers' market/farm market is one of the strong growth areas in retailing in the new millennium.

Cities and towns around the world once again have thriving farmers' markets. As a guide there is one farmers' market to every 100,000 of the population in many parts of the first world. Reducing 'food miles' are now buzz words.

In the USA, due in part to the increased interest in healthier foods, a greater desire to preserve local types of cultivars or livestock and an increased understanding of the importance of maintaining small, sustainable farms on the fringe of urban environments, farmers' markets in the USA have grown from 1755 in 1994 to 5274 in 2009. New markets appear regularly and existing markets – some well over a century old – are seeing renewed growth in both North America and Europe.

Farmers realize that to obtain customer loyalty they have to attend a market with their produce every week. Others still rely on participating at a market once a month, but this timeframe encourages consumers to use supermarkets during the off weeks, an undesirable marketing strategy. We believe monthly markets will change as the farmers' market become a natural part of shoppers' weekly experience and culinary adventure.

New York was one of the earliest cities to have farmers' markets and now has over 300 markets located around the city. In 2005, the Farmers Market Federation of New York produced a paper for the markets on what they needed to do as the '10 Principles of a Successful Market'.[1] The ten principles are:

**1.** A time, location and season that coordinates the needs of farmers, consumers and the local community. We have visited markets in the middle of winter in Germany where there have been two stallholders shivering in the winter snow. In the spring there have been numerous stallholders. It would be better to close the market and launch it with refreshed vigour rather than provide an inconsistent offer to consumers. In milder climates a weekly market is essential.

**2.** A central, visible and permanent location. Visitors are creatures of habit, the market needs to be visible to attract the first-time consumer and then permanent so they keep coming back. We know of markets located in school yards and town squares. Location is key, location in the town square means that other local businesses benefit and often there is a richer experience for the visitor.

A survey in Australia reported in 'New Generation' Farmer's Markets in Rural Communities by Max Coster and Nicole Kennon[2] found markets were located as follows:

- Town square: 33%;
- Showgrounds: 24%;
- Car parks: 9%;
- Community centres: 9%;
- School grounds: 9%;
- Packing sheds: 6%;
- Racecourses: 6%;
- Farms: 4%.

**3.** The market has a diverse range of products and producers. Consumers want a wide range of produce. In our experience one of the conflicts is often a question of whether there should be duplication of produce sold. Our view is competition is healthy and as long as there is not over-dominance of one specific produce then duplication of choice for the consumer should be good for the market. In the Farmers Market Federation of New York paper[2] the vendor numbers were as follows:

- Rural town: 10–30 vendors;
- CBD: 50–65 vendors;
- Regional market: 10–25 vendors;
- Suburban market: 20–40 vendors.

**4.** Fair and enforceable rules and regulations. The golden rule here is do not write it down if you cannot or are not willing to enforce a regulation as a manager or committee.

**5.** A strong market manager who is passionate about the market. We have been involved in the setting up of markets in Australia and served on committees to manage markets and the role of the manager is critically important. It is our view that this role should be a paid position. A market manager will have to put in more effort than they are often rewarded for, but they need to know this when they are appointed. They need to be able to work with stall-holders, the public, often a management committee and at the same time keep everyone happy.

**6.** A management structure that allows vendor input. Whether you have an advisory board or fully incorporated management board, the majority of this board should be from vendors. It is their market and they need to feel they are engaged in its management.

**7.** A marketing plan that clearly defines the target audience and has a strategy to reach that audience. Once you know the market you can then plan the education and entertainment that will work with that target audience.

**8.** Funding. Market fees will provide income, but there will be a need for seed money to get the project established.

**9.** Involve the community. A successful market needs to engage with the Chamber of Commerce, senior groups, schools, youth groups, Lions Clubs, Rotary Clubs, Men's Sheds and other local groups, and surveys will ensure standards are maintained. Success is about offering a consistent product to visitors.

We have been consultants to farmers' markets for many years and set up our local farmers' market. In those years we promoted the fact that farmers' markets are the 'social church'.

It used to be that the church was the meeting place for the community and where the community bonded. In many western societies, less and less of the community go to church and a new bonding place was needed. The high street used to be a place of bonding, but the demise of the high street has seen that venue decline as a social bonding place.

For many communities, the farmers' market is one of the new bonding venues. Hence the term 'social church' and the need for the market to be more than a place just to sell produce.

## Farmers' market objectives

The main objective of a farmers' market is to sell local produce to the local community; the challenge is what is 'local'? In some British farmers' markets, for example, you can come across farmer's stalls from France and other parts of Europe, which in some ways defeats the original objective.

Markets will evolve over the next few years and we will continue to see them multiply. They will become a lot more progressive and the retailing

**Fig. 4.3.** Mindil Beach Sunset Market, Darwin, Northern Territory, Australia is a major tourist attraction for the city.

skills of those involved will become more professional. This does not mean that they will become more like supermarkets. The reverse is true. They will clearly define their own niche and character.

The key issue is keeping the market true to its values. A farmers' market should sell local produce and the sales team should be from the local farm. Alas, many farmers' markets are starting to lose sight of those values. We have been to farmers' markets in Canada that sell plastic flowers from China and markets selling fresh produce that cannot be grown in that country during that time of year.

Many farmers' market organizations around the world are developing strategic plans to enable them to define their governance and structure. Guidance is needed on what an authentic farmers' market is, and what it is not and which stallholders, farmers and their agents are eligible in a market.

One result of this is that many countries have now developed an accreditation scheme for farmers' markets. The aim of accreditation is to guarantee market integrity, trading success and long term sustainability. The main aim is to provide a 'best practice' market that the consumer can continue to trust. The successful farmers' market keeps to its values. The market is not just about selling local produce.

As far as the farmer is concerned, a farmers' market should be an incubator where they can test new ideas. On a visit to Manjimup Farmers Market in Western Australia we discovered local farmers doing taste testing with consumers on new varieties of apples, a great way to engage the consumer.

## Create the experience

Consumers need more than just produce sellers. Consumers attend farmers' markets for the experience as well. They are looking for entertainment as well as food. They are also looking for education and one of the key performance indicators is how long the consumer lingers at the market. We are aware of markets where consumers just go to do the weekly shop and leave. However, there are other markets that become true local community hubs and tourist attractions, with locals and tourists spending half a day at the market and enjoying the experience.

One of the questions we are often asked is how often should a market be held.

We know towns that have two markets a week, weekly, two-weekly and monthly markets. Consumers buy weekly so they should have access to a market every week, two in the same week is overdoing it. Ideally the market should be in the same location and preferably in the town centre rather than a location outside of the retail hub.

In smaller communities we can see the logic in rotating the market around local towns. Remember farmers' markets are retailing experiences and the rules of retailing apply to the market. The following tips should be implemented by farmers' market managers to develop profitable retail skills by a farmers' market stallholder.

It was Tom Peters,[3] the American management guru, who is quoted as saying 'If you are still doing what you are doing now, in five years' time your business will be dead.' This is as true for farmers' markets as it is for other businesses. Retailing in farmers' markets is changing too.

## Who shops at farmers' markets?

Successful farmers' markets take a close look at who they are trying to attract. What do they look like? We do not mean how do they dress, but how old are they? In the western world, in marketing terms consumers are split into a number of generational marketing segments. These are:

- Spoodles: 0 to 5 year olds;
- Pester Power: 5 to 10 year olds;
- Generation Y/Millennials: born 1985 to 2004;
- Generation X: born 1965 to 1984;
- Jones Generation: born 1955 to 1964;
- Baby Boomers: born 1945 to 1955;
- Greying Tigers/Silent Generation: born 1925 to 1944.

Today, the generation with the most spending power in society in most countries is Generation X. The generation that is most price-conscious is the Greying Tigers. To be successful you need to appeal to Generation X upwards, but we have been to some farmers' markets where the average age of consumers has been in the sixties and they have had a desperate need to down-age their consumer profile. Farm market managers should research the age of the consumers in the catchment area and the age of potential tourists. They should then do a study of their own farmers' market consumers and question if they are the same percentages based on the local and visitor demographics. If not then some marketing needs to be done to attract the missing consumer group.

The ideal farmers' market consumer profile is a woman aged between 35 and 49, often with a college degree and with a household income of more than US$40,000 a year. In general retailing that profile is also the biggest spender and therefore an ideal target. A detailed profile of a farmers' market consumer can be obtained from 'A Profile of Farmers' Market Consumers and the Perceived Advantages of Produce Sold at Farmers' Markets'.[4]

## Setting up a farm stall at the market

Most farmers' markets charge a stall fee and a percentage of that fee goes to a marketing budget. As a general rule 2% of the market's turnover should be invested in marketing. Some of this should come from stallholders' fees and producers may also need to invest some money to promote their specific market stall.

The marketing aim of any market should be to get at least 20% new consumers into the market every time a market is held and this is where the culinary tourist becomes a major target market. If a market is not achieving that, the marketing is not working effectively and the long-term future of the farmers' market is very questionable.

The challenge for a market may not be to make a profit. It may be to down-age the consumer profile first and then make a profit. The challenge may be to look at how the market can:

- add value for the visitor experience;
- provide a quality experience for consumers;
- provide superior customer service; and
- make consumers feel comfortable at the market.

## Team effort

A farmers' market is a unique form of retailing. In other forms of retailing the business owner is in control of their own destiny with little influence from other retailers. In a farmers' market the standards set by everyone affect the profitability of each individual stallholder and the market in general.

Let us give you an example.

We were recently at a farmers' market that opened at 8 am and closed at 4 pm. At 3 pm there were stallholders who were closing their stores. As a result every stallholder's business in the market suffered. When we questioned why this was occurring, one participant said 'I have to go and feed the pigs.' When we mentioned that he was letting consumers and other stallholders down his reaction was the pigs were more important!

This sort of attitude towards retailing will affect every business in the market. A business owner is in control of their own destiny, but we do not think they have the right to affect other people's business destinies in a negative way. Farmers' markets that work well have ground rules and are operated as a team. Those that do not work effectively, have groups of individuals with stalls. As one person mentioned in a workshop, 'Why don't they close the market at 3 pm?' A logical conclusion, but alas management were not prepared to make that decision.

Farmers' market surveys carried out in the USA indicate stallholder sales per week can vary enormously. Figures can be as low as US$50 a week or as high as US$2500 a week per stall. A stallholder needs to make sure they participate at the winning markets.

## What makes a successful farmers' market?

Consumers are the ones who make a farmers' market successful or not. Visitors look for a location where they can park the car easily and find quality produce. But there is more to a successful market than that. Subconsciously, consumers make decisions on the following criteria:

**1.** Is the market compatible? This means is there the right mix of retailers based on the consumer's shopping habits? A supermarket nearby may be part of the compatibility mix in their mind as they still have to go shopping for those necessities that the market does not sell. A coffee shop may also fall into this bracket, but make sure the coffee is the best quality; a poor cup of coffee could be detrimental to persuading consumers to linger longer at a market.
**2.** Are the stalls complementary? Consumers expect to get all their food needs in one location. A butcher therefore complements a fruit seller. A successful market needs the butcher, fishmonger, baker, egg supplier and possibly an organic pet food supplier.
**3.** Can consumers comparison shop? Farmers may want to be the only stall owner who sells what they do, but consumers enjoy comparison shopping. They want to compare quality and price of the same produce. Having competitors who sell the same produce can be a plus for the overall market success.

In the research carried out by the Sustainable Food Center[5] in Texas, consumers mentioned that the core purpose of going to a farmers' market was for fruit and vegetables, but they would impulse spend on breads, jams, cheeses and other added value products.

They were prepared to spend between US$21 and US$50 during a 30 min stay at the market, but it must be within a 15 min car journey from home. Convenience is a key factor in a successful market.

Texas consumers also said they preferred a weekly Saturday market, 24.6% said it should be a morning market and 18% wanted an afternoon market.

Consumers visit a farmers' market for the experience and therefore the farm market brand is critical to the market's success. A brand is not a logo; it is not even what management say it is. It is about the people, experience and the whole package. A brand is a unique identification of the business from the consumers' perspective.

According to research carried out by Martin Lindstrom in 2005,[6] a customers' memorable journey is based on:

- Sight: 58% of those surveyed thought this was critically important;
- Smell: 45% of those surveyed thought this was critical;
- Sound: 41% thought this was important;
- Taste: 31% thought this was important;
- Touch: 25% thought this was important.

We must stress this research was carried out across a wide area of retailing. If it had been done in a farmers' market we expect that taste would have had a higher score. However, it does highlight how important all the elements of the senses are in creating the best experience for the visitor. The position of the baker and fishmonger can affect the total experience for the consumer.

## Market stall skills

Retail is detail and it is always the little things stallholders do that make the big differences. The following tips from our e-book '27 Ways to improve Your Farmers Market Stall'[7] are literally that; they are tips that can make a big difference to the bottom line.

### 1. Catch the wave
Farmers may not think they are in the fashion industry, but we would argue that they are.

Consumers want suppliers to be in tune with them, their desires, needs and to know what they feel is important. Producers have to put themselves in the shoes of a 35-year-old female consumer and ask what that shopper would want the supplier to do.

Waves are constantly rolling in, but are always changing.

They also come from some unexpected places, for example, 10 days before Christmas 2006 Jonathon Ross, a chat show host on UK evening television, introduced his guest Nigella Lawson, one of the UK's leading celebrity chefs. As he introduced her live on TV, he mentioned that when he was a child his mother roasted potatoes covered in goose fat and that he felt it was the best way to roast potatoes. He asked where he could get some goose fat.

The result of that one sentence was that farmers' markets were inundated over the next 10 days with consumers trying to buy goose fat. Those that had the product in stock experienced a sales increase of over 400%. That was a 10-day wave. It was an unexpected wave, but still a wave.

Waves can be based on:

- Yearly events such as Valentine's Day;
- charity causes;
- sports events;
- women's causes; and
- instant waves generated by broadcasters.

### 2. Branding is essential

Successful farmers' market stalls stand out from the crowd. We recently met a farm market stallholder in the USA, who gave us his business card and on it said he was 'the King of Corn'.

We asked what type of crown he wore at the market; he asked if we were serious. Of course we were. If you call yourself the 'King of Corn', you have an opportunity to stand out in the crowd and really get noticed. He felt he would look foolish wearing a crown; our reaction was that in that case he was using the wrong name to brand his business.

Successful producers make sure their dress code stands out from every other stallholder in the market. The aim is to be noticed and remembered. That is part of the rules of retailing and an integral part of the brand strategy.

Ideally the salesperson could match what they wear to what they sell. For example, if you sold corn you could wear a yellow shirt with a slogan on it, if it was strawberries a red shirt or, based on one we saw recently, a farmers' market stallholder selling tomatoes wore a red shirt with the slogan 'Red Plump and Juicy' written across it.

### 3. Name badges build trust

A farmers' market is part of 'experience retailing' and consumers want to get to know about the personalities at the market. They want to form a relationship. Research carried out by Shoppers Anonymous in Perth, Western Australia, shows that retailers who wear a name badge are perceived as providing 15% better customer service than those who do not wear a name badge.

Name badges for stallholders in farmers' markets should be compulsory. They can make so much difference to relationship-building with customers. Not every customer will be bothered about names, but others find it a nice touch and will want to use the team member's name. The name badge need only be the first name. The name should be in lower case and be in large enough type-face so customers can see it at a glance.

Local badge supply companies provide a range of different styles of name badges. Choose a style that suits the business and get at least three of each name done. It is guaranteed someone will lose their badge.

### 4. Brand the business in the sightline

Branding a farmers' market stall is something that is important. The business needs to get 'mind recognition' in the consumer's brain and this can only be achieved by maintaining a consistent image.

Everyone can describe a McDonald's hamburger outlet even if they have not been inside one. Consumers should be able to do the same concerning a farmers' market stall.

Where you place the business name is critical. Stallholders want the customer's eye to stop at the back of the stall. They do not want the eye to wander into the background, especially if the stall backs on to other stalls or shops. This backdrop position is an ideal place to promote the brand. It should not reflect the same style type as a supermarket, although it is equally as important to put the business branding in front of the customer.

This may be the company name or what the producer does. Pictures are stronger than words, ideally a stallholder should not make it look similar to the glossy photography that is now being used in supermarkets. Branding is equally important and should reflect the company's beliefs and style.

### 5. Three-benefits signs grow sales

Take a walk around a farmers' market the next time one is open and look at the signage. One of the easiest ways of increasing sales in a farmers' market is to change the way signs are written.

There has been a tremendous amount of research carried out into what signs work and what signs do not work. Alas, many farmers' market stall-holders assume consumers know more than they do. We were recently at a farmers' market and saw a sign that just said 'Yukon Gold'. Imagine how confused some consumers are when faced with Yukon Gold, Tomatillos, Daikon or Cassava and all they are told is the price.

In order to make a sale, a product sign should tell consumers the name of the product, three benefits and the price. Three benefits is enough; do not give any more information or consumers will become confused. The stallholder has less than 10 seconds for the consumer to take in the message of a sign.

Research indicates the sign should be written in lower case without joined up letters. It is easier for consumers to read that way. Do not write the sign in red ink as red is often associated with cheapness and that is the last message that should be portrayed to the consumer.

### 6. Tastings are essential

Having a tasting session at a farmers' market is one of those non-negotiable rules of retailing in this industry.

Research reported in our book *Just About Everything a Retail Manager Needs to Know*[8] showed that in the food industry 70% of consumers will sample food that is offered by a professional food demonstrator. If a business positions the demonstrator strategically next to the stall, 30% of those that taste will buy. That is an excellent conversion rate by anyone's standards. Tasting should start, from a consumer's perspective, about one-third of the way through a shopping experience. Therefore the location of a tasting stall in the market is critical. The consumer needs to take in the ambience of the market and feel comfortable before they start tasting.

The key is to not over-pressurize the taster. It is far better to locate the food for sale that is being tasted about 1 m (1 yard) away from the sample station. This gives the customer both thinking and breathing space and as a result sales should increase.

Apart from the tasting itself, this is a wonderful opportunity to engage the customer. By this very factor alone the farmer is able to show they are an expert and gain the confidence and trust of the consumer.

### 7. Retailing is about always being consistent

It does not matter if a producer is excellent or bad at what they do, they can still be successful. What annoys customers is inconsistency in standards. Customers want to feel comfortable with the business they are dealing with and its team; they can only feel comfortable if the producer is consistent at what they do.

Think about all the franchise companies out there. They all started as one site businesses, but they managed to multiply because they set a standard and then kept to it. They know that the formula for success is consistency.

How do they achieve that? They have checklists and they check standards all the time. They do this because they are aware that if they leave it to chance they will become store blind and miss the obvious things that the customer will pick up.

A successful farmers' market must have a checklist that sets the standard for all stallholders to abide by and organizers should be checking those standards every time the market opens.

Having said that, we would not recommend that it is left to chance. Every stallholder should have their own checklist that they use. Once they have finished building the stall, they should get the checklist out, give it to one of the team and get them to check the standards to ensure the company is providing a consistent standard. The following is an example of a checklist.

|  | YES | NO |
|---|---|---|
| STALL | | |
| Clean | | |
| Floor clean | | |
| Produce labelled | | |
| Waste bins empty | | |
| Linked sales obvious | | |
| Produce well displayed | | |
| Signage in place | | |
| Skirt clean | | |
| Litter-free zone | | |
| TEAM | | |
| Name badges on | | |
| Uniforms worn | | |
| POINT OF SALE | | |
| Change available | | |
| Bags ready | | |

### 8. Wear a skirt

We do not mean that your team has to wear a skirt, but we do believe that stalls should wear a skirt. Most stalls are created using pallets, crates, trestle tables and the like. This is normal practice and the easiest method available to create an instant shop.

The seller wants the customer to focus on what is on offer, not the framework of how the builder built the display. Therefore hide the building materials. The easiest way to do this is to install a skirt around the front and sides of the stall. It will improve the appearance enormously and make the stand look a lot more professional.

The skirt is part of the branding and may reflect the business colours. It can be made of cloth to enable it to be easily rolled up, washed and stored ready for the next stall-building session. Clip the skirt to the framework of the stall using table cloth clips as used by many outdoor restaurants.

### 9. Tell the tourist you are a local

**Fig. 4.4.** 'Buy Local' billboard on Vancouver Island, British Columbia, Canada.

Tourists love to buy and try new things from a local, especially when they are exposed to new culinary products. The key is communicating with the consumer.

Messages that work in a farmers' market include:

- 'New';
- 'Harvested today';
- 'Just arrived';
- 'These carrots were in the ground last night';

- 'Freshly harvested';
- 'In season now';
- 'Locally grown';
- 'Grown by me'.

The key is to develop 'action signs'. Signs focus the consumer and a call to action will increase the average sale per customer.

Do not smother the stall with this type of signage. Focus on one new produce item every time the stall is built. This creates a reason for the consumer to come back next week.

Farmers know they are local, but often the tourist does not know. The stall-holder may say it is obvious, but take a look around the market from a customer's perspective. Recently in the UK there were farmers from France with stalls and stall owners with Polish and German accents. The consumer had no idea who was a local. Stallholders need to tell the consumer via signage that they are a local farmer. Put up a picture of the farm as a form of reassurance to the consumer.

Food miles are becoming increasingly important and farmers can use food miles to provide a local message. For example:

- The supermarket cabbages have travelled 1000 miles; these cabbages travelled 10 miles from our farm.
- These carrots were still in the ground yesterday, they are local and they are fresh.

Do not assume the consumer knows who you are and where your farm is located.

### 10. Tilted displays increase sales

The aim is to present produce in the most eye-appealing way. Tilting the product towards the customer makes the product look more appealing. This is easy to achieve. All the retailer need to do is to raise the rear of the display using slats of wood, cardboard boxes or anything else that can do the trick. This is a simple technique that could increase sales per linear foot or metre.

### 11. The strategic positioning of red

Look at the colours in the fruit and vegetable department in a local super-market. The chances are, if the manager of the department is astute, produce such as red apples and red capsicum are positioned in the middle of the displays. This did not happen by chance – they were strategically positioned there.

As a producer of the product with a selection of green vegetables that were laid out along the full length of the display, the chances are that more are sold at the ends of the linear display and less in the middle. Consumers tend to purchase at the ends. The aim is to maximize sales along the whole shop fixture. Therefore red is used in the middle of the bench to attract the consumer and lift sales. Why red? Red has hidden messages in a consumer's mind. It can indicate danger, stop, passion or sexiness. Whatever the subliminal message, red stands out and attracts the eye to it. The aim is to draw the consumer's eye to the middle of the display. It works; give it a try on a stall.

Put a red product in the middle. If red product is not available, use a red drape or backing colour in the centre of the display to achieve the same result.

### 12. Indenting sells

People love to shop where they feel comfortable and hesitate to shop when they are not comfortable. If a consumer comes up and congratulates a retailer on a display and keeps walking, then the display has failed; the retailer did not engage the consumer. The key is to build the stall display and then spoil it, take a product away, make it looked 'shopped'; it makes consumers feel more comfortable to make a purchase rather than be the first.

When the majority of people go to a coffee shop to purchase a coffee and a slice of cake, they will select a slice from a cake where there has been a slice removed already. They feel someone has already taken a slice and therefore it is okay to select another slice. The cake where all the slices are still in place will be a slower moving cake until the first slice has been removed.

This is exactly the same in a market. This law of indenting applies to rounds of cheese and other items; build the display and then spoil it by 'removing a slice'.

### 13. Provide solutions and ideas

McDonald's do not sell hamburgers and Starbucks do not sell coffee. The consumer goes to the store for the core product, the hamburger or the coffee, the company representative's role is to then provide the solutions and ideas to make the relevant add-on sale. Why not sell the add-on herbs with the core produce? An example could be to promote a recipe book that has been produced by the farmer and local customers.

### 14. Provide simple cooking instructions

We visited our local market recently and visited the new butcher who sold quail eggs, crocodile meat, venison, kangaroo and ostrich meats. Great, interesting products, but what do you do with them, how do you cook them? The sales representative had not tried any of the produce on sale and was therefore unable to advise us.

If a consumer did purchase, the majority would go home and look in the recipe book under crocodile or go to Google and check on crocodile recipes. Wouldn't life be wonderful if the butcher offered a series of recipes himself for his favourite crocodile dishes?

The role of the stallholder is to provide solutions for the customer, not just sell produce and products. Stallholders need to provide their favourite solutions and ideas. Stallholders often assume too much when it comes to products. Stallholders could ask customers to provide their favourite recipes, which can be offered free to consumers during the year. At the end of the year the stallholder can combine all the recipes in a book and sell them back to his customers. Each recipe owner should be given credit for the recipe in the book and thereby make customers the heroes.

Keep recipes simple and easy to understand. The producer is the expert and should be providing the complete solution and ideas.

### 15. Newsletter

Every business in the world has to do some form of marketing to ensure it builds loyalty and gets new customers. The best form of traditional marketing that works in a farmers' market is a newsletter. In today's world, this can be the most effective marketing tool you can use. Ask customers for their e-mail address and then circulate the newsletter very cheaply.

The newsletter should go out weekly from the market. Keep the newsletter brief; if it takes longer than 7 minutes to read then it is too long for today's consumer and it will not be read. According to many retail gurus the best newsletter in the world comes from Trader Joe's,[9] the food retailer in the USA. Trader Joe's newsletter is a very casual newsletter and is an ideal model to use as a source of ideas. Another successful newsletter is from Farrington's Farm Shop in Somerset, UK. Farrington's newsletter[10] is produced along a similar style and works exceptionally well with their clientele.

Newsletters are an ideal marketing tool whose production can be delegated to a member of the team. It is important that someone is focused on producing the newsletter as it is such an important part of the business.

The following ideas will help construct the newsletter:

*   What is happening on the farm;
*   What produce is in season;
*   Stories on produce that are more unusual;
*   Topical news that affects the industry from a consumer's perspective;
*   Your favourite recipe;
*   Consumer profile of the newsletter;
*   Meet one of the team;
*   Customers' favourite recipes;
*   Positive market gossip.

You can also include an offer, i.e. bring the newsletter to the stall on 'x' day and receive a complimentary 'y'.

Customers love to read an entertaining, light-hearted newsletter, so make it fun. Once you have finished it, do get someone to proofread it before it goes out. The worst thing is a newsletter with spelling mistakes or bad grammar.

### 16. Do not put items in plastic bags

The world is going 'green' and shoppers expect farmers' markets to be 'green'. Many politicians around the world have joined the 'green' movement. This is not a fad; it is a trend that will not change for many years to come. Consumers are aware that they should be doing their bit to change their habits to help reduce the 'greenhouse' effect, and so should the market stallholders. In Ireland, for example, there is now a tax on plastic bags and in South Africa the plastic bag has been removed from shops in order to improve the country.

Portland, Oregon is one of the greenest cities in the world and has a recycling policy. Local farmers' markets should be following the guidelines of cities like Portland and become 'green' retailers. Consumers attend a farmers' market because they feel they should be green and support local communities and the environment. Market managers and stallholders owe it to them to be just as sensitive to the environment and to offer an alternative to the plastic bag. There are a number of alternatives on the market. Some retailers prefer hemp bags while others are using biodegradable bags that are made from tapioca or corn starch.

### 17. Network the market

The average British person at 4 pm has no idea what they will have as a meal that evening. This is an opportunity to sell them their evening meal. That may mean that a group of stall owners could get together and sell them the complete meal. Network marketing is an opportunity to sell the consumer a solution. Why not have the meal of the week where a group in the market promotes a specific meal based on produce available in the market. These products could be identified with a recipe that all the stall owners hand out, plus a special flag label on the specific produce to identify it. The opportunities to network within the market are exciting, but most markets tend to trade as a group of individuals and as a result they and the customer miss out on the opportunities.

Developing a network market, possible with a market loyalty card, would lock the customer into the market and create a unique marketing opportunity for the stall owners. To develop such a scheme all the stallholders concerned have to have confidence in each other and feel that all will benefit from such a campaign. It would need some planning, but the consumer would benefit and so would the market.

### 18. Promote TV and local chefs

Jamie Oliver, Rick Stein, Heston Blumenthal...the list goes on. Not only do these chefs have a national reputation, they now have a global reputation as the stars of food. Their books are sold around the world and their TV programmes are syndicated around the food channels of the world. They have a huge following. If you are a farmer selling anything that has been promoted recently on TV by celebrity chefs then you must tell the customer. All you need to say on a sign is 'As seen on TV' and you will have jogged the consumer's mind and sales will increase. This does mean that your team have to be watching the cooking programmes, and there are a lot of them out there. Share the watching of the programmes out between the team and have everyone report back on what should be promoted as a result of what has been mentioned on their selected programme.

Do not underestimate the power of the media. The media can be a powerful advocate for what you are doing and you need to be in tune with what consumers are watching.

## The threat to farmers' markets

Farmers' markets have had a wonderful few years of growth around the world. However, we should also consider what are the threats to farmers' markets in the future. These were summarized well by Max Coster and Nicole Kennon in *'New Generation' Farmer's Markets in Rural Communities.*[2] Coster and Kennon found the main threats are the following.

1. Maintaining grower commitment to the market.
2. Overcoming the lack of product diversity.
3. Achieving a year-around product range that fits in with the value of the market.
4. Securing the correct market infrastructure to ensure long-term viability.
5. Ensuring the funding is maintained.
6. Dealing with restrictions, especially in our view, food hygiene regulations.
7. Developing effective marketing strategies.

Supermarkets are aware of the impact farmers' market have had on their businesses; they have experienced a reduced market share. As a result we are aware of at least two supermarkets that have set up their own 'farmers' markets' to counteract this competition. In the early days of markets the 'big' end of town did not take farmers' markets seriously. Now they do and that could be the biggest threat to farmers' markets. Management teams in farmers' markets will have to be prepared for negotiating with large corporate companies in the future.

Farm market management committees cannot simply rely on the 'nostalgia' elements of farmers' markets; large supermarkets are learning to create the same experience for consumers, they have funds to spend on it and are learning quickly.

Farmers' markets are still one of the key ingredients of culinary tourism. A well-operated farmers' market can be a major tourist attraction and help promote other culinary events in the area as well as local shopping experiences. They can be the linchpin to develop food tourism in a region.

# Night Markets

Many Asian cities have night markets, which have become major culinary tourist destinations for locals and international visitors; these can be farmers' markets or sell a range of products, but are held in the cooler part of the day. Some of them can still be open at midnight. The idea is not unique to Asian cultures, the night market in the Dordogne in France is a major tourist attraction.

One of our favourite night markets is in Manila, the Philippines. Each region of the country has its own stand selling local food from that region. The region is clearly identified on the stand and the tourist can literally take a culinary journey around the market.

## General Food Markets

Not all farmers' markets are farmers' markets in the true sense, some offer a wider range of produce. One market that has to be mentioned in a book on food tourism is Borough Market (www.boroughmarket.org.uk) in London. Borough Market is a true tourist destination and a backdrop to many films and music videos. The market is located on Southwark Street in London. To reach it one needs to get off the Underground at London Bridge and then walk straight into the market.

This market was set up in 1276, although the locals will argue it was actually 1014. In 1754 it became so busy that there was an Act of Parliament to close the market. Once it was closed the locals set it up again down the road. The existing market was established in 1851 and is a great example of how food can become an iconic tourist attraction providing fresh food from producers around Europe.

Their webpage describes it best:

> Borough Market is London's most renowned food market; a source of exceptional British and international produce.
>
> It is a haven for anybody who cares about the quality and provenance of the food they eat – chefs, restaurateurs, passionate amateur cooks and people who just happen to love eating and drinking.
>
> But it's not just the sheer quality of the food on offer that makes Borough Market special – it is also about the people and the place.
>
> Start your visit by meeting our traders, find out about what's happening in the Market, take a look behind the stalls or sample the fine food.

Their magazine, *Life,* is one of the best newspaper-style market newsletters anywhere in the world. It provides quality articles on food, chefs and farmers involved in the market.

We all have our favourite markets. One that is a must-visit is La Boqueria in Barcelona, Spain. This city is famous for Gaudi, Picasso and Catalonian cuisine. One of the best places to experience that cuisine is at the markets halfway down the famous La Ramblas. This 13th-century market started outside the city walls, arriving at its present location in 1914. Many stallholders are now third and fourth generation.

## Christmas Markets

In recent years two of the fastest growing weekend vacation destinations in Europe in the month of December have been Germany and Prague in the Czech Republic; the Meccas of the Christmas markets. Many other towns around the world have also picked up the idea and Birmingham in the UK now has one of the biggest Christmas markets in Europe.

Christmas markets have bolstered the economy of many traditional businesses at what was traditionally a more quiet time of the year. The markets sell gifts and a wide range of items but local food is also an important element of the Christmas markets.

Hot mulled wine is one of the essential ingredients of a European market. This can be accompanied by almond cake, gingerbread and trdlo (grilled rings of sweet bread dipped in ground almonds and sugar). Local chestnuts are often roasted as is a pig placed on a spit along with local sausages. Many local producers will also make up food hampers full of local foods and gifts.

## The best Christmas markets in Germany

### Dresden Striezelmarkt
This is Germany's oldest Christmas market. It started in 1434 and is where the traditional Stollen cake comes from. A 3500 kg cake is made and cut into pieces and slices are sold.

### Lübeck Christmas market
This town is known as the marzipan capital in Germany. The Lübeck market started in 1648 and takes place at the medieval Heiligen-Gelst Hospital.

### Rothenburg Christmas market – Reiterlesmarkt
This market is considered one of the most romantic Christmas markets in Germany.

## Community Gardens

> I'm a big believer in community gardens both because of their beauty and for their access to providing fresh fruits and vegetables to so many communities across the nation and the world.
>
> Michelle Obama

Community gardens are starting to be promoted alongside farmers' markets as a food tourism activity. A community garden is where local residents set up a garden to provide food for themselves and their neighbours. Many would argue the largest community garden in the world is in Havana, Cuba where the food economy over many years has relied on organic community gardening. The system seems to work as the average Cuban lives as long as the average American and Cuba does not have a health care system that would compare with their near neighbour, the USA.

The value of community gardens in Cuba was highlighted in the 2006 documentary, The Power of Community: How Cuba survived Peak Oil. After the fall of the Soviet Union in 1990 Cubans developed community gardens when oil imports halved.

John was raised in Birmingham in a terrace house where the only way to garden was to apply for an allotment. These allotments were where locals could grow their own food on land that was owned by the council. Over time the allotment became less desirable; home owners started their own gardens, originally dedicating a part of the garden to food production. But as people

**Fig. 4.5.** Kalamunda Community Garden, Perth, Western Australia, was developed in 2013 as a community project.

became more affluent and time poor, they dedicated more of their garden to ornamental plant growing.

We have now come almost full circle; more and more city people are moving to apartments with no gardens and having to rely either on local retailers to provide them with fresh food or to grow their own in community gardens... the modern allotment.

Community gardens are now a common feature in urban communities around the world. They are still often on council land, but are managed by enthusiastic locals who care about growing their own food.

Community gardens can be split into four different types of gardens:

- Neighbourhood Community Gardens: these are a development of the traditional allotment;
- School Gardens: as this suggests, gardens developed to educate school children on food production;
- Blooming Branches: this is a programme developed in Illinois, where the local libraries provide a venue for a series of garden talks;
- The Green Youth Farm Program: this is another American initiative where students can learn about organic farming and then sell their produce at a farmers' market.

In 1979 the American Community Gardening Association (www.communitygarden.org) was founded to recognize that community gardens in the USA improved people's lives and were a catalyst for neighbourhood development. They were also recognized as a means of reducing the family food budget and creating an opportunity for education.

In Australia there is the Australian City Farms and Community Gardens network (http://communitygarden.org.au).

'The Kitchen Garden Foundation'[11] developed by Stephanie Alexander, a celebrity chef in Australia, has proved to be highly successful in getting schools engaged in fruit and vegetable gardening. This initially started in the State of Victoria schools, but has now gone nationwide.

To find out how to develop community gardens we recommend *Local Food, How to Make it Happen in Your Community*.[12] In this book the authors introduce the seven principles required to set up a successful Local Food Movement. Their seven principles are the following.

1. A group with positive vision.
2. The garden should help people access good information and assistance.
3. Include all local people and have openness.
4. Enable sharing and networking.
5. Build resilience.
6. It is a safe place for sharing.
7. The garden is organized and decision making is taken at the appropriate levels.

## Open Kitchen Gardens

In Richard Benfield's book *Garden Tourism*,[13] he states that garden visits are an increasingly popular tourist activity with more Americans today going on garden visits than to the Disney vacation spots and Las Vegas. Private gardens open to the public around the world are often in the Open Garden Scheme of participating countries. Culinary tourists should look out for Open Kitchen Gardens, these are private gardens open at selected times to the public that are dedicated to food production.

The top kitchen gardens to visit in the world[14] include:

1. Patrenella's, Houston, Texas.
2. Chez Painisse, Berkley, California.
3. Filk, Warsaw, Poland.
4. De Kas, Amsterdam, the Netherlands.
5. L'atellier de Jean-Luc Rabanel, Arles, France.
6. Chateau de la Bourdaisiere, Loire Valley, France.
7. Tangerine Dream Cafe, London.
8. Petersham Nurseries, London.
9. Longueville House, Mallow, Ireland.
10. Silvertree, Cape Town, South Africa.

## Victorian Walled Gardens and Potagers

The ultimate food garden for many people to visit is the Victorian-style walled garden. The walled garden was traditionally part of a large country estate.

The wall was a protection from weather and wildlife and the food for the county house was grown within the four walls. Victorian walled gardens had their own staff and the head gardener was one of the most important people on the estate.

During the most part of the 20th century Victorian walled gardens fell to ruin. This was partly because gardeners were sent to fight in the two world wars and partly due to the high cost of maintaining the estate and the garden.

The walled garden had a revival in the 1980s due to the BBC TV programme and book *The Victorian Kitchen Garden*.[15] Where possible, walled gardens were restored in the UK as tourist attractions; these included West Dean in Sussex, Heligan in Cornwall and Chilton Foliat in Berkshire.

In France, the same style kitchen garden is called a potager and built along similar lines as kitchen gardens in the UK. Many chateaux still have a well-kept potager and these are major tourist attractions.

The French potagers have had intermingled vegetables, fruits, flowers and herbs since medieval times. Potagers are more popular than ever in France; a government survey taken in 1994 revealed that 23% of the fruit and vegetables consumed by the French are home-grown.

In France today, the potager, often called the *jardin de curé*, or country curate's garden, has an informal or romantic design. Its inspiration is a complicity with nature rather than a desire to impose order, and this fashion has been fed by the growing influence of organic gardening in France over recent decades.

## Urban Orchards/Community Orchards

Most people's impressions of a community garden is that it is a plot of land situated in suburbia where the locals raise fruit and vegetables.

The UK is well known for its orchards growing a range of different fruits, yet 90% of the fruit consumed in the UK comes from outside the country. One of the results of this is a decline in fruit growing in counties such as Wiltshire where they have lost 95% of their orchards in the last 40 years.

One result of this decline is that urban or community orchards are increasing in popularity.

Urban orchards in city centres are growing in popularity. One example of this is the Perth, Western Australia Urban Orchard in the city centre. The main cultural precinct in Perth does not have ornamental flower beds and trees, it has an urban orchard. The petunias have been replaced by kale and the plane trees by apple trees. During the busy lunch-time period city workers have their lunch surrounded by an urban orchard. Local residents maintain the garden and this is a real example of bringing fresh food to the community, it cannot get fresher. Vandalism has also declined.

**Fig. 4.6.** The fruit and vegetable garden created in the Cultural Centre Precinct in central Perth, Western Australia.

In Nelson, New Zealand, The Open Orchard Project[16] aims to plant, tend and harvest fruits from trees in public places. This was established in 2008 and now has over 40 active members.

In Bohemia and Moravia in what is now the Czech Republic, toward the end of 19th century the government introduced a programme of improvement of nourishment and raising welfare of the community by a supported planting of fruit trees and care of them along roadways. Tourists can still travel the roads of the Czech Republic and pick fruit from roadside trees.

## Foraging

Many older readers may remember going out into the countryside on an autumn weekend and picking wild blackberries or other fruit from hedgerows. This is foraging, and it has been done for generations in autumn in Spain, France and Italy to collect wild mushrooms.

Foraging may now be trendy, but it was the way many cultures fed themselves in the past. In 1424 Aeneas Sylvius, Pope Pius the Second visited Scotland and reported that the locals peeled the bark of the pine trees and used the inner bark to make bread; Lapps were making bark bread up until the last century. The American slippery elm, *Ulmus rubra*, kept early settlers alive in America and herb products are still sold based on this tree.

Collecting and eating plants from the wild is once again increasing in popularity and can take place in any season and in almost any rural location including the beach, where seaweed can be collected as food.

In many countries nuts were the easiest to forage. Cobnuts or filberts were harvested as were hazel followed by sweet chestnut (*Castanea sativa*) in temperate climates, and the Romans ground them and called the flour polenta.

The key to foraging is the harvester must know what they are picking. For example there are numerous poisonous mushrooms that look very similar to edible mushrooms. In countries such as Hungary, once a harvester has picked the mushrooms they are encouraged to take them to the local market where they can be inspected for free by a government inspector to make sure they are edible.

In Australia the term 'Bush Food' is used to describe wild food. The local aborigines have a far better understanding of the food in the bush than most settlers and it is advised that tourists forage with a local expert.

The latest trend is urban foraging, where tourists can forage in cities such as downtown New York or London.

Television programmes such as Valentine Warner's 'What to Eat Now'[17] in the UK and celebrity chefs such as Jamie Oliver have promoted local edible delights that can be found on a community's doorstep.

### London's hunter-gatherers

A growing number of groups, including Abundance (www.abundancelondon.com) and Hackney Harvest (http://hackneyharvest.com), are promoting free, pick-it-yourself forays, with maps of fruit trees in the area to start locals off foraging in the city. Nick Saltmarsh, who was the chef at Le Gavroche in London, now organizes one day Food Safaris[18] in central London.

### New York's hunter-gatherers

'Wildman' Steve Brill (www.wildmanstevebrill.com) provides 4 h foraging walks around central New York.

Ava Chin[19] writes a blog and articles for the *New York Times* on foraging opportunities in the city.

### Sydney's hunter-gatherers

In Sydney, Australia, 'scrumpers'[20] search for herbs and berries that thrive in the sunny, coastal climate. Diego Bonettoa, a local naturalist, leads foraging excursions in and around the city.

## Providores/Specialist Food Retailers

It's really exciting to find out what makes a good shop tick.

Rick Stein

**Fig. 4.7.** Gourmet food shop in northern Italy.

**Fig. 4.8.** Specialist mushroom retailer at Orta S Giulio, Italy.

Providores are literally providers, although the term is used extensively for the providers of fresh produce. Many growers will select the retailers that they want to distribute their produce and as a result these shops can become tourist attractions for the foodie tourist as these retailers become recognized as 'gourmet' retailers.

These tourist attractions are generally not owned by growers or farmers, but by independent retailer operators who purchase food through the normal distribution channels. They often label the produce to tell the consumer the exact location of where the produce came from and some promote the growers as well as the location.

These stores are normally exceptionally well designed by retail design consultants to encourage the consumer to explore and spend time discovering new produce. As a result the impulse sales are often far higher than in most traditional food outlets.

A number of books have been written on gourmet retail outlets and two we recommend are:

- *Fabulous Food Shops* by Jane Peyton[21]; and
- *Gourmet and Specialty Shops* by Martin M. Pegler.[22]

Speciality food stores that should be visited as a tourist include the following, which comprise our top ten:

- Andronico's Market, Danville, California;
- Borough Market, London;
- Falorni, Greve, Italy... plus many more in Italy;
- Food Emporium, New York;
- Fortnum and Mason Food Hall, London;
- Harrods Food Hall, London;
- Kowalski's, Woodbury, Minnesota;
- Nature's Northwest, Portland, Oregon;
- Whole Foods Stores in USA;
- Zagara's, Jenkintown, Pennsylvania.

## References

[1] Farmers Market Federation of New York (2005) 10 Principles of a Successful Market. Available at: http://extension.psu.edu/search?SearchableText=10+principles+of+a+successful+market&x=0&y=0 (accessed 22 February 2014).

[2] Coster, M. and Kennon, N. (2005) 'New Generation' Farmer's Markets in Rural Communities. RIRDC Publication No 05/109, USA.

[3] Peters, T. and Waterman, H.R. (1982) *In Search of Excellence*. Profile Business, USA.

[4] Wolf, M. McGarry, Spittler, A. and Ahern, J. (March 2005) A Profile of Farmers' Market Consumers and the Perceived Advantages of Produce Sold at Farmers' Markets. *Journal of Food Distribution Research* 36(1).

[5] Sustainable Food Center in Texas. Central Texas Foodshed Assessment. Available at: www.sustainablefoodcenter.org/about/Central%20Texas%20Foodshed%20Assessment_English.pdf (accessed 22 February 2014).

[6] Lindstrom, M. (2005) *Brand Sense, Sensory Secrets Behind the Stuff We Buy*. Crown Publishing.

[7] Stanley, J. (2009) 27 Ways to Improve your Farmers' Market Stall. E-book from John Stanley Associates webpage (www.johnstanley.com.au).

[8] Stanley, J. (2003) *Just About Everything a Retail Manager Needs To Know*. Lizard Publishing, Australia.

[9] Trader Joe's newsletter: www.traderjoes.com/soapbox.asp (accessed 22 February 2014).

[10] Farrington's Farm Shop. Available at: www.farringtons.co.uk/about/news (accessed 22 February 2014).

[11] Kitchen Garden Foundation: www.kitchengardenfoundation.org.au/about-us (accessed 22 February 2014).

[12] Pinkerton, T. and Hopkins, R. (2009) *Local Food, How to Make it happen in Your Community*. Transition Guides, Silver Spring, Maryland.

[13] Benfield, R.W. (2013) *Garden Tourism*. CAB International, Wallingford, UK.

[14] *National Geographic*. Food Journeys of a Lifetime, Extraordinary Places to eat Around the Globe.

[15] Davies, J. (1987) *The Victorian Kitchen Garden*. BBC Books, UK.

[16] The Open Orchard Project, Nelson, New Zealand. Available at: www.stuff.co.nz/nelson-mail/features/lifestyle/going-green/3776317/Free-fruit-and-nuts-for-all-to-enjoy (accessed 22 February 2014).

[17] What to Eat Now, Valentine Warner TV Programme. Available at: www.bbc.co.uk/programmes/b00lpbxs (accessed 22 February 2014).

[18] Food Safaris in London, UK. Available at: www.edibleexperiences.com/p/608062/Food-Safari/1002/A-Taste-of-the-Wild (accessed 22 February 2014).

[19] Ava Chin, New York Times Blogger: www.avachin.com/tag/urban-forager (accessed 10 February 2014).

[20] Sydney 'Scrumpers'. Available at: www.smh.com.au/news/entertainment/good-living/ripe-for-the-scrumping/2009/11/30/1259429332120.html (accessed 11 February 2014).

[21] Peyton, J. (2005) *Fabulous Food Shops*, 5th edn. John Wiley & Sons, West Sussex, UK.

[22] Pegler, M.M. (2001) *Gourmet and Specialty Shops*. Visual Reference Publications, New York.

## Websites

Abundance: www.abundancelondon.com (accessed 22 February 2014).

American Community Gardening Association: https://communitygarden.org (accessed 22 February 2014).

Australian City Farms and Community Gardens Network: http://communitygarden.org.au (accessed 22 February 2014).

Borough Market, London: www.boroughmarket.org.uk (accessed 22 February 2014).

Dresden Striezelmarkt: www.dresden.de/striezelmarkt

Hackney Harvest: http://hackneyharvest.com (accessed 22 February 2014).

Lübeck Christmas market: www.luebecker-weihnachtsmarkt.de

Polyface Farms in Swoope, Virginia: www.polyfacefarms.com

Rothenburg Christmas market – Reiterlesmarkt: www.rothenburg.de

Wildman Steve Brill, New York: www.wildmanstevebrill.com (accessed 15 February 2014).

# 5 Agri-Entertainment or Agri-Tourism

> I want the family farm, the backbone of our country's heritage – to thrive and survive for future generations.
>
> Jane Eckert, Agri-tourism Marketing Professional, USA

## Introduction

Agri-entertainment or agri-tourism is basically entertainment on the farm, which may or may not include a culinary element in the tourist offer. Agri-tourism is one of the fastest growing tourism activities in the USA and Canada and is now being developed by progressive farmers around the world. In California alone 2.4 million people visited agri-tourism sites in 2008.[1]

It is estimated that over 87 million Americans visited a farm in the USA, 20 million of these were children under the age of 16. This means there are huge opportunities for agri-tourism ventures, but where do you start? One valuable guide is 'Promoting Tourism in Rural America'.[2]

In many countries there is a lack of comprehensive database research on agri-tourism and all the research comes from the USA. Even in the USA over half of the agri-tourism ventures did not exist 10 years ago.

The definition of agri-tourism as defined by the University of California[1] is 'a commercial enterprise at a working farm, ranch or agricultural plant conducted for the enjoyment or education of visitors, that generates supplemental income for the owner.'

This means that farm shops and farmers' markets that are primarily retail do not actually fall into this definition, although some authorities do include retailing as an agri-tourism function.

The majority of agri-tourism activities included in reports are:

- Hosting school trips, 51% of agri-tourism activity;
- U Pick or Pick Your own;
- On-farm tours and classes;
- Fairs and festivals on the farm;
- Pumpkin Patches; October is the biggest month in USA for agri-tourism;
- Weddings;
- Youth camps;
- Orchard dinners;
- Barn dances;
- Hunting and fishing.

The objectives of agri-tourism, and therefore the support by government in the USA and Canada, is for six main reasons.[3]

**1.** Long-term investment in future generations of farmers who will carry on historical family traditions.
**2.** Conserve prime farmland for farming.
**3.** Preserve valuable resources so that future generations will have access to the same natural wonders.
**4.** Promote sustainable growth.
**5.** To encourage innovation by farmers.
**6.** Give character to a region or farm that sets it apart.

The Californian research[1] shows that a farm needs to be near to a city of a minimum population of 10,000 to participate in recreational activities. According to research carried out in South Carolina, half the trips are made within a 300 mile radius and one-third within a 150 mile radius.

The consumer drivers for agri-tourism are:[4]

- Convenience;
- Diversity of the attraction;
- The opportunity to purchase value added products on one site.

Samantha Gross identifies these key trends.[5] Agri-tourism is becoming so popular because of:

**1.** Increased travel by cars.
**2.** Desire for new and different experiences.
**3.** Short trips planned at the last minute.
**4.** Strengthening of family relationships.

Many farm communities are now ready to develop agri-tourism. Success is often based on marketing around a 'hero' product or facility on the farm. The Garlic Farm in the Isle of Wight, UK, is a model of what can be achieved.

## Promotion by farmers in the USA

The research carried out by Ellen Rilla at the University of California[1] indicates that agri-tourism ventures promoted themselves as follows with the following results:

- 97% response from word of mouth;
- 81% response from signage outside farm;
- 78% webpage;
- 76% business cards handed out;
- 63% newspapers;
- 63% agricultural promotions;
- 55% paid advertising;
- 46% chamber of commerce;
- 39% visitor bureau;
- 39% direct mail;
- 32% newsletter.

The same report asked farmers why they wanted to participate in agri-tourism and the results were as follows:

1. Economic competition with corporate farms encouraged them to diversify.
2. Extra earnings as basic farming did not cover operational costs.
3. Direct sales to the consumer were more profitable.
4. A means of promoting the farm and its unique features.

## Impact on farms

California Agri-tourism Operations at the University of California[1] looked at the economic impact of agri-tourism on the farming community. They found the following:

- It supplements the farm production activities;
- Provides full employment of farm assets;
- Farms engaged in agri-tourism employed more local people and created jobs.

Note: In California in 2007 agri-tourism generated US$35million in revenue.
In summary, according to the University of California research,[1] the main benefits of agri-tourism are as follows:

- Experience: the success of agri-tourism is based on a farm that has a history and provides a unique farm experience;
- Land stewardship: conservation of natural resources;
- Partnerships: new found opportunities for partnering with government entities for the improvement of the community;
- Self-pride: agri-tourism promotes the region and helps agricultural heritage.

When it comes to the culinary tourist and agri-tourism we can split the market into two groups: (i) connoisseurs who know about food and are looking for a 'true' food experience; and (ii) those that want a day in the country and who would not classify themselves as foodies but are interested in the farm experience. The majority of the population would fall into the second group.

This group needs more than the food experience; they need to be entertained on the farm and during that experience hopefully they will learn more about local food production. This is where agri-entertainment comes into its own.

## Target market

The key target market is young families and therefore the facility needs to be child friendly, but what exactly does that mean? Penrith City Council[6] in the UK developed a child friendly strategy for the city and their guidelines also work for farmers:

- Engagement – utilizing a range of activities to engage with children directly;
- Health and wellbeing – emphasizing the importance of fun and engaging activities, and services and places that are accessible to children;
- Safety – including fostering positive attitudes towards children;
- Personal development – focusing on stimulating, interactive environments where there is a range of opportunities for free and independent play on the farm;
- Community development – including the importance of strong connections with local communities and schools;
- The farm is a place where children can engage in healthy and active play;
- Children are independently mobile and able to move safely around a designated farm area;
- The farm provides opportunities for exploratory and imaginative play;
- Children have access to nature, the farm and green spaces;
- It is a safe and secure environment for children, which also reduces the stress of parents.

## Agri-Entertainment Activities

Entertainment on the farm can either be a year-round activity, seasonal or 1- or 2-day events. Year-round events need to be covered as usual business activity and be planned with the local government as per any business activity.

More and more farms are being used for short period events and these events need to be organized well in advance.

When budgeting for an event the following need to be considered:

- Public liability insurance;
- A temporary event notice;

- A premises licence;
- Site costs;
- Infrastructure;
- Sanitary provisions;
- Security;
- First aid;
- A health and safety consultant;
- Car parking on site;
- Vehicle access to the site.

Cornwall Council[7] in the UK have prepared an excellent guide to traffic management when holding an event and this is a valuable guide for all event organizers.

## Traffic management for large events

Event organizers will need to draw up a traffic plan, a failure to do so means that an event may be cancelled.[7] When an event takes place near the highway it is normally the responsibility of the event organizer for public safety.

A traffic management plan will need to consider the issues below.

### Location

- How will visitors get to the event, e.g. bus, coach, train, walk, cycle, car?
- How will you organize traffic control on the roads to the site and on the site itself?

### Roads, public rights of way

- Which roads and paths may be affected by the event traffic?
- Will they be able to accommodate the extra traffic from the event without causing delays?
- How will the organizer deal with breakdowns or collisions on the roads leading to the event site?
- Will there be a need to apply for any road closures?

### Road closures

It is normal if road closure for the event is required to allow at least 3 months for an application to be processed.

- Identify which roads or sections of the road will need to be closed;
- Where will traffic be diverted?
- Are temporary traffic lights required?
- Will the closure clash with any road works or other activity on the roads near the event?

### Directional signage

Directional signs will be required on the highway if there will be a large number of drivers visiting the event who are unfamiliar with the area or if specific routing is needed.

- What directional signage will be used and where?
- What will the signs say?
- Who will erect and maintain the signs? This will normally have to be done by an accredited contractor with appropriate public liability insurance.

### *Public transport*

- Will the organizer need to contact public transport operators to see if extra buses or trains with more carriages can be arranged?
- Will the organizer need to arrange free buses?
- Will the event need park and ride or park and walk facilities?

### *Car park closures*

- Will any car parks need to be closed to traffic because they are being used as event venues?
- What alternative parking is available?
- What arrangements will be made to replace any disabled parking spaces if a car park has to be closed?

### *On-street parking*

- Does on-street parking need to be restricted to allow better access to the event site?

### *Parking*

- What parking is available for organizers, visitors and emergency services at the event site?
- Is there enough car parking on site for the number of visitors you are expecting?
- How will the organizer deal with breakdowns that block access to parking?

## On-Farm Entertainment Activities

The list of activities that can be operated on the farm is endless and we cannot cover all the activities in this book. If you can think of an idea, we will guarantee that a farmer has tried it somewhere in the world.

In 1969, Max Yasgur was a dairy farmer in Bethel near White Lake, New York. He probably invented the most famous agri-entertainment of all time. He held Woodstock, the music concert that changed the music world and a generation.

In 1970, Michael Eavis, a farmer in Pilton, Somerset, UK also decided he would do the same thing and the Glastonbury Festival is still a highlight on many UK concert-goer's calendars. We are sure neither farmers believe they are in agri-entertainment, but they are two of the founding fathers and many farmers have learned of the opportunities from these two entrepreneurs.

Concerts on the farm are now a feature in many countries, but most farm entertainment is more easy to plan and manage.

## Petting zoo or animal farm

Animals are always an attraction for children, especially young farm animals. Young children love to pet them and it starts to give children an understanding of what actually happens on the farm.

In recent years *E. coli* has been a scare in farm petting locations and this is bound to be raised again in the future. It is recommended that children under the age of 5 should not pet farm animals and that older children should scrub and wash their hands when they leave the farm. The farm should provide these facilities to ensure they stay within the guidelines of local regulations. The main problem is gastroenteritis in humans due to the bacteria *Salmonella* and *Campylobacter* and the protozoan parasite *Cryptosporidium* that are carried by animals. The main way humans get gastroenteritis is by handling animals and then putting their fingers to their mouths.

This can be overcome and the farm must supply hand sanitization points and suitable signage advising visitors to wash their hands before and after they have petted animals. Farmers are now providing mobile petting farms that visit schools, parties and farmers' markets. In this situation where washing facilities may not be available, then provide a 70% alcohol-based hand rub or gel to clean hands after handling the animals.

### Signage at petting farms
Look at the movement of visitors and erect signage with public health advice in locations where they will be seen. These include:

- The entrance of the farm;
- Entrances and exits of petting area; and
- Entrances to designated eating areas.

The following should be on the sign:

- Wash hands thoroughly after touching or visiting animals;
- Wash hands thoroughly before eating, drinking or smoking;
- Eat or drink in designated areas only;
- Hand washing facilities are located at XXXXX.

The sign should finish on a positive note and say:

- We hope you enjoy your visit;
- The above advice is in the interest of your health.

Farmers should not be put off by these restrictions; children love to go to the farm and pet animals. Nothing is as memorable as children seeing their first lamb or stroking farm animals.

## The maze – or is it maize?

The word maze is said to have originated in the 13th century when elaborate living jigsaw puzzles were developed as an elaborate plant arrangement using yew (*Taxus baccata*) to entertain guests at stately homes. When they reached the centre of the jigsaw the guest was said to be 'amazed' and this is where the term maze originated.

A maze should not be confused with a labyrinth, they are two totally different things. A maze has a complex of branching routes to give the traveller a choice of routes whilst a labyrinth is a non-branching route.

Mazes or plant labyrinths have been around a long time. Remains have been recorded in ancient Egyptian and Greek culture.

The mazes used by farmers to 'amaze' their guests tend to be mainly constructed from maize plants, a maize maze. Where the mazes you see at the stately homes of Europe took years to mature, the farmers' maize is grown in a season and the next year a new labyrinth can be planned. The farm maze originated in the USA as an agri-entertainment feature on the farm, and is especially popular at Halloween. Organizations now exist to help farmers develop elaborate maize mazes that can be changed yearly to provide the visitor with a different experience.

*Valuable contacts*
UK: The Maize Maze Association: www.maize-maze.com
USA: Corn Mazes America: www.cornmazesamerica.com

## The pumpkin patch

In the USA, think of October and many culinary tourists think of Halloween and pumpkins. This is one of the few times that many Americans actually think about visiting a farm. The pumpkin patch is a major tourist draw in many states. Farms have developed pumpkin activities to include Pick Your Own pumpkins, Halloween festivals based on the pumpkin, pumpkin carving, pumpkin recipes and autumn festivals. Pumpkin festivals on farms in the USA celebrate the harvest season and are now big business for many farmers.

Competitions are also held to see who can grow the biggest pumpkin and these events often get major local and national media cover.

*Spookley....The Square Pumpkin*
Spookley started life in New York State, and was created by children's author and lyricist Joe Toriano when his young son Nicholas wanted a bedtime story about pumpkins. Spookley can now be found in farms in Ireland, UK and across the Americas (www.spookley.com).

The story of Spookley is that he is the only square pumpkin in the field and gets bullied because he is different to all the round pumpkins in the

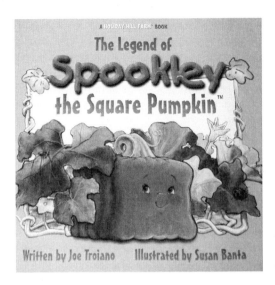

**Fig. 5.1.** The Legend of Spookley the Square Pumpkin – farm books have been written to help develop the marketing campaign.

field. Then one night there is a big storm when all the round pumpkins get blown by the wind and roll towards a hole in the fence at the edge of the field and a cliff. Spookley the square pumpkin reaches the gap in the fence first and because he is square he is able to block the hole and save all the round pumpkins. This is the outline of the Spookley story, which is available in book form and as a Disney-produced TV programme for children. The author of Spookley joined forces with Holiday Hill Farm in New York State and a number of farm activities and merchandise are now offered under the brand. Spookley's story is used to help prevent bullying at schools and has resulted in him being the 'Official Spokes-Pumpkin' for National Bullying Prevention Month in October in the USA.

How does Spookley fit into food tourism?

Licensed Spookley farmers and garden centres engage with their local school to help prevent bullying, especially in the autumn when the pumpkin crop is ready. This creates a tourism opportunity revolving around one product that is attractive to children and helps a cause close to many people's values. In the USA 100% of the sales of 'Dare to be Square' shirts from the month of October goes to PACER's National Bullying Prevention Center.

Spookley allows farmers to interact with visitors by developing story times, interactive activities and exposing them to a seasonal food. It introduces new consumers to food tourism as well as entertaining and educating consumers.

### Lavender farms

Lavender may not be considered by many as a food crop, but it is used in making tea and the flowers can be used in cooking as well as many other herbal products. Lavender farms are temperate climate enterprises. The Australian Lavender Growers Association (www.talga.com.au) has set up a lavender tourist trail that stretches across the country. Tourists can also go to the lavender fields at Xuelangshan in Jiangsu Province in China. The advocates will tell you that if you are looking for the best or 'fine' lavender the place to visit is Provence in France where lavender grows wild as well as cultivated.

Provence, France in July and August has lavender roads and lavender festivals, the key festivals being:

- La fête de la lavande in Valensole;
- La lavande en fête in Esparron-du-Verdon;
- La fête de la lavande et du miel in Riez (lavender and honey);
- Les journées lavande in Digne-les-Bains;
- La fête de la lavande in Barrême;
- La fête de la lavande in Thorame basse.

Lavender is a good example of how one product can be developed into a key tourist attraction. In this book we talk about 'heros'. Lavender has its own hero with an interesting story.

The story starts at Bridestowe Lavender Estate (www.bridestowelavender.com.au) in northern Tasmania where they developed 'Bobbie the Bear', a microwaveable bear that turns into an aromatic hot-water bottle. Bobbie the bear became a hot accessory for Chinese model and actress Zhang Xinyu who endorsed his qualities on Facebook. Bridestowe received over 45,000 orders for Bobbie and was unaware of what was causing the influx. The team at the farm tells of busloads of Chinese each leaving with a bear, and tears when they find they are unable to buy more for friends and family.

'He's now the must-have object in southeast Asia,' Mr Ravens the farm owner said. 'Every lady under 30 wants one'. Bridestowe has put on four extra staff to help hand-stuff the bears, believed to be the only ones in the world containing fine lavender. Adding value and using the Internet as a major marketing tool, sometimes the success can come before the farmer knows what is happening as is the case with 'Bobbie the Bear'. This story highlights the opportunity that can occur to many products sold in the food tourism category.

## Herb gardens

Herb gardens have received a popularity boost in recent years. The sale of herbs in garden centres has increased with the surge in edible landscaping. Herbs and spices grow in all the countries involved with food tourism and herb gardens are a popular food tourist destination. Many locations have a herb festival and it is a festival where the community can get involved as many gardeners grow herbs.

In 1991 the International Herb Association[8] launched 'Herb of the International Herb Week'. The herbs that have reached International status are:

- 1995 Fennel;
- 1996 Monarda;
- 1997 Thyme;
- 1998 Mint;
- 1999 Lavender;
- 2000 Rosemary;
- 2001 Sage;
- 2002 Echinacea;
- 2003 Basil;
- 2004 Garlic;
- 2005 Oregano and marjoram;
- 2006 Scented geraniums;
- 2007 Lemon balm;
- 2008 Calendula;
- 2009 Bay laurel;
- 2010 Dill;
- 2011 Horseradish;
- 2012 Rose;
- 2013 Elderberry;
- 2014 Artemisia;
- 2015 Savory.

## Tea plantations

Think of tea plantations and the mind goes to terrace fields in Sri Lanka or India. Tea, *Camellia sinensis,* will grow in many parts of the world. In Western Australia there is one plantation; an example of a grower being an entrepreneur and developing a product line that is different and the potential to create a tourist attraction.

## Birthday parties

We have one farmer client in the UK who went into providing children's birthday parties. He tells us it is the most profitable venture he has ever been involved with. Birthday parties used to be at a child's house and then many moved off site to places like McDonald's. Parents today seek out more unique venues and the farm can be the unique venue they are looking for.

A barn can be converted into a dedicated birthday venue and a farm team can put a birthday package together that includes everything from the cake to the party trimmings. A farm team can also introduce unique features such as a hayride and petting zoo activity that other venues cannot offer. This is an opportunity to introduce children and their parents to food tourism and many parents will become advocates of the farm.

## Off-Farm Entertainment

More and more farmers have realized they can combine the rural setting, interest in food tourism and development of off-farm entertainment to generate income. The options are as wide as you can think, the major ones to consider include the following.

### Events, shows and festivals

**Fig. 5.2.** Ludlow Food Festival.

The Country or State Agricultural Show has been a feature of the rural community for many years. It has always been an event where city and rural communities get together to celebrate farming and agriculture in the local community. This need not just be a yearly event and may be held on-farm or off-farm depending on the location and desire.

The USA is the place for events and festivals and we can learn a lot from that part of the world where festivals are one of the fastest growing events to attract tourists and one of the premier tourist attractions in the country.

The definition of a festival is 'a celebration that takes place over a period of time.'[9] That period of time is usually 3–5 days and includes the weekend.

Festivals, and especially food festivals, are prime tourist attractions. They appeal to travel agencies, coach tour operators and primary tourist providers. Outside of the festival providers of local accommodation, food services, transport and souvenir shops all benefit as well as the secondary providers such as food producers, petrol or gas stations, security providers, local service suppliers and general retailers.

Donald Vaughan and Eric Peterson's book *Amazing Festivals, 100's of Hometown Celebrations*[10] is a starting point to look at the different ideas and opportunities in developing food festivals.

### Planning a festival

Festival planning is a skill in its own right. It takes a year-long commitment to plan an annual festival event. A committee is needed and organizers need to be prepared to delegate. The best way to develop a festival is to have sub-committees that are focused on set tasks such as:

- Fund raising;
- Festival security, this is becoming more important each year;
- Vendor planning;
- Entertainment;
- Guest hospitality;
- The parade;
- Partnerships;
- Marketing;
- Onsite services.

A festival will have a range of activities and someone needs to be prepared to manage each one along with the support of a committee. The Government of Western Australia[11] has produced an excellent guide on festival planning and we recommend any event organizer to use this as a template for planning their own festival.

### Concessions/vendors

To be successful, a festival will have to include other businesses providing attractions and food that cannot be provided by the event organizer. This is where concessions and vendors become an important part of the mix. Festival crowds will expect a variety of food for sale and a variety of retail activities, whilst the organizer can look at these as an extra source of profit.

Vendors can come from the non-profit sector via local clubs and charities or from the profit sector. There is often a ready local source of small businesses who would want to be a part of the success.

A festival organizer will need to produce an application form and set a fee schedule for the event. Being flexible in the fee structure is often a mistake. Set a fee and keep to it is the secret to success.

**Fig. 5.3.** Concession stallholder at Ludlow Food Festival.

The application form must have a return date on it to enable the organizer to effectively plan the event. Apart from the standard information of name, address etc., the form should request whether water and power will be needed and if the vendor is setting up a self-contained unit or not. The fee is normally based on size of site required and a fee for every 1000 visitors that come to the festival, plus extra charges for 'hook ups' to power or water if required.

Local health authorities will set the ground rules for a festival and those rules need to be clearly stated to the vendor. They do vary around the world, but in our experience health inspectors do come and check on standards at events and an organizer needs to be prepared.

Our experience has shown that the rules must state by what time a vendor stand must be set up, the earliest they can take their stall away, and where they can park vehicles and come on site with vehicles.

If the event has plenty of food vendors then the event will also need plenty of garbage cans or rubbish bins around the food area and these will need to be emptied on a regular basis. This will help keep the festival looking clean and save time cleaning up at the end of the event.

### Festival income

The business objective of a festival is to generate income and vendors are one source of income. Clearly an entry fee for visitors is a major source of income. Some events will charge extra to park cars at the venue. We personally feel this leaves a 'bad taste in the mouth' and would recommend the parking fee is costed into the entry ticket.

Programmes provide income in two ways: (i) the event organizer can sell advertising space in the programme; and (ii) the programme can be sold to festival guests. According to Patricia Mestern who organizes festivals for the food industry in Canada and author of *So you Want to Hold a Festival, The A-Z of Festival and Special Event Organization*,[12] you will need 1,000 programmes for every 10,000 guests. Sales of programmes can be increased if a competition is promoted and built into the programme. Patricia suggests then you will sell 6,000 programmes to every 10,000 guests.

Other income can come from special events inside the festival. For example, the event organizers may organize a Saturday night concert and charge extra for the concert.

The other main source of income can be from souvenirs. This can be challenging as the organizer has to invest in souvenirs well before the event and it is exceptionally difficult to decide what will sell. We know many organizations that have boxes of souvenirs that have not sold.

### Festival ideas

Food festivals come in all shapes and sizes. The aim should be to create a unique festival for your area rather than copying something that someone else has done.

One of the biggest attractions at many shows is the heaviest, biggest or longest fruit and vegetable. Who can grow the largest pumpkin is a favourite competition for local domestic vegetable growers. This can be the largest in the community or the largest in the world.

At the time of writing the global record holders include:

| Vegetable | Weight | Country |
| --- | --- | --- |
| Heaviest sweet potato | 11.2 kg | Lebanon |
| Largest marrow | 65 kg | Norfolk, UK |
| Heaviest jackfruit | 34.4 kg | Hawaii, USA |
| Largest green cabbage | 34.4 kg | Alaska, USA |
| Largest watermelon | 122 kg | USA |
| Largest pumpkin | 76.6 kg | Massachusetts, USA |
| Longest cucumber | 1 m | Bath, UK |

**Fig. 5.4.** The world's biggest pumpkin.

*Examples of food festivals*
*USA*
Maine Lobster Festival
Milford Pumpkin Festival, New Hampshire
Vermont Maple Festival
National Cranberry Festival
Potato and Corn Festival, North Branford, Connecticut
National Buffalo Wing Festival, Buffalo, New York
Maryland Seafood Festival
World Biggest Fish Fry, Paris, Tennessee
North Carolina Pickle Festival
Vidalia Onion Festival, Vidalia, Georgia
National Grits Festival, Warwick, Georgia
Windsor Zucchini Festival, Windsor, Florida
Alabama Butterbean Festival,
Louisiana Sweet Potato Festival, Yambilee, Louisiana
Dandelion Festival, Dover, Ohio
… and the list goes on.
There is always something or a local product that a region can celebrate.

*Around the world*
There are numerous festivals celebrating food around the world, far too many to list here. The following are some of the festivals we recommend.

*Australia*
The Margaret River 'Gourmet Escape' Weekend (www.gourmetescape.com.au) is one of the best new examples of how food tourism has developed in recent years. The weekend is held in the south-west of Western Australia and is located at Margaret River, one of the remotest places you can find for a food tourism event. It highlights what can be achieved with vision and is now an important event on the state events' calendar.

The keys to success are:

*   Attract celebrity 'Food Thinkers' and develop an educational programme around food. The celebrity food thinkers in the past have included Heston Blumenthal, Rick Stein as well as other international and national chefs, food critics and celebrities;
*   Involve all the local food tourism destinations and promote the region rather than the venue;
*   Develop a Gourmet Village where suppliers of food and cooking utensils and equipment can provide information, tips and products;
*   Visitors are encouraged to use 'GEM's, which are the official currency of the event and used to purchase food and drinks on site. This allows control over the consumption of food and alcohol on the site.

The LiveLighter Araluen's Fremantle Chilli Festival[13] is held in the port city of Fremantle in Western Australia in March each year. It is now in the

*Guinness Book of Records* as the largest chilli festival in the world. It is a festival that highlights how quickly an event can go from a minor tourist attraction to a major culinary festival.

Tasting Australia (www.tastingaustralia.com.au) is a festival held around Adelaide in South Australia over a week in late April and early May. It shows how festivals are changing from a one-venue location to a celebration of a region with a variety of activities. The event across the city includes wine-tasting sessions, an Origins Dinner where international celebrity chefs prepare local food, town square kitchen workshops, producers picnic and spotlight events.

### Ireland

Every country has festivals and food tourism can learn from all of them. The city of Galway in Ireland holds the oldest oyster festival in the world (www.galwayoysterfest.com). This was started by the entrepreneur Brian Collins in 1954 when he was the manager of the Great Southern Hotel (now the Hotel Meyrick) and wanted to attract more guests to his hotel in September. A festival that started with 34 people now attracts over 22,000 people.

The elements to this festival that make it a success include a festival marquee, a crowned Oyster Pearl who presents the mayor with the first oyster of the season – a traditional *ab initio* – a Festival Food Village where local restaurants provide oyster dishes, The National Oyster Opening Championships (the winner represents Ireland in the World Oyster Olympics), a seafood music party and the oyster 'Mardi Gras'. The festival shows what can be achieved by thinking 'outside the box'.

### Italy

The Slow Food Festival, Turin (www.salonedelgusto.com) was mentioned earlier in the book and is probably the one festival that is a must see for all culinary tourists who are searching out local foods. It is held every other year (http://salonedelgustoterramadre.slowfood.com).

### UK

The Ludlow Food Festival (www.foodfestival.co.uk) has been so successful that they now have a spring and September festival.

### Taste festivals

Eighteen cities around the world hold Taste Festivals in their cities once a year. These cities are selected as being cities well known for their food and wine. The cities are Amsterdam, Auckland, Cape Town, Dubai, Dublin, Durban, Helsinki, Johannesburg, London, Melbourne, Milan, Moscow, Mumbai, Perth, Rome, Stockholm and Toronto, plus a Christmas Festival. This event started in London 10 years ago and the event has become a major part of the food calendar for many tourists (www.tastefestivals.com). The event is held in one location in each city and is promoted as 'The World's Greatest Restaurant Festival'. The aim is to expose local tourists to local food and what is available in local restaurants and from local suppliers.

**Fig. 5.5.** Ludlow Food Festival logo.

According to the Organic Authority[14] the top ten food festivals in the world are:

**1.** Hokitika Wildfoods Festival: this festival takes place on the west coast of New Zealand's South Island, and celebrates the weird side of food. Try dishes like wild snails, worm milkshakes, flower wine, huhu grubs and more (www.wildfoods.co.nz/index.cfm).

**2.** The Taste: sponsored by the *Los Angeles Times*, this event at the Paramount Studios features all-you-can-eat-and-drink passes for only US$65. This 3-day festival has a huge collection of exhibitors: local restaurants, wineries, bakeries, brewing companies, distilleries and more (http://events.latimes.com/taste).

**3.** La Tomatina: this Spanish festival celebrates the red tomato with the biggest food fight on the planet. Held in the town of Buñol, this party starts with a rush to climb a ham-topped greasy pole. Once the ham is grabbed, several truckloads of tomatoes drive into the city and the crowd goes wild throwing them at each other and creating a massive mess of marinara (www.latomatina.org).

**4.** Maine Lobster Festival: held in the New England town of Rockland, the Maine Lobster Festival is a celebration of the crustacean that the state is known for. The event features live music, carnival rides and a floating lobster crate race, as well as lobster prepared in more ways that you could ever imagine (www.mainelobsterfestival.com).

**5.** Melbourne Food and Wine Festival: many people call Melbourne Australia's cultural capital. It has hosted this 20 day festival for 20 years as a showcase of the continent's culinary mastery through cooking demonstrations, special tours and food tastings throughout the city (www.melbournefoodandwine.com.au).

**6.** Aspen Food & Wine: hosted by *Food & Wine* magazine, this food festival takes place each June and features a full weekend of cooking demonstrations and samples prepared by celebrity chefs (www.foodandwine.com/classic).

**7.** Gilroy Garlic Festival: one of the biggest food festivals in the USA, this festival in Gilroy, California, celebrates the aromatic allium known as garlic. Visitors discover garlic cooking demonstrations, garlic braiding classes and an array of garlic-infused food, including garlic ice cream, garlic popcorn and garlic mussels (http://gilroygarlicfestival.com).

**8.** Cayman Cookout:[15] the Caribbean's biggest culinary event, this food festival on Grand Cayman Island celebrates all the flavours of the islands – cooked outdoors in paradise. Guests find cooking showcases by famous chefs, culinary tours of the island, catamaran cookouts and more.

**9.** Hatch Valley Chile Festival: New Mexico's Hatch Valley is known for its production of spicy Hatch chiles, and these red firecrackers take centre stage at this spicy celebration. Chile eating competitions, cook-offs, carnival rides and a huge assortment of spicy food to sample (www.hatchchilefest.com).

**10.** The World Gourmet Summit:[16] this gourmet festival takes place in Singapore each year. Sample the most sought-after flavours in the world, from fine wines to ethnic specialities, and attend celebrity cooking demonstrations and workshops taught by master chefs.

### Annual festivals with a food opportunity

Every year there are hundreds of local festivals celebrated around the world that have a food tourism opportunity. The astute food marketer will develop these as part of their marketing package.

The key is to understand the 'essence' of what the festival should achieve. Recently we attended an annual Cherry Festival. Our expectation was that the 'essence' of the festival would revolve around the cherry. The festival was busy and must have had over 100 stallholders. There were three stalls selling cherries and we could find no education or storytelling focused on the fruit. This missed opportunity meant the festival was a 'me too' festival and did not encourage the visitor to come again the next year.

Festivals that do not take the opportunity to make the 'product' the hero will be short-lived festivals. They may make a short-term profit, but food tourism is about enriching the consumer experience, not selling boxes of produce.

Festival opportunities include the following.

### Halloween

This has been a popular festival season in the USA for many years and many think it was developed as an American festive event. This is a misconception as the event is based on early Celtic harvest rituals. Some believe it goes back earlier than that and is based on Italian farming rituals.

This seasonal event also has its own trade show held in January every year in the USA. The trade show provides all the novelty items required to make a festival event and should be attended by anyone planning to make this a festival on the farm. www.halloweenpartyexpo.com

*Valentine's Day*

Products could revolve around a love theme or even aphrodisiac foods. Imagine the fun that could be generated around a festival that included anchovies, apricots, asparagus, avocados, beans, blueberries, cabbage, chocolate, clams, figs, honey, quince and watercress. All these produce could provide ecstasy for the consumer as they are classed as aphrodisiac foods.

## Icon Food Tourism – The Giant Pineapple to Gillie Racing

**Fig. 5.6.** The Karlgarin gilgie races sign in Western Australia.

We realize that culinary tourist advocates will criticize the fact that we have covered 'icon' food tourism in this book. Food tourism is about engaging tourists in local food activities, not all tourists are foodies and not all tourists look for the same thing. Disney-style tourism related to food works and should be considered as one way of engaging the consumer.

The Big Pineapple is recognized as one of the most successful food-related icon structures. The first one was erected in Hawaii by the now Dole Food Co. This was a stylized water tower and was removed in the 1930s.

The most famous existing Big Pineapple (www.bigpineapple.com.au) is located in Queensland, Australia, on the Bruce Highway. In 1971, Mr and Mrs Bill Taylor purchased a pineapple farm and erected the 16 m high pineapple and developed train rides, a petting zoo and other activities around the farm. In 1972 the attraction was the first to be awarded recognition by the Australian National Travel Association.

In 2010 the pineapple farm was purchased by the Bowden family with the aim of developing the tourist attraction. The Big Pineapple is a wonderful example of how an iconic structure can engage tourists that would not normally engage in food tourism. By entertaining the visitor they have been able to start to educate the tourist in local foods and especially the growing of pineapples.

A farmer in the Bay of Plenty in New Zealand has created a similar icon tourist attraction based around the Big Kiwi, a commonly grown fruit in that area.

Other 'icon' food statues include the Big Banana, which was erected in 1964 in Coffs Harbour in New South Wales, The Big Lobster at Kingston, South Australia, and Giant Rams at Goulburn, New South Wales and at Wagin, Western Australia.

You will see from this list that Australia is a Mecca for 'icon' statues and the postal service even produced a series of stamps on them in 2007.

World news picked up on the fact that the Big Mango in Bowen in Queensland, Australia was removed overnight in February 2014 as a guerrilla marketing tactic by the fast food chain Nandos; an example of how 'loved' this type of icon can become in communities.

Special mention should be made of the Gillie. This is where an icon can make a difference. The Giant Gillie is on a sign at Kargalin in the Western Australian wheat belt. This community is so small that if you Google the name it does not come up. There are about three properties there with three farming families, but each year they have Gillie racing. Gillies are a crustacean reared by one of the farmers as a delicacy and each year they have a race to attract tourists. This shows how 'out of the box' thinking in a small remote community can provide an event each year to attract tourists off the beaten track.

## Traditional Crafts, Foods and Cooking Techniques

> Till St Swithin's Day be past. The apples be not fit to taste.
> Notes and Queries 1870

The desire to preserve traditional crafts is not a new trend. Herbert. L. Edlin wrote *Woodland Crafts in Britain*[17] in 1949 with the aim of keeping alive the old traditional crafts of Britain. Many festivals now include demonstrations and exhibitions of the old crafts and they have become a tourist attraction in their own right.

### Make tradition a tourist attraction

Many tourists visit Stratford on Avon in Warwickshire in the UK to view Shakespeare's birthplace. Not far from his birthplace is Mary Arden's Farm. Mary Arden was William's mother. This has given the charity that operates the birthplace an opportunity to develop a Tudor farm, which is open from March until November and provides a wide range of tourist activities. Team members dress in Tudor clothes and the farm includes rare farm breeds, birds of prey and Tudor entertainments.

Williamsburg, Virginia and Old Sturbridge Village in Massachusetts have developed similar themes as a tourist attraction.

Monselice near Padua in Italy holds a Medieval fair every September. The village already had a weekly farmers' market, but once a year it sets up a medieval fair when all the villagers dress up in medieval clothes and practise the old farming and food-preparation techniques.

Nostalgia is a big tourist draw, as tourism and culinary tour venue operators try to search out the traditional values they remember from their youth. Many of the traditional agricultural skills are being lost and need to be preserved to ensure the skills are passed on to the next generation.

Many culinary tourists are looking for traditional ways of food production. Traditional methods may be more expensive and time consuming, but particularly the older consumer is prepared to pay for the real experience. There are a number of ways we can preserve the traditions.

### Promote the seasonal calendar

Farming communities live by the seasons and understand the seasons, whereas visitors from the city have less understanding of the seasons. Modern food distribution means that many urban dwellers assume strawberries are harvested all the year round from the same field, as they are available as a year-round fruit on the supermarket shelf.

Most farming communities work on a four season calendar, but this not always the case. In Australia the aborigines rely on a six season calendar.

The authors live in the Noongar Aboriginal region of Australia and the seasons are Bunuru (February–March), Djeran (April–May), Makuru (June–July), Djilba (August–September), Kambarang (October–November) and Birak (December–January). Promoting these seasons and how they affect what is grown creates further interest in food tourism and encourages tourists to return in different seasons to experience how the land and crop production has changed.

### Historic harvesting and adding value techniques

Today the visitor is familiar with modern machinery travelling across the field and often controlled from a satellite. They are less familiar with a Clydesdale horse travelling across fields as the original 'horse power' and this can be an event in itself. Visitors are fascinated to learn how butter, cheeses, cider and other foods were prepared on the farm in days gone by. How food was prepared before the industrial kitchen was invented is something that will be discussed on Facebook and Twitter when a family returns home.

The Tullamore Farm Show in Ireland is one of the biggest events in the country and thousands of visitors go to see more traditional farming activities.

### Traditional festivals

Many counties have traditional festivals based around food. In the UK, cheese often appears as the reason for a festival. In Randwick, Gloucestershire[18] they have the May Day Cheese when three Gloucester cheeses are decked with garlands and paraded around the village. The cheese are then rolled around the church and distributed between villagers.

One traditional festival using Double Gloucester cheese has achieved a global audience and now attracts visitors from around the word. Cooper's Hill[18] just outside the village of Brockworth in Gloucestershire, has been used to roll cheese down since the 15th century. This tradition has promoted the village and it has now become a world famous event. During the food rationing years after the war, between 1941 and 1954, a wooden cheese was used.

In our modern world, the event breaks health and safety regulations and authorities have tried to ban it. Alas, the cheese is often now a plastic cheese and Diana Smart, a local cheese-maker has been banned from selling any cheese that has been rolled down the hill due to health and safety regulations. As a result of the publicity, the fastest cheese chaser down the hill has been won by an American and a Japanese and there is now a separate women's event (details can be obtained on www.cheese-rolling.co.uk). Even negative publicity can be a positive when it comes to tourism exposure.

## Cooking techniques

**Fig. 5.7.** Consumers in a cooking class at the Ludlow Food Festival.

Many food preparation and cooking techniques are being lost and food tourism is a means of reviving and preserving these techniques. There are numerous examples around the world where the skill is being lost.

Tourism in New Zealand has helped preserve and develop traditional Maori cooking. The Hangi or earth oven has been used in traditional Maori cooking for hundreds of years. The technique involves digging a hole in the ground and heating volcanic stones in the pit, which will not split or splinter as they heat up. Manuka or tea tree wood is then added which helps flavour the food. The first thing after that to go into the pit is a basket of meat, which is covered with a wet cloth and then dirt. The water on the cloth turns to steam and the heat helps cook the meat. Cooking time is around 7 hours and because of the preparation and cooking time the art has become less popular, but the food is worth the wait. Prepared Hangi meals are often part of a Maori cultural evening in New Zealand and the art has been preserved.

## Food Factories and Museums

Museums and factories can get involved in food tourism. Think of Atlanta, and most people will also think of it being the home of Coca-Cola. They have the world of Coca-Cola as a Disney-style tourist attraction for guests. Think of Dublin and most people will also mention Guinness, and a tour of a working factory and watching the drink being made is on many tourist itineraries.

Ferran Adrià has closed his world famous restaurant in Spain and opened a museum and visitor centre called ElBulli 1846 (www.elbulli.com). This celebrates the 1846 dishes created at his elBulli restaurant and the year that Auguste Escoffier was born. The museum aims to attract some 200,000 people a year. The elBulli Foundation draws inspiration from the Cirque du Soleil, Salvador Dali and his museum in nearby Figueres, and MIT's Media Lab. The capital to build this venture was €6 million and it takes €3 million a year in revenue, which proves the confidence that Ferran has in the future of food tourism.

According to *Food Journeys of a Lifetime*,[19] the top ten food factory museums to visit are:

1. Ben and Jerry's, Waterbury, Vermont.
2. World of Coca-Cola, Atlanta, Georgia.
3. Mount Horeb Mustard Museum, Wisconsin.
4. Shin-Yokohama Raumen Museum, Japan (Raumen is the Japanese noodle).
5. Museum of Bread Culture, Ulm, Germany.
6. Pick Salami and Szeged Paprika Museum, Hungary.
7. Museo del Peperoncino, Maiera, Italy.
8. Alimentarium, Velvey, Switzerland (Nestlé's Museum).
9. Museum of Cocoa and Chocolate, Brussels.
10. Bramah's Museum of Tea and Coffee, London.

Factories can be developed on a smaller scale and still prove to be successful. It can be as simple as a gingerbread-making shop, fudge-making shop or a local chocolate-making facility.

## Old-Fashioned Candy Stores

The sweet shop that older readers may remember from their youth has now disappeared from the majority of high streets around the world, but in place of the sweet shop a piece of nostalgia has appeared. Many high streets and many tourist attractions now have old traditional candy stores that provide their guest with traditional old fashioned handmade sweets. These tourist shops not only provide nostalgia in the range of handmade sweet products, but also in the way they merchandise and display the product, bringing back the traditional sweet jars and loose sweets.

Some of the traditional sweet shops that survived have become national icons as tourist attractions such as Ali Muhiddin Haci Bekir in Istanbul in Turkey. This shop was actually set up in 1777 and is still owned by the original family.

## Further Information for Agri-Tourism

Arizona
Profile Of Visitors To Fresh Farm Produce Outlets in Cochise County, Arizona. Julie Leones, Douglas Dunn, Marshall Worden and Robert Call. Available at: http://ag.arizona.edu/arec/pubs/dmkt/AProfileofVisitors.pdf (accessed 22 February 2014).
California
Agricultural Benefits Agriculture in San Diego County. Available at: http://sfp.ucdavis.edu/agritourism/Case_Studies/agritourSD (accessed 23 February 2014).
Obstacles in the Agritourism Regulatory process in 10 Californian counties. Available at: http://aic.ucdavis.edu/oa/brief22.pdf (accessed 23 February 2014).
University of California Cooperative Extension – Small Farm Research Brief. Available at: http://sfp.ucdavis.edu/food_safety (accessed 23 February 2014).
Colorado
Agritourism: A potential Economic Driver in Rural West. Available at: www.agmrc.org/media/cms/edr0601_cda89b9a1e15e.pdf (accessed 23 February 2014).
Georgia
Considerations for Agritourism Enterprises in Georgia. Available at: www.agmrc.org/media/cms/Agritainmentpdf_263439021F9DA.pdf (accessed 23 February 2014).
Hawaii
Introduction to Agri-tourism. Available at: www.ctahr.hawaii.edu/agtourism (accessed 24 February 2014).
Hawaii Agricultural Statistics. Available at: http://hdoa.hawaii.gov/add/hawai'i-agricultural-statistics (accessed 23 February 2014).
Illinopis
Agritourism. An Economic Opportunity for Illinios. Available at: http://web.extension.illinois.edu/agritourism/business_opportunity.cfm (accessed 24 February 2014).
Iowa
Agritourism Briefing for Iowa. Available at: http://www.agmrc.org/commodities_products/agritourism/technical_reports_on_agritourism/reports_by_state/articles (accessed 23 February 2014).
Kansas
Agritourism: If we Build it Will They Come? Available at: www.uvm.edu/tourismresearch/agtour/publications/Kansas%20State%20Study.pdf (accessed 23 February 2014).
Michigan
Direct Marketing of Agricultural Products to Tourists. Available at: http://michigan.gov/documents/mda/MDA_guide_335948_7.pdf (accessed 24 February 2014).

Nevada

Agritourism: Opportunity for farm diversification in Nevada. Available at: www.
unce.unr.edu/publications/files/ag/2005/fs0538.pdf (accessed 23 February
2014).

New Hampshire

New Hampshire Department of Agriculture Marketing research report. Available
at: www.agmrc.org/media/cms/strategy_DF542FCDD40E4.pdf (accessed 23
February 2014).

New Jersey

Income Distribution Comparison on Farms with Innovative Activities. Available at:
www.agrisk.umn.edu/Library/Display.aspx?RecID=2304 (accessed 25 February
2014).

New York

Agritourism in New York: A Market Analysis. Available at: www.agmrc.org/media/
cms/agtourmktfs_1CB11950FA839.pdf (accessed 25 February 2014).

Agritourism in New York 'Management and Operations'. Available at: http://njsus-
tainingfarms.rutgers.edu/agritourismwp/_pdf/Agritourism_Mgt_Operations_
NY_2001.pdf (accessed 22 February 2014).

Agritourism 'Market in New York'. Available at: www.agmrc.org/media/cms/
AgAndEconomy_8FB184E838C3F.pdf (accessed 23 February 2014).

Considerations for Agritourism Development. Available at: www.uvm.edu/tourism-
research/agritourism/research/agritourconsid.pdf (accessed 22 February 2014).

North Carolina

North Carolina Agritourism Survey Results 2005. Available at: www.ncagr.gov/mar-
kets/agritourism/documents/2005SurveyWithLetter.pdf (accessed 24 February
2014).

Oregon

Agri-Business Council of Oregon Agri-Tourism Workbook. Available at: www.
landcarecentral.org/References/Agri-Tourism%20Workbook.pdf (accessed 23
February 2014).

Tennessee

A Snapshot of Tennessee Agritourism. Results from the 2003 Enterprise Inventory.
Available at: www.agmrc.org/media/cms/PB1747_1109766D4376E.pdf (accessed 24 February 2014).

Considering an Entertainment Enterprise in Tennessee? Available at: https://
www.clemson.edu/public/ciecd/focus_areas/agribusiness/programs/agri-
tourism/agritourismresources/agtritainmententerprises.pdf (accessed 25
February 2014).

Targeting School Groups for Agritainment Enterprises. Available at: https://utexten-
sion.tennessee.edu/publications/Documents/pb1669.pdf (accessed 25 February
2014).

Vermont

Agritourism Diversification Critical Success factors. Available at: www.uvm.
edu/~snrvtdc/agtour/publications/Agritourism%20Report.pdf (accessed
24 February 2014).

Vermont Agric-Tourism Survey 2003. Available at: www.uvm.edu/~snrvtdc/
agtour/publications/VT%20Agri-Tourism%20Survey%202003.pdf (accessed 25
February 2014).

Virginia

Virginia Cooperative Extension Agric-Tourism Publication. Available at: http://pubs.
ext.vt.edu/310/310-004/310-004.html (accessed 23 February 2014).

# References

[1]  Rilla, E., Hardesty, S.D., Getz, C. and George, H. (2012) California agritourism operations and their economic potential are growing. Research article. Available at: http://ucce.ucdavis.edu/files/repositoryfiles/ca6502p57-85601.pdf (accessed 23 February 2014).

[2]  Promoting Tourism in Rural America (2013) USDA National Agricultural Library. Available at: www.nal.usda.gov/ric/ricpubs/tourism.html#tourismdevelopment (accessed 23 February 2014).

[3]  Braganza, C., Coventry, M. and Fontana, G. (2011) Agritourism: Designing Your Marketing Strategy. Presentation at Fresno Convention Centre, California, on 7 July 2011. Available at: http://sfp.ucdavis.edu/files/144800.pdf (accessed 22 February 2014).

[4]  Brown, D. and Reeder, R. (2007) Farm-Based Recreation: A Statistical Profile. USDA ERS Economic Research Report No. ERR-53, 28 pp.

[5]  Gross, Samantha. USA Today. Traveling To Eat: Food Tourism grows in USA. Available at: http://usatoday30.usatoday.com/travel/destinations/2007-02-19-food-tourism_x.htm (accessed 22 February 2014).

[6]  Penrith City Council – A Child Friendly City Strategy: Available at: www.penrithcity.nsw.gov.au/uploadedFiles/Website/Children/ChildFriendlyStrategyReport.pdf (accessed 22 February 2014).

[7]  Cornwall Council Traffic Management for Large Events. Available at: www.cornwall.gov.uk/default.aspx?page=28020 (accessed 19 February 2014).

[8]  The International Herb Association: www.iherb.org/hoy.htm (accessed 24 February 2014).

[9]  The Free Dictionary, definition of a festival. Available at: www.thefreedictionary.com/festival (accessed 26 February 2014).

[10]  Vaughan, D. and Peterson, E. (2011) Amazing Festivals, 100's of Hometown Celebrations. Publications International, Lincolnwood, Illinois.

[11]  Government of Western Australia. The Western Australian Government Event Management Plan Checklist and Guide. Available at: www.gdc.wa.gov.au/uploads/files/Event%20Management%20Plan%20-%20GDC%20Toolkit.pdf (accessed 26 February 2004).

[12]  Mestern, P. (2002) So You Want to Hold a Festival, The A-Z of Festival and Special Event Organization. OATI, Guelph, Ontario.

[13]  LiveLighter Araluen's Fremantle Chilli Festival, Western Australia: www.araluenbotanicpark.com.au/araluen-fremantle-chilli-festival

[14]  The Organic Authority top 10 festivals. Available at: www.organicauthority.com/top-10-tastiest-summer-food-festivals

[15]  Cayman Cookout: www.caymanislands.ky/eventsoffers/caymancookout.aspx

[16]  The World Gourmet Summit: www.worldgourmetsummit.com/wgs2012/main.php

[17]  Edlin, H.L. (1974) Woodland Crafts in Britain. David & Charles, Newton Abbot, UK.

[18]  Cooper's Hill Cheese-rolling and Wake. Available at: http://en.wikipedia.org/wiki/Cooper's_Hill_Cheese-Rolling_and_Wake (accessed 14 February 2014).

[19]  National Geographic (2009) Food Journeys of a Lifetime, 500 Extraordinary Places to Eat Around the Globe. National Geographic, Washington, DC.


## Websites

Aspen Food & Wine: www.foodandwine.com/classic

Bridestowe Lavender Estate, Northern Tasmania, Australia: http://bridestowelavender.com.au/pub (accessed 26 February 2014).

Cheese-rolling in Gloucestershire: www.cheese-rolling.co.uk

Corn Mazes America: www.cornmazesamerica.com

ElBulli Foundation: www.elbulli.com/home.php?lang=en (accessed 25 February 2014).
Galway Oyster Festival, Ireland: www.galwayoysterfest.com
Gilroy Garlic Festival: http://gilroygarlicfestival.com
Hatch Valley Chile Festival: www.hatchchilefest.com
Hokitika Wildfoods Festival: www.wildfoods.co.nz/index.cfm
La Tomatina: www.latomatina.org
Ludlow Food Festival, UK: www.foodfestival.co.uk
Maine Lobster Festival: www.mainelobsterfestival.com
Melbourne Food and Wine Festival: www.melbournefoodandwine.com.au
Slow Food Festival Tasting, Turin, Italy: www.salonedelgusto.com
Spookley the Square Pumpkin: www.spookley.com (accessed 26 February 2014).
Tasting Australia, Adelaide, South Australia: www.tastingaustralia.com.au
The Australian Lavender Growers Association: www.talga.com.au (accessed 26 February 2014).
The Big Pineapple, Nambour, Queensland, Australia: www.bigpineapple.com.au (accessed 26 February 2014).
The Margaret River 'Gourmet Escape', Western Australia: www.gourmetescape.com.au
The Taste: http://events.latimes.com/taste
UK Maize Maze Association: www.maize-maze.com

# 6 Accommodation

When you get into a hotel room, you lock the door, and you know there is a secrecy, there is a luxury, there is fantasy. There is comfort. There is reassurance.

Diane von Furstenberg

## Introduction

The aim of a culinary region should be to persuade the culinary tourist to stay for at least a few days in a location and therefore accommodation is an essential part of the promotional package. The challenge is providing what the guests want.

We could dedicate a book to accommodation and the range of offers available; the food tourist tends to have specific needs and will, if possible, avoid the 'chain' accommodation if alternative accommodation is available.

Having said that, many larger hotel chains have identified the marketing opportunity of attracting culinary tourists and have started to organize culinary weekends where a celebrity chef is invited to either prepare meals, speak to the guests or do both.

Tourists will search out suitable accommodation that enhances the experience. This is where search engines such as Trip Advisor, booking.com, Agoda.com and other accommodation search engines can be a great help for both the tourist and accommodation provider. It is also advisable for accommodation owners to monitor comments on these websites and to react when necessary. These websites should not be a one way process, they should encourage engagement between hotel team members and potential and past guests.

Accommodation can also be one of the challenges for the traveller. On a recent out-of-season tour of Italy we found accommodation was a major challenge. Many hotel owners were only interested in staying open for the main tourist season even though our farmer clients had their facilities open to the public. Food tourism allows hotels and other accommodation to extend the season past the traditional accommodation period. However, this only works if the hospitality providers work together with local food tourism organizations.

Ideally they want sustainable accommodation. Many of the culinary tourists of today are looking for accommodation that minimizes the impact on the environment. Sustainable friendly accommodation is often preferred.

Sustainable accommodation must usually meet the following criteria:

- Dependence on the natural environment;
- Ecological sustainability;
- Proven contribution to conservation;
- Provision of environmental training programmes;
- Incorporation of cultural considerations;
- Provision of an economic return to the local community; and
- Sustainable kitchen.

According to research reported in the Guardian,[1] each UK family throws away the equivalent of 24 meals a month, while according to research reported in the Hospitality and Catering News in the UK[2] 56% of consumers are prepared to pay more for sustainable food.

The sustainable accommodation developer needs to think about the following.

**1.** Low energy input. The carbon footprint gets more important as each year passes.

**2.** Low water bills. Many countries are facing the challenge of changing the current water management policy to help improve the health of water and to conserve water.

**3.** Low waste bills. It is estimated that 50% of food produced in the first world is wasted. In the UK 20% is wasted in the food service industry.[3]

**4.** Improved labour productivity and value to the consumer.

Sustainable accommodation can cover anything from a hotel to a Mongolian-style yurt on a camp site.

Accommodation can be split into a number of different segments for this style of tourism.

## Hotel Accommodation

There are plenty of examples of culinary hotels; hotels that promote the food of the region as part of the offer. Culinary hotels differ from the standard hotel in a number of ways:

- They promote local foods from the region and tell the story of the local foods as part of the guest experience;

- They support local business and have a responsible sourcing policy between farm gate and hotel plate;
- They often are associated with cooking schools on or off the premises.

Many tourist associations promote culinary hotels. Two in particular
have caught our attention: (i) Good Food Ireland (www.goodfoodireland.ie)
also has the Culinary Hotel of the Year Awards; and (ii) www.myswitzerland.
com, which also lists culinary hotels in that country.

We all have our favourite hotels. One that has caught our eye is Sooke
Harbour House situated a few kilometres to the west of the village of Sooke
on Vancouver Island, British Columbia, Canada (www.sookeharbourhouse.
com). The hotel is ideally situated overlooking the Pacific Ocean and a great
place for whale spotting amongst other things. The hotel is surrounded by
a wonderful edible garden containing over 230 herbs, edible flowers and
vegetables. Guests also have the opportunity to taste native edible plants
while staying at the hotel. The rooms as well as the menu are also a culinary
adventure. You can stay in the Herb Garden room or Edible Blossom room
as well as dine on local food, most of it coming from the garden and picked
that day. On John's visit the menu contained locally caught oysters, octopus,
mussels and clams from the Pacific Ocean. From the island itself came elk or
duck, all served with vegetables from the garden. The hotel also does garden
tours for guests and visitors. Vancouver Island is in itself a magical culinary
adventure and this hotel is an ideal starting point for that adventure.

## Bed and Breakfast

We have spent many an evening at bed and breakfast establishments around
the world. Staying at bed and breakfast accommodation is an opportunity to
get to know real local people and share local stories rather that stay in one
of the chain hotels, where you can often wonder what country you are in as
they often seem the same.

The definition of bed and breakfast changes around the world. In general
terms, an inn provides evening meals as well as a bed and breakfast, whilst
a bed and breakfast does not provide an evening meal. The majority of bed
and breakfast operations are run as local family businesses.

Bed and breakfast is an ideal accommodation for the culinary tourist as
travellers get to appreciate the region they are travelling through. Bed and
breakfast is like hotel accommodation in some ways, there are the places you
want to linger longer and there are the places where you cannot wait until
you can leave and travel to the next location.

Although bed and breakfast is a growth sector in many economies, the
research on the industry is dated and therefore it is difficult to gauge what is
happening in the industry at present. It is a market where the perception of accommodation is changing. It is no longer the source of cheap accommodation;
the sector has matured and consumers are prepared to pay for the experience.

What makes a successful bed and breakfast location for food tourism?

Any successful business revolves around people and this is never more true than in the accommodation industry. The host must enjoy engaging with people as they are in the people industry and bed and breakfast is very much a people industry.

There are many skills required to be a successful bed and breakfast operator. The aim of this book is not to advise on how to set up and operate a bed and breakfast facility. There are plenty of books already available, one we would recommend is 'Become a Bed & Breakfast Owner'.[4] The information in this book will provide you with the knowledge needed to develop skills to build the business.

Like any other business, one of the keys to success is marketing. A survey carried out in the USA as far back as 2001 by CNN Money[5] asked people how they found out about bed and breakfast accommodation and the response was 49% via the Internet, 18% via word of mouth and 6% via printed marketing. This was over 12 years ago, before Booking.com and similar services were established. It indicates that if you are operating in this market sector, you had better be Internet savvy. This also includes having complimentary Wi-Fi for your guests.

Bed and breakfast is often preferred by guests who are empty nesters, young couples and parents having a break from the children. In other words this style of accommodation is often not suitable for young families.

The target guest is looking for privacy and pampering. They select accommodation that is located in an attractive location often with an attractive garden and house and look forward to home-style cooking either at the accommodation or at a local restaurant.

The following checklist may sound like common sense, but can make the difference between a memorable bed and breakfast and just another forgettable night's accommodation:

- When guests arrive, welcome then with a local food dish or drink. First impressions are so important and can influence how the whole stay will be measured in the eyes of the guest;
- Make sure the breakfast is made up of local foods and explain the source of the ingredients on the menu. This is a great opportunity to network with local producers and promote that the breakfast is made up of food that was grown and raised within a set mileage from the accommodation. Why not call it a '20 mile breakfast' and promote this as a key reason to stay at your location?
- Recommend restaurants that use local food for the evening meal. This is all about networking within the local culinary region;
- Have a notice board in the accommodation that promotes local culinary activities in the community. Plus, make sure there is literature in the room on local culinary activities that the guest can read at their leisure;
- In the bedroom provide a history of the area and recommend local walks that the guests can do in an evening and provide a map with highlights along the way. Promote local farmers and foods;

- Provide a guide of what local flora is in flower and the names of local birds recently spotted the area;
- Have vouchers available for local culinary, ecotourism activities in the area.

## Farm Stay

Farm stay is very similar to bed and breakfast, but as the name suggests the accommodation is on a working farm and the visitor experiences a unique agricultural experience. Some farms, often due to remoteness, will provide an evening meal as part of the package whilst others prefer the bed and breakfast route. As a guest to the region this is a real opportunity to get to know the farm, the farmer and to understand how the farming community works in the region. It is important for the farm stay owner to identify and understand what they offer is the real point of difference between a bed and breakfast model and staying on the farm. Some farmers also allow camping on site either in a tent or caravan.

Talking with farmers, we have found that the key issues in establishing a farm stay include:

- Establishing the right accommodation and fitting out the rooms with good quality linen and furnishings to establish a different accommodation experience;
- Ensuring access roads to the accommodation are suitable for urban visitors;
- Ensuring that there are adequate water tanks and sewage facilities;
- Adequate electricity to the site and a spare generator available;
- Using local produce when providing meals;
- Providing guidance on how the visitor should act on the farm; not every visitor assumes gates should be shut once they have entered a field;
- Being registered in the farm stay directory.

    Valuable references include:

- The UK Farm Stay Directory: www.farmstay.co.uk
- The Australian Farm Stay Directory: www.australianfarmstay.com.au

## Glamping

When John was younger in the British Isles he can remember the fun of camping. John lived not too far from Glastonbury in Somerset and recalls thousands of music fans going to the annual 3 day festival. Festival goers would hope for a sunny weekend as they would be camping rough and if it rained they were left to cope with the mud.

The die-hards still look on Glastonbury the same way, but many visitors now go glamping at Glastonbury. Glamping is still camping, in that you sleep under canvas, but that is where the similarity finishes. Glampers sleep in a proper bed with fine linen, en suite toilet, carpet or decking and all the facilities.

This new style of luxury camping is becoming increasingly popular, especially in countries like Botswana and South Africa where campers can go and see the wildlife and then retreat to a camp and enjoy first world comforts under canvas.

Glamping allows the sustainable tourist to be just that, whilst still enjoying their creature comforts. In fact in countries such as Botswana it has become a major source of attracting tourist dollars.

## Setting up glamping

Setting up a glamping site is basically the same as a traditional camping site, with a few variations. This is not about getting as many camp sites on a piece of ground as possible. The guest is prepared to pay more than a traditional camper and the site must reflect that. Make sure the tent is situated where the best views are located and that the glamper, ideally, cannot see or hear other glampers – they are looking for isolation. Where possible create furniture made by local artisans using local materials, and be prepared to invest a bit more to create a unique experience for your guests.

Remember the key point of difference is that the tent contains a bed with fine linen, not a mattress on the floor; create a decorated hideaway. Consumers expect each tent to have an en suite, veranda and at least a Queen-size bed, and include breakfast and possibly dinner depending on the isolation of the site.

Be as sustainable as possible. There are now many unique solar devices on the market designed especially for camping, to create power, lighting, hot water and flushing toilets.

Get to know what your guest is looking for early on in the transaction. Is it solitude or do they want you to engage with them and provide meals as well?

Solar barbecues can provide an eco-friendly cooking experience.

Glamping is a way that visitors can spoil themselves on a budget. Having said that, at the top of the range glamping destinations, visitors spend thousands of dollars a night.

Darts Farm (www.dartsfarm.co.uk) in Devon in the UK has taken an interesting approach to glamping. Once a year they offer their customers a 'Family Camp'. This coincides with the end of the tent show in Exeter, their local city. For one weekend they provide a camp. For a fee of £15 per adult and £9.50 for children they provide a field, BBQ and dessert, bush crafts, nature walks, camp fire sing-a-long, toasted marshmallows and breakfast. All the visitor has to do is bring their tent or hire one for £5. This makes glamping an affordable family event – they provide few luxuries, but it gives families a taster of the potential of glamping.

Here are some other glamping ideas:

- Wild Luxury in an Apple Orchard in Norfolk, UK: www.wildluxury. co.uk
- Hobbit-style accommodation in Cornwall, UK: www.classicglamping. co.uk
- Tree tents in Wales, UK: www.sheepskinlife.com
- Medieval themed bell tents at Warwick Castle in the UK: www.warwick-castle.com
- Eco-tents in Australia: www.ecostructures.net.au

One of the keys to success is accommodation. However good the accommodation, the culinary experience should exceed expectations, that is a critical factor in success.

## Valuable references

- The Sustainable Restaurant Association: www.thesra.org
- The Carbon Trust Hospitality Guide. Available at: www.carbontrust.com/media/39220/ctv013_hospitality.pdf (accessed 27 February 2014).[6]

# Country Houses

Large country houses are part of the rural scene in many European countries. The challenge for many landlords is the rising costs of maintaining a large country house. As a result entrepreneurial owners have ventured into various activities to obtain the income required to maintain these properties.

In the past belonging to an organization like the National Trust in the UK meant that the house could be opened to the public for an entry fee. Visitors today expect more and as a result owners now seek out new ways to attract more consumers and glean extra income.

Providing high quality food in a grand setting is not a new trend. Gidleigh Park (www.gidleigh.com) in Devon, Hambleton Hall (www.hambletonhall.com) in Rutland and Le Manoir aux Quat'Saisons (www.manoir.com) in Oxfordshire, UK, have been providing excellent local meals to patrons for many years. More and more country house owners are now looking at the opportunity of employing a celebrity chef and offering local foods.

Country house cooking in the UK has also obtained extra media exposure with the TV programme 'Country House Cooking Contest'[7] held in the 13th century Maunsel House in Somerset.

Accommodation is a key part of food tourism and one of the keys to success is networking between tourism authorities, farmers, farmers' markets and other food tourism organizations along with accommodation providers to ensure the complete package can be offered to visitors.

# References

[1] Rebecca Smithers, consumer affairs correspondent. Food waste report shows UK families throw away 24 meals a month. *The Guardian*, Thursday 7 November 2013. Available at: www.theguardian.com/environment/2013/nov/07/uk-households-food-waste (accessed 25 February 2014).

[2] Diners want restaurants to tell them about their sustainability actions – and will pay a premium. *Hospitality & Catering News*, 20 August 2013. Available at: www.hospitalityandcateringnews.com/2013/08/diners-want-restaurants-to-tell-them-about-their-sustainability-actions-and-will-pay-a-premium (accessed 25 February 2014).

[3] Sustainable Restaurant Association – Consumer Report 2013. Available at: www.thesra.org/wp-content/uploads/2012/01/Consumer-Report-2013.pdf (accessed 27 February 2014).

[4] Become a Bed & Breakfast Owner. Available at: www.fabjob.com/bedandbreakfast.asp (accessed 27 February 2014).

[5] CNN Money 2001. Available at: http://money.cnn.com/2001/05/14/sbstarting/q_bandb (accessed 10 January 2014).

[6] The Carbon Trust Hospitality Guide. Available at: www.carbontrust.com/media/39220/ctv013_hospitality.pdf (accessed 27 February 2014).

[7] Country House Cooking Competition, UK. Available at: www.lifestylefood.com.au/tv/country-house-cooking-contest (accessed 13 January 2014).

## Websites

Darts Farm, Devon, UK: www.dartsfarm.co.uk (accessed 9 January 2014).
Eco-tents in Australia: www.ecostructures.net.au
Gidleigh Park, Devon, UK: www.gidleigh.com (accessed 1 January 2014).
Good Food Ireland: www.goodfoodireland.ie (accessed 14 February 2014).
Hambleton Hall, Rutland, UK: www.hambletonhall.com (accessed 2 January 2014).
Hobbit-style accommodation in Cornwall, UK: www.classicglamping.co.uk
Le Manoir aux Quat'Saisons, Oxfordshire, UK: www.manoir.com (accessed 14 January 2014).
Medieval themed bell tents at Warwick Castle in the UK: www.warwick-castle.com
Sooke Harbour House, Sooke, Vancouver Island, British Columbia, Canada: www.sookeharbourhouse.com (accessed 11 February 2014).
The Australian Farm Stay Directory: www.australianfarmstay.com.au
The Sustainable Restaurant Association: www.thesra.org
The UK Farm Stay Directory: www.farmstay.co.uk
Tree tents in Wales, UK: www.sheepskinlife.com
Wild Luxury in an Apple Orchard in Norfolk, UK: www.wildluxury.co.uk

# III Food Tourism – The Wider Picture

Food tourism can take the form of many different activities, it is more than enterprises developed by farmers and the food community. Each year new food-related festivals and tourist activities are developed to explore the way food can be used as a tourist activity.

The evolution of these activities can also be intriguing. For example, in Finland, it has been difficult legally to set up 'pop up' food offers like those seen as street food in Asia. The result of this has been a movement to fight the legislation and the development of 'Restaurant Day' where anyone can open their doors to the public and provide food. This one-day event is held four times a year in Finland. Although it has only being going for 3 years, in 2011 it was awarded the Cultural Act of the Year. In May 2013 local residents opened their doors to the public and offered food, 527 of them were in Helsinki, and the event is now a major tourist attraction and spreading across the globe.

Restaurant days are held in Iceland, Columbia, Ivalo in Lapland, Singapore, Jerusalem, Poznan in Poland, San Diego, Lisbon and Yekaterinburg in Russia.

This event was declared the Food Event of the Year in 2013 in Copenhagen, Denmark and is an example of how novel ideas are spreading the message of local food as well as becoming a major tourist attraction.

Food tourism is one of the fastest growing tourist activities. Tourists want to discover more unusual food, find out how their food is grown and produced, discover new ways of cooking and enjoy the experience.

# 7 Independent Garden Centres and Nurseries

What is a weed? A plant whose virtues have never been discovered.

Ralph Waldo Emerson

## Introduction

During the 1980s and 1990s independent garden centres were a major tourist attraction in many countries. They can still attract large tourist crowds in season. An independent garden centre specializes in retailing garden products rather than growing plants on site, plus, as the name suggests they do not belong to a national chain retail organization.

Although their popularity in many first world countries as a destination has waned over recent years, they still have an important role to play in the garden and food tourism experience.

Many countries have seen the spending in the home garden market decline by as much as 50% over the last decade. There are number of reasons for this: (i) gardens have become a lot smaller in urban areas; (ii) there is more time pressure on people's lives and the garden has for many become a lower priority; and (iii) today's consumer is not as well educated in gardening as the generations that came before them.

However, in recent years there has been a major shift in home-owners' attitude towards gardens and gardening. The home garden in years gone by used to be about beautification and annual shows of flowers. This home garden beautification was a major income source for garden retailers during the spring months. Increasing number of consumers today want to establish their own edible garden and, as a result, more vegetables and fruit trees are being planted. As a consequence, the edible plant category has grown in importance in garden centres.

**Fig. 7.1.** Czech garden centre displaying pumpkins and plants together in late summer.

Successful garden centres over recent years have had to rethink their retail model; what was a successful retail model in 1980 is not a successful model in 2015. The retail garden industry developed by selling products, the consumer of today buys 'dreams', hence the garden retail model has had to change completely. Many traditional garden retailers have found this difficult to understand and to adapt their business model to meet the new consumer demands.

Progressive independent garden centres found they had to introduce some of the following additional activities to appeal to the changed consumer needs:

• Farm shops, which are in competition with farm shops on the farm. Examples of successful food offers in the retail garden sector include The Hole Enjoy Centre in St Albert, Alberta, Canada and Barton Grange Garden Centre and Farm Shop near Preston, Lancashire, UK. The garden centre food offer tends to be a food hall rather than a farm shop, although some garden centres have managed to create genuine farm shop retail offers. According to research carried out by Readex Research in the USA in July 2013,[1] 10% of American garden centres have or are looking at including a farmers' market (farm shop) in store within their centre;

• Restaurants that serve local foods. The prepared food sector of the garden industry can now be as large in turnover as the garden sector. The early adopters of the food offer in the industry often served standard processed food with little consideration for quality or food sourcing. This has now changed and many garden centres have established an authentic regional food offer. Others still have a long way to go in gaining credibility with the discerning food tourist, but it is rapidly changing;

- Kitchen utensils as a new retail category. As the food and gardening categories come closer together it is inevitable that kitchen utensils will become part of the product mix. To a garden centre operator there is no difference between a garden tool, such as a spade, and a kitchen tool such as a cheese slicer. Both provide the total solution to today's consumer;
- The development of the edible garden department rather than rows of plants laid out using botanical names. This helps create the experience the consumer is looking for. Plus the average sale per customer tends to increase as consumers can see a range of products at the same time that appeals to their specific buying needs.

This means that forward-thinking independent garden centre operators are now becoming part of the culinary food tourism journey as more and more garden centres introduce food as an important part of their retail mix.

The leading independent garden centres belong to IGCA (The International Garden Centre Association; www.intgardencentre.org). These centres will often have the IGCA logo displayed at the entrance to their garden centre. The logo indicates they are recognized by their peers as one of the best independent garden centres in the world.

# The Value of Independent Garden Centres to Food Tourism[2]

Food tourists are often keen gardeners and often have an edible garden at home in some form. During the last few years they have probably converted more and more of their garden over to edibles and reduced the amount of ornamental plants. They like to be able to go into their garden to gather the freshest fruit, vegetables or herbs for a meal.

As food tourists they visit many of the activities mentioned in this book, but not only do they want to purchase produce they often also like to take a plant home and grow that produce in their own backyard. In the consumer's mind the garden centre is part of the food adventure and a visit to a local garden centre will often be included on their itinerary to see what edible plants they might find there. Astute independent garden centres take advantage of this trend and use it as a marketing opportunity.

They will consider the following strategies.

## Marketing outside of the business

- Promote their business in local tourist food magazines;
- Network with the local producers to develop cross-marketing opportunities;
- Cross-promote venues at other food tourist destinations; and
- Partner with local food activities, whether that be a community garden or farmers' market.

**Marketing within the business**

Create an edible section in the garden centre where all edibles are located together. In the USA one of the biggest trends is combining ornamental and edible plants in containers for consumers. Edibles are the second biggest plant category in the USA at the time of writing and experienced a 27% increase in sales in 2013.

- Highlight the local, more unusual produce they have for sale within the edibles department;
- Hold food-growing classes that can be attended by locals and visitors;
- Network with local celebrity chefs and provide recipes next to the produce;
- Introduce locally made kitchenware and utensils where they are available; and
- Ensure the restaurant in the garden centre serves locally sourced produce.

# Nurseries

Purists would define nurseries as operations that grow the plants on their premises and either sell directly to the public or sell to retailers who then sell to the public. This means that some wholesale nurseries will not be interested in food tourism and will actually deter visitors from coming to their nursery.

In the 1950s and 1960s, many nurseries were started by farmers who changed from growing food crops to growing ornamental plants as at the time that strategy proved to be more profitable. Those plants often ended up in independent garden centres.

As we have said, the market has changed again and many of those growers have now reverted back to growing food plants, often to be sold in farmers' markets or garden centres. They have gone the full circle, and have to relearn the growing skills of producing food plants for the new consumer.

Food tourists are only interested in retail nurseries. Retail nurseries are nurseries that grow plants and open their gate to the public who can buy direct from the grower. In theory this should guarantee that the plants are locally grown, but remember some growers buy in plants from other nurseries, sometimes in other countries and then 'grow them on' in their own nursery for sale. Retail nurseries may allow the food tourist to buy local fruit and vegetable plants grown by the local grower and therefore get extra advice and know that the plants are authentic to the area. When considering nurseries food tourists may also consider mail order nurseries and online nurseries; these can often be an excellent source of more unusual plants.

# References

[1] *Garden Center News* 17 October 2013. Research carried out by Readex Research July 2013.
[2] Stanley, J. (2002) *The Complete Guide to Garden Center Management*. Ball Publishing, Chicago, Illinois.

## Websites

International Garden Centre Association: www.intgardencentre.org (accessed 2 January 2014).

# 8 The Food Offer

You go to a restaurant to eat what you cannot prepare at home.

Sat Baines, Chef at NG7, Nottingham, UK

## Introduction

In many people's minds food tourism is about eating food, the consumer expects to experience and digest the best food a region has to offer. The first culinary tourist restaurant was probably when Mr Lyons opened his tea and cake shop in the UK in 1870. The shop was so successful that it became an institution and Lyons Tea Shops spread across the country over the next century.

Another major change in eating habits came in the 1960s when many small cafés were replaced by fast food outlets with the result that many cafés closed down.

Fast food was controlled by speed and price and most street corners today seem to have a selection of fast food outlets.

Some restaurant icons remained. Bettys in Harrogate in Yorkshire has remained as an institution to this day and is a major tourist attraction. Bettys tearoom was opened by Frederick Belmont in 1919 who was a Swiss confectioner. To this day, nobody knows who the original Betty was; it is part of the magic of the place.

Today's culinary tourists want to linger longer in independent local food outlets and we have come full circle in the food offer to the consumer.

## Where do Food Tourists Start?

### Airport restaurants

Many culinary tourists will start their journey at an international airport. Historically airport restaurants have not been recognized as providing quality food experiences, but that is changing.

**Fig. 8.1.** Giraffe Restaurant in Bath, Somerset, UK.

John Torode and Gregg Wallace, two of the UK TV Masterchefs, have been appointed as the official food tasters at Heathrow Airport in London. The philosophy at Heathrow Airport today is to promote and provide food based on British culinary talent. In July 2013 Heathrow Airport Ltd launched a magazine *Food on the Fly*, which is available to all terminal users. Heston Blumenthal has opened a restaurant at Heathrow Airport's Terminal 2. This is an indicator of how airport restaurants will join the food tourism market over the next few years.

Copenhagen Airport in Denmark has developed 'pop up' restaurants, CPH Nordic Dining, and uses three leading Danish chefs to prepare and promote local Danish food.

Many airports now have a local retail food offer as one of the retail offers in the departure lounge.

When a gourmet culinary tourist starts planning their journey they will often start their restaurant search in one of two ways.

### *The MICHELIN Guide to Restaurants and Hotels* or the 'Red Guide'

*The Michelin Guide* was started in France by the makers of car tyres, Andre and Edward Michelin, when they wrote a guide in 1900 for French car drivers on the best hotels and restaurants in Europe.

In 1926 they developed a star points system to grade the top restaurants and Michelin star rankings have become the 'Oscars' of the restaurant industry. The stars are divided into three groups:

- One star – very good restaurant;
- Two star – excellent restaurant;
- Three star – exceptional restaurant.

Food connoisseurs search out Michelin restaurants in Europe. Michelin rankings are now in other countries as well. The Michelin 'red book' (www.michelin-travel.com) has become the culinary tourists' 'bible' of the restaurant industry.

### Top restaurants guides

Magazines and the Internet also now provide lists of the top restaurants in the town, county, country, or the world and have become a major reference source for culinary tourists. Restaurant owners should have as one of their aims to get on to at least one of these lists, for example *The Good Food Guide*[1] in the UK, which lists the 50 best restaurants.

## Present-Day Food Tourism

Food tourism today, like other types of tourism, can be divided into two groups: businesses who are the primary provider of the offer and secondary providers. In general food tourists often carry out less prior research than gourmet culinary tourists and will find venues as they travel a region. Food tourists will often select from the following two options.

### Primary food providers

Primary food providers are businesses that are food destinations in the consumer's mind. They need to provide excellent food and service and are the main reason for the tourist visiting the region. The food they provide is critically important to the consumer experience.

### Secondary food providers

This group often do not see themselves as being in the tourist industry, but in the visitor's mind they are just as important. They are the providers who offer food in petrol or gas stations, cafés along the way and accommodation providers providing breakfast who are not part of the primary destination. However, it is our experience that it is these providers who can so often provide negative experiences for the traveller.

Providing the best local food and best experience should be a major priority for all who engage with tourists on their journey.

# Restaurants

The restaurant sector is a sector that is changing rapidly. It is also one of the fastest movers; businesses come and go, plus, food fashions are constantly changing. What is trendy in one part of the world may not be trendy in another region.

The 'true' food tourist is interested in restaurants that focus on local foods and local traditions. Conventional restaurants would not fit into the food tourism category.

A 'true' food tourist restaurant includes restaurants such as Sat Bains in Nottingham in the UK (www.restaurantsatbains.com). Sat Bains is a Michelin chef who will only source food that is grown or raised within the local postal code.

## Food trends

The latest information on eating habit trends was produced in September 2013 by 'Growth Delivered' (http://acgrowthdelivered.com), an American consultancy company. Their report indicated that the trend in 2013 was NOT to eat around the table and snacks were blurring with meals, e.g. soups are now looked on as a snack.

In the USA, 47% of the food spend was in restaurants, although 21% of the population called themselves opportunist eaters, or having a snack on the run when they could and if it was available.

## Restaurant categories

Restaurants fall into a number of different categories as far as consumers are concerned:

- Exotic restaurants. This is where consumers want to experience food from a culture other than their own;
- Bar-style restaurants where casual dining is the norm;
- Quick low-budget eating establishments. These are family dining restaurants such as the many fast food restaurants scattered around the world;
- Fine dining restaurants. These are restaurants where the finest local food is served and guests normally book a table for the evening;
- Generation Y restaurants, such as Jamie Oliver's restaurants where young consumers tend to browse eat several times a day.

Tourists visit restaurants for a number of different reasons and this is high-lighted in the research carried out by Jason Guenther and Barry Zimmerman in a report by Professor James Potter titled 'Restaurant Research.'[2] Guenther and Zimmerman concluded the choice of restaurant is based on different reasons, but primarily, in priority sequence, they are:

1. **Quality of food: 70%.**
2. **Customer service: 70%.**
3. **Restaurant atmosphere: 20%.**
4. **Price of the meal: 5%.**
5. **Location of restaurant: 5%.**
6. **Speed of food delivery.**
7. **Healthiness of the food offered.**
8. **Networking opportunities.**

## Customer service

Around the world the general view is that customer service is declining in all retail establishments. Research in the restaurant industry covered a number of areas of customer service.

### Team visual appearance

- 70% of customers polled felt team visual appearance was very important when choosing where to eat;
- 20% of customers felt it was important;
- 10% felt it was not important.[2]

This identifies how important team training is in the restaurant industry. Team members need to know where the food served came from, they need to understand how the meal is prepared, they need to understand the ingre-dients and must be able to advise customers with allergies etc. In addition, they must have the personality skills and empathy to know how much en-gagement the customer wants whilst dining.

### Restaurant atmosphere

The key ingredients that make up the atmosphere in the consumer's mind are:

- Lighting: fast food restaurants tend to focus on using fluorescent light-ing. Their aim is persuading patrons to eat their meal quickly as 'table' turns are important to making a profit; the more tables they can turn in a session the more money the restaurant makes. Whereas upmarket res-taurants rely on 'mood' or accent lighting to relax patrons and will often allow the guest to book a table for the whole evening;
- Privacy: some patrons are looking for privacy within the restaurant whilst others want a more public location to share with friends and to be seen. Generation Y restaurants are all about being seen in the right

establishment as a guest, while Baby Boomer restaurants are more likely to provide secluded booths where guests can dine with some privacy;

- Comfort: the style of furniture used and especially the chairs is a major comfort factor. The faster the restaurant's desired turnover of guests, the less comfortable the chairs that are provided;
- Vegetation is used in a number of ways. Vegetation can indicate a 'green' or 'sustainable' business as well as offering colour, intimacy and image building. The important issue is that vegetation is maintained to a high standard. A dying *Ficus* or rubber plant in the corner of the room does not inspire a guest to feel the food is fresh;
- House architecture: this creates the overall image of the dining experience. It can create nostalgia, old, young or fresh and help attract specific consumer groups;
- Colour affects how consumers feel and it plays a role in eating behaviour. It can make consumers eat quickly, McDonald's red is an example of this, or slowly using more relaxed colours.

## Trends

Every year the *Australian* newspaper publishes the 'Hot 50 Restaurants' and look at trends in Australia. In 2013 it identified the following trends of which food tourism restaurants should be aware:

- The best managed restaurants tend to be small focused restaurants; the owners are more passionate and can relate to the local environment;
- Fine dining is becoming less popular as consumers seek better value;
- Local and unusual ingredients are been sought by consumers. In Australia this includes nettles and palm hearts, homemade butters, homemade curds and handmade smoked products.

According to Rene Redzepi, the chef and owner of Noma, the Copenhagen restaurant that is considered to be one of the best restaurants in the world, the menu of the future will focus on locally grown and seasonal fruit and vegetables and have less emphasis on meat.[3]

All these trends are relevant to food tourism-focused restaurants.

- Wine-friendly foods are in vogue plus the wine is an added value opportunity for the restaurant.

## Theatrical eating

Culinary tourists seek an experience, as a result a number of theatrical restaurants have appeared around the world.

Biribildu, for example, is a souvlaki restaurant in Athens, Greece, designed by Greek architect Minas Kosmidis (www.minaskosmidis.com), and planned to look like a circus ring. Once inside patrons are exposed to carousel horses with the kitchen designed to look from the outside like a circus ring. Patrons visit this restaurant for the fun experience.

Eating habits also change with age. Generation Y are changing the way restaurants are developing, Generation Ys look to more tapas-style eating and expect to be able to eat whenever they want. They want funky restaurants with a less formal atmosphere.

## Culinary Tourists Want To Eat Local

Culinary tourists want to eat local food. Providers of food should know what is local and what is in season. Alas, many food providers often fail the customer in this key area.

There are many books written on how to set up and manage restaurants and this is not the aim of this book. We will focus on the aspects that are specific to food tourism.

We all have our favourite restaurants and it is well worth visiting them both physically and online to see what tips you can pick up. One of our favourites is Babylonstoren (http://babylonstoren.com/food) near Cape Town in South Africa. This is a great example of how a restaurant can develop a food tourism niche. This restaurant offer includes its own edible garden food.

### It starts with the menu

The first exposure to the food offer for the majority of consumers is the menu. Consumers will make a decision on the whole food experience just by looking at the menu. Planning a menu is critical to the success of the business and we advise, if you are about to provide a food offer from scratch, you start with the menu.

The following vital factors should be taken into consideration:

- Consumers are looking for healthy, nutritional food in a relaxing environment, that has been prepared either locally or on site;
- Find out what local produce is available seasonally and decide how it can be incorporated into the menu design. Consider how seasonality of produce will affect the menu design;
- How often will the menu need to be changed to keep the seasonality and variety of the menu?
- What menu balance will be required and what nutritional qualities will consumers be looking for?
- Have a variation to cope with consumer allergies, dietary requirements, calorie counts and different eating habits;
- What do potential diners want to eat; are they coming for a snack or a full menu?
- What are the gaps in the market place that you have discovered and how can you cater for them?

- Are you expecting young families or more mature tourists and when do you expect them to visit your restaurant?
- What gross profit and net profit do you want to achieve? You need to work backwards to decide what your menu price structure will be;
- What catering equipment do you have already and what will you need to purchase? The decision on what equipment you need will be based on what is offered on the menu;
- What skills will be required by the catering team to meet the needs of the menu and what time allocation will the visitor tolerate between ordering and serving?
- Design the menu so that it reflects the image of the business and acts as a promotional tool for the business. Use the menu to sell the story of the local produce and the local growers;
- Keep it simple. Long lists of different food offerings confuse consumers as well as it means you will have to purchase more produce and this could result in waste produce at the end of the day;
- Create a 'signature' dish that is unique to the restaurant. We recently visited a coffee shop in Manjimup in Western Australia that offered Rustle-berry Pie. It promoted itself as the only coffee shop in the region that served the unique local berry in a pie. A great example of a simple but effective 'signature' dish. In Western Australia, Buy West, Eat Best, the State promotional body for promoting regional food, launched a competition in 2014 to develop a Western Australia signature dish using local foods. This state-wide competition aimed to promote local signature dishes.

Once you have designed a menu, be prepared to change it. The consumer will decide what is the ideal menu and we guarantee that you will need to alter it to meet the consumer needs.

The menu ideally should go on a website where the catering team can edit the menu daily and drive customers to the website. Richardson Farms near Baltimore, Maryland (www.richardsonfarms.net) does this very successfully and it indicates to the consumer that they are a farm in the 'fresh' industry.

## Opening a culinary food offer

Before opening a café or restaurant, visit other food offers in the region. Be objective in looking at what they are doing, get to understand their menu and what they are offering and why. Do they promote local foods and local food offerings, how many people do they seat and when do consumers visit them? What decor are they using and why? Create a SWOT analysis of each business visited and then use the combined SWOT analyses to develop your own business SWOT plan.

Before venturing too far into a food offering check on the local legal requirements, they differ from country to country and region to region. The regulations will include:

- Planning Acts;
- Building Regulations;
- Food and Drug Acts;
- Public Health Acts;
- Food Hygiene Regulations;
- Fire Prevention Regulations;
- Trade Description Acts;
- Regulations related to less able persons; and
- All the other regulations and laws that apply to setting up a local business.

## Designing a restaurant or café

There are numerous consultants who specialize in this area of expertise and depending on what you are aiming to achieve we advise that you consult with a consultant with skills in this field.

There are a number of rules you should be aware of to help you get the best out of the advice and set your business up. The design of the catering operation will depend on what you are aiming to achieve.

The following should act as a guideline only:

- Café: eating area 90% of space; preparation area 10% of space;
- Self-service offer: eating area 75% of space; preparation area 25% of space;
- Waiter service: eating area 65% of space; preparation area 35% of space.

The preparation area will again be divided up into working area and storage area and the workflow must provide a logical work sequence. The sequence should be delivery, storage, preparation, cooking and serving and then washing up and refuse disposal.

## How big should the restaurant be?

One of the biggest mistakes we have seen in restaurant facilities is that they were not big enough at establishment. The minimum seating arrangement should be 60 seats, below that it becomes difficult to make a profit. The challenge is how to optimize the table and chair arrangement.

Research carried out in the UK[4] recommends the following for a 106-seater restaurant:

| Group size | Number of tables | % |
|---|---|---|
| One | 13 | 26 |
| Two | 26 | 52 |
| Four | 4 | 16 |
| Six | 2 | 12 |

The space allocated to each diner also varies depending on the shape of the tables.

- Square tables for two: 1.7–2.00 m² per diner;.
- Square tables for four: 1.3–1.7 m² per diner;
- Circular tables for four: 0.9–1.4 m² per diner.

We prefer the look of circular tables, although there is a trend towards long tables where everyone mixes together and this could be the image you are looking for. It encourages people to interact with each other and provides the Italian family-look to the facility.

Space between tables should be at least 900 mm and 450 mm between chairs, although this does change with different cultures; for example, Asian diners will sit closer together than New Zealand diners. As a general rule provide 16 ft² per diner.

When it comes to designing the kitchen most catering supply companies have a consultancy service and it is well worth using this facility, it can save a lot of money.

## Manage to make a profit

Restaurants and coffee shops can be profitable ventures, but they do require a large amount of capital to set up. One of the biggest challenges is managing food costs. Most small restaurants aim for about 30% of costs to be on food, although this will vary depending on the offering to your patrons.

The following formula will help you determine what you need to price a food item at to achieve this goal:

Cost of portion × 4 = selling price, including sales tax

The restaurant owner should always be looking at plates when people have finished their meal. The last thing the owner wants to see is food left on the plate; this could be an indicator that the meal size is too large and shows potential profits that are going in the waste bin. It also means that it is difficult to add-on sell and offer a dessert to a consumer who is already full. The ideal scenario is where the consumer has room for the highly profitable dessert that the team have prepared.

The real challenge in running a restaurant is controlling food costs. Food costs can only be controlled when the problem is known. Read and understand the stock sheets and make sure the team who need to, can do the same. The answer is usually evident if you understand what the numbers are supposed to look like.

Once a problem has been identified, suitable action can be taken. The following list includes areas that can be controlled and monitored:

1. Theft: cash or stock.
2. Portion control: over-portioning to customer or over-portioning to staff.
3. Waste: in preparation, overproduction, incorrect storage, receiving in poor condition or food drying out on hot plates.

**4.** Staff meals: eating more than their allowance or eating high-cost food items.

**5.** Pricing: incorrect prices charged, items not charged for or incorrect pricing of new recipes.

**6.** Purchasing: bought at too high a price or purchasing from unauthorized suppliers.

**7.** Deliveries: are they being checked in correctly, are quantities correct, are you not receiving some stock and are there substitutes at a higher price?

**8.** Sales mix: producing and selling a high percentage of products that have a high food cost.

**9.** Recipes: recipes not being followed, resulting in higher usage of raw food items.

**10.** Stocktaking: incorrect stocktaking may produce a higher food cost if stock is not counted.

Other costs also need to be taken into consideration. Staff wages are always one that needs to be monitored. In a small restaurant wages should be around 20% of turnover and overhead costs around 20% of turnover.

There are numerous consultants in the restaurant industry. Before venturing into catering we strongly advise that their advice is sought. This could save a lot of capital investment and ongoing costs in running the operation.

## Keep to the values

The important message with any food offer is that the owner keeps to the values of the business.

One of our favourite restaurants in London is Canteen. The company has strong values that it communicates to the visitor. Canteen sources British food from a good provenance. Meat is additive free and fish delivered daily. They use seasonal fruit and vegetables and fish from sustainable fishing practices. Beef comes from Sussex and Red Devon animals that are hung for up to 4 weeks to improve the flavour and texture, and jams are home made.

We realize that there will be readers saying that they are also doing this and we know that many are. The difference with the Canteen is that they are upfront with the message and promote this to their guests in the restaurant. The 'values' are clearly evident as soon as the visitor walks in the restaurant.

## Coffee – Make it Easy

It is a saying that we often hear 'that life is too short for bad wine and bad coffee'. It is well worth investing in a good coffee machine and attending a Barista course. If an operator can supply a great coffee it will be amazing how much of a magnet the coffee can become for the coffee-thirsty tourist. When possible select Fair Trade coffee beans, but also consider what you put the coffee into. It is easy to buy takeaway coffee cups, but consider what happens to them. Consumers today appreciate their coffee in a sustainable container.

In Australia, for example, 1 billion takeaway coffee cups and lids are thrown into the countryside every year to litter the environment. As a result of this, the 'Responsible Cafes' Programme[5] was developed with the incentive to use reusable coffee cups. In the food tourism market, providers should care about the environment and should consider a scheme such as this.

Most disposable coffee cups and lids are not recyclable. We have travelled around Portland, Oregon, where it is compulsory that all utensils used by all food providers are compostable, but this is not the norm in other cities. Portland is one of the greenest sustainable cities in the world and lessons can be learned in their city for all food tourism operators.

More and more coffee retailers see the need for a sustainable future and many organizations have started to get involved in the development of 'green' coffee offers.

In Australia one approach has been an incentive that has been built into the coffee offer. Customers are offered a discount if they bring the coffee cup and lid back, or bring in their own cup; this varies between 30 and 50 cents a cup.

Not only does this allow the coffee retailer to handle the cups more effectively, it also increases customer loyalty and attracts new customers. Plus, a new income stream for the retailer is developed. Reusable cups are sold at often a 60% mark up to a professional recycling company. The above scheme is operated in Australia by Take3, the Two Hands Project, Tangaroa Blue, The Australian Marine Debris Initiative and Transition Bondi.

Consider how you can make your coffee a green sustainable offer that cannot be refused.

## On-Farm Restaurants

Setting up a restaurant is a major decision for any farmer. It is a completely new business and will need its own dedicated team to manage it. One of the challenges is that you cannot start small and make a profit. To justify the capital outlay and development cost, the restaurant will need to sit a minimum of 60 people; some of the seating can be outdoors to reduce the capital outlay, but the challenge is still there.

One extra challenge over conventional restaurants is the offer is on the farm; many farms have flies or other insects and insect screening may be needed if outdoor eating areas are designed into the plan. This is critically important in some parts of Australia where flies can be a major nuisance.

## Pop Up Food Offers

One of the fastest growing sectors of food tourism is what is known as 'pop up food.' Pop up food is where a food offer literally 'pops up' when and where it is needed.

'Pop up' is not completely new. The fish and chip van used to appear in many towns and still does in many areas on a Friday evening. The new trend in pop up food started in Los Angeles where street vendors would appear for the lunchtime workers or evening theatre trade.

Pop up retailing of food in the past was often avoided by the food tourist as they were often dubious about the quality of food offered. Today, however, we have the emergence of excellent quality food offers popping up in cities around the world. The pop up vehicles are often becoming celebrities in their own right. Marketing is often carried out via social media with the on-board chef sending a Tweet out to the local client base just before the arrival of the van. Pop up food retailing now takes many forms, and new ways of 'pop up' are developing all the time.

## Food Trucks

In 1866 Charles Goodnight identified that cattle drives and the cowboys that drove them in the USA needed a feed at the end of the day. He obtained a United States Army wagon and converted it into a food wagon. The first food truck was on the road, except then it was called the 'Chuckwagon'.

The 'Chuckwagon' evolved and wagons often visit factory sites delivering food; these wagons often go under the slang name of 'roach coaches'.

Now food trucks have evolved to places where you can get trendy food. A food truck in Perth in Western Australia sells truffles amongst the delicacies on offer. Most cities now have food trucks providing high quality food that are now part of the tourist scene.

Tampa, Florida has the world's largest food truck rally with 99 trucks arriving at the rally. Sydney, Australia, has introduced the trucks as a tourist attraction as have other cities who often have dedicated webpages, (www.sydneyfoodtrucks.com.au).

One of the fastest growing franchisees in the USA is Gourmet Streets, which franchises food trucks.

## Street Food

One of the pleasures of going to Asia is to enjoy the food. At the end of the day in most cities street food vendors set up their kitchens. They bring along fresh ingredients straight from the markets, set up a small stove and cook the food in front of the client. This traditional source of food for the workers has become a major tourist attraction.

In Jogjakarta, Indonesia, a major tourist attraction is Lesihan breakfast held on the pavement of many of the streets. Lesihan was traditionally provided as a cheap breakfast for students at the many universities in the city. Today students and tourists alike use Lesihan as a major point for a social gathering.

## Field Kitchens

**Fig. 8.2.** A floating restaurant at Stratford on Avon, Warwickshire, UK.

Mention field kitchens and most people will think of a rough kitchen set up on an army camp or scout camp. These kitchens still exist, but the development of pop up retailing has also moved into the kitchen market. The modern culinary traveller expects to be able to taste the food and enjoy a meal made from local foods.

As a farmer or grower, the thought of setting up a kitchen may be challenging, especially with the capital cost and legislative hoops to go through to get a restaurant off the ground. For many growers the capital and ongoing costs are prohibitive.

The field kitchen may be the solution.

The majority of tourists tend to visit farms on a weekend looking for a more rustic experience. Set up a pop up kitchen and a few tables for when you need them. Often a local food supplier is willing to work with a venue to establish such a kitchen and the cooking can be done on a series of barbecues.

Thinking 'outside' the box may solve your problem.

Google 'field kitchen' and you will see a wide range of options that could be considered to provide a catering experience for your guests. Most can be set up and dismantled easily, some can be rented or you may want to consider getting your own kit.

Whilst looking at the 'pop up' opportunities, you may want to consider offering picnic baskets to your guests.

In British Columbia, Canada we came across Locavore, a pop up food outlet developed by a local farmer. This is a trailer kitchen that goes to events to provide local foods. Pop-up food outlets are common, but this is the first time we have seen a farmer develop one to sell his own produce direct to the consumer.

## Food Tourism Cluster Food Offers

A common question asked by new entrepreneurs to the industry is should they be a standalone business or should they cluster with other businesses who provide a similar offer.

We often refer them to the scenario that if you pull off a freeway in the USA you are met with a number of different food offers in one location; many of them selling either a hamburger, chicken or pizza. These food retailers know that cluster, or a community of food offers, works in the best interest of all concerned; it provides a destination that gives the consumer choice. These are food tourist destinations that do that exceptionally well.

In shopping centres now we see the development of the food hall as an important part of the site's retail offer. Numerous self-service and food retail offers are located, often in a semi-circle, around a large seating area for consumers to make a choice and then sit together with family or friends.

This means that each family member can eat a different dish from a different part of the world, but still eat as a family unit. Many pundits may not look on this as part of food tourism, however for those who have visited Asian cities, eating in a food hall is a major evening social activity and must surely be grouped as a tourism activity. Food halls often do not start to become busy until after 8 pm in an evening and can still be exceptionally busy at midnight. They provide an entertainment zone, often in air-conditioned centres where locals and tourists can enjoy an evening in a pleasant and comfortable environment.

Farmers' markets often have a number of vendors offering the same offer and competition is healthy and beneficial to all in situations like this. Cluster businesses become a destination in their own right.

If the business is a standalone, it has to have special attributes to encourage tourists to make a special journey to visit them. Many businesses do not have that special factor to be successful as standalones. If they do, the inevitable happens and other businesses start clustering around them. An example of this is 'The Eden Project' (www.edenproject.com) in Cornwall in the UK; the Eden Project is situated in one of the remote parts of the country, yet Eden is the most visited attraction of its type in the UK. As a result, it is now surrounded by other businesses that are thriving as a cluster as a result of the vision of the developer of the Eden Project, Tim Smit.

However, it is recommended that ideally a business should locate where the tourists and the cluster of like-minded businesses are already located. This formula has worked for businesses for many years and will not change in the forseeable future.

## Chinatown

A unique national food cuisine environment that has established itself as a tourist destination in its own right around the world is Chinese food offered in Chinatown. Chinatown is often located near a city centre and many cities in the world have their own Chinatown. Most Chinatowns that we have seen are highly decorated and have become tourist destinations in their city.

The oldest Chinatown outside of China was founded in 1594 in Manila in the Philippines. The area known as Binondo is famous for its Chinese quarter, which can be visited by calesa, a horse-drawn trap. One of the favourites in this area is spit roasted pig or Lechon, which is a local delicacy.

Chinatown offers an experience where the visitor is transported to another country within the confines of the town. This must be one of the true culinary journeys that is common around the world. No other national cuisines have managed to make this transition of providing a unique cultural experience. Chinatowns can be found in Canada, the USA, Australia, Europe and most Asian countries.

The top ten Chinatowns in the world according to National Geographic's *Food Journeys of a Lifetime*[6] are:

1. Manhattan, New York. This is one of the world's largest Chinatowns: www.explorechinatown.com
2. Vancouver, Canada: www.vancouverchinatown.ca
3. San Francisco Chinatown, USA: www.sanfranciscochinatown.com
4. Havana, Cuba: www.cubatravel.cu
5. Singapore: www.chinatown.org.sg
6. Binondo, the Philippines: www.tourism.gov.ph
7. Jakarta, Indonesia: www.jakarta-tourism.go.id
8. Brisbane, Australia: www.visitbrisbane.com.au
9. London, based around Soho: www.chinatownlondon.org
10. Manchester, UK: www.visitmanchester.com

## EatWith and Cookening

Tourists venture increasingly into more remote places and want more local food experiences. To accommodate this trend, new opportunities are appearing, one of which is EatWith, which allows the consumer to experience food tourism by eating in local people's homes. EatWith started in Tel Aviv, Israel; visitors can now go to local residents' homes and have a meal with the family by logging on to 'EatWith' (www.eatwith.com).

Cookening (www.cookening.com) is a similar programme in Europe, where home owners share a meal with travellers.

## 'Comedy of Errors' Restaurants

It is often difficult to decide where to draw the line between food tourism and pure entertainment. Some restaurants provide great food and bad service – on purpose. Comedy restaurants are places where customers go expecting bad service, often provided by trained comedians. Guests willingly pay for a 'Basil Fawlty' experience and come away smiling.

### Silent eating as a tourist attraction

One of the complaints of many restaurant goers is that the restaurants are getting noisier. How about a silent eatery? One of the tourist attractions in Brooklyn, New York is EAT. For around US$40 a meal, guests eat in silence. If a guest breaks the rules they are asked to go outside. Silent eating is a unique tourist attraction. eatfreenpoint.com

## Picnics and Food Hampers

Historically the picnic was a moveable feast that the medieval wealthy indulged in during hunting events in Europe. Victorian gentry then developed the picnic concept (where it was known as a *fêtes champêtres*) as we know it today. Every guest contributed food and the 'picnics' were quite lavish.

With the introduction of the car, the picnic evolved into a family event when travelling. Food was prepared and placed in a hamper or basket and a spot in the countryside was selected for casual family dining.

The origin of the word 'picnic' is believed to come from the southern part of the USA and has a derogative background that thankfully has been lost as time has progressed.

The food hamper was developed in England over 300 years ago by Fortnum and Mason, who still promote that they provide the best hampers in the world. The origin of the hamper was to provide the aristocracy of England with a food basket that they could take with them on their journeys. It also evolved into a food hamper that was sent to the troops during the war.

**Fig. 8.3.** Picnic arrangement at the Leeuwin Estate, Margaret River, Western Australia.

The Victorian era was when the food hamper really came into its own because of the 'London Season' when all the main events took place around the city. This was where the 'must-be-seen' wealthy had to go to be seen, the events included the Harrow and Eton cricket match, Henley Regatta, Cowes Regatta and the Epsom Derby. Fortnum and Mason supplied picnic hampers for these occasions, many of them being collected on the day from the store.

Hampers traditionally were wicker baskets, but now a range of containers are used; we recently had a meal on a train and the meal was in a cardboard box that was called a 'hamper'.

The picnic has evolved; not all food tourists want waiter service and sit-down meals, some want to sit in the countryside and admire the view and have a picnic. This is also a cost-effective way of providing food as a catering offer.

Picnics can be set up on rustic tables or a provider can do something different. It is amazing what can be achieved with an old tractor tyre as a table, wooden seats, large cushions and a rug. All of a sudden you have a boutique picnic offer that is memorable and unique.

Some guests will bring their own food in a hamper whilst others will want you to provide food. The most effective way of doing this is to provide food hampers of various sizes and with a range of ingredients. The hampers should contain all local food and can also be sold as gifts or for consumption off site.

Many farm retailers now create specific hampers custom-made for their patrons.

## Food Trails

**Fig. 8.4.** Flavour Trail sign on Vancouver Island, British Columbia, Canada.

A recent and rapidly growing food tourism attraction is food trails. Government and tourist organizations alike are developing food trails as a new tourist marketing opportunity. The modern food trail is based on a travel habit that is centuries old. Early explorers went on food trails to the Spice Islands and other regions of the world. Many early food trail explorers were on a walking mission to discover new edible plants and foods. Today the modern food trail can still be a walking tour, but it can also be on a bike, car, coach, train or boat.

When one researches food trails on the Internet, the discovery is that almost every region of the world has a food trail that can be explored.

A food trail means the region can build the reputation of the location as a source of quality food, plus provide a complete package to tourists and promote both accommodation and visits to local food destinations.

Today's tourist and consumers do not want to travel long distances to visit one venue in that location; tourists want to discover a number of different locations in one area and this is why food trails are growing in popularity. A food trail should promote a specific region and the food offer within that region.

To be successful, there are a number of important elements that need to be in place on a food trail.

## Cooperating producers with the same goal

A group of growers and added value food operators need to agree to cooperate and have the same goal before a trail can be developed. Experience shows that this is easy to say and more difficult to implement. All participants need to have similar values and believe in the opportunities in the region.

The first stage is to get all interested stakeholders to meet to discuss the opportunities and to define what is unique about the region. If there is an overlap in what people produce this is not a problem, there are very successful trails that focus on wine or whisky and even lavender, so a multiple of growers doing the same thing can be an asset to the venture.

The distance between sites on the food trail needs to be discussed. Having them too close together means that it is not a trail in the true sense, but have the venues too far apart and visitors will get disillusioned and leave the trail. Ideally the consumer travelling by car should be able to reach at least three venues in a day.

Once the primary stakeholders are committed then include the broader stakeholder community. This could include:

- Regional tourism organizations;
- Development commissions;
- Wine Industry Association;
- Tourism councils and associations;
- Department of Agriculture;
- Department of Fisheries;
- Department of Transport;
- Restaurant associations;
- Local authorities;
- Local Chambers of Commerce;
- Events organizations; and
- Key businesses and industry representatives.

## Branding

A food trail does need to be branded to enable the visitor to identify who is a genuine food trail member and who is not. The brand, via a logo, must be clearly visible to travellers. The food trail is the key brand in the consumer's mind, not the name of the individual enterprise and this can cause some conflict in some growers' minds.

The objective is to get tourists to the region and the overall brand has to be the 'hero'. Tom O'Toole is a conference speaker and the owner of Beechworth Bakery (www.beechworthbakery.com.au) in Beechworth, a remote town around 3 hours' drive from Melbourne in Victoria, Australia. Tom has the most successful standalone independent bakery in the southern hemisphere. His motto has always been 'My job is to get them to Beechworth, once I have got them to Beechworth, I can then sell them bread.' The same thinking should be behind food trail development.

The aim of the marketing campaign should be to encourage the culinary tourist to the region, not to individual businesses.

## What are the objectives?

Food trails need to be thought through thoroughly before development commences. Consider why the trail is being developed and what are the objectives.

The Gascoyne Food Trail (www.gascoynefood.com.au) in Western Australia is an extremely well organized food trail and the organizers have developed clear objectives:

- Maximize the opportunities for the local primary producers and to increase their sales and profits;
- Sell directly to the public and to attract more consumers to the region;
- Stimulate added value opportunities for local produce;
- Showcase the local producers in the region. These local producers can include cafés, restaurants and eateries that use local food, producers, local food events, food markets, value-adding food producers that use local produce, regional food retailers and retailers in hospitality;
- Ensure the food trail has a positive impact on the region;
- Increase the awareness of, and then the consumption of, food grown in the region;
- Encourage positive interaction between producers and visitors; and
- Encourage food diversity in the region.

Experience has shown that a food trail needs to be structured professionally. The group involved will need a coordinator and a management committee to ensure the food trail is a success. Members should pay to join the group and adhere to the rules of the group.

To become a member in most food trails the producer has to fit into one of four groups:

**Case Study: Genuinely Southern Forests, south Western Australia**

Manjimup in Western Australia was traditionally a lumber town, but with the decline of the timber industry the local residents needed to reinvent the area to guarantee a viable future. It is a region where more products are grown than almost any other part of Australia. It was already well known as being the home of 'Pink Lady Apples' and 'Black Truffles'. The farming community decided to group together to develop a marketing brand that would allow them to promote the region rather than individual farm enterprises.

The brand slogan is 'Genuine fresh local produce from Genuine down-to-earth locals'.

The first stage was to develop a brand that all parties could agree to and from that a brand mark or logo was designed that could be used by all members of the community whose produce adheres to a brand code of practice or brand criteria that was established to ensure brand integrity was maintained. This provided the group with a united brand presence in the market place and the opportunity to develop a reputation for quality and diversity of their produce, as part of this united brand. The marketing is evolving to an internal/external approach both within the region and beyond, and to date has included broader marketing including billboards on the major highway to the south-west tourist area, a magazine insert in the state newspaper with a circulation of over 300,000 copies, regional radio and television advertising to build local passion and involvement. Marketing has also commenced with retailers, including smaller independent and the larger supermarkets, with the aim to build the brand and promote the amazing produce to consumers who will enjoy the produce and then ultimately look to discover the region as 'food' tourists. In the future the plan is to develop a food trail for visitors based on the brand amongst many other aspects, and to create a world class culinary tourism destination.

www.southernforestsfood.com

**Fig. 8.5.** Southern Forest Food Group cover of newspaper insert in *The West Australian* newspaper in March 2014.

**1.** A local grower in the region.
**2.** A company that is adding value to food produced in the region. This means that a local restaurant can become a member as well as a business making for example local jams and chutneys.
**3.** A non-edible producer in the region.
**4.** A company that is adding value to edibles grown in the region.

Some food trails have associate members such as bed and breakfast and restaurant providers who need to be kept in the loop to build the success of the trail.

To become a member a company needs to show that it has public liability and food safety standards as relevant to the region in which the trail is operating.

## Marketing

Members will need to pay a fee to employ a coordinator and to develop the marketing strategy. Marketing should include the development of a webpage and phone app, a brochure and signage that can be located on the trail and at the farm. The coordinator will also need to liaise with travel companies, tourist bureaus and tourist organizations to generate visitor traffic.

## Member commitment

A food trail is only as good as its members and the weakest link in the membership. Consistency between a group of individual businesses is hard. As a result there have to be member rules and they have to be adhered to. Growers who fail to implement the rules should be asked to leave the group.

Members 'MUST' rules should include the following.

**1.** The farm must be maintained in a manner that it is safe for the public to walk around the designated area.
**2.** The member will abide by the objectives of the group.
**3.** Customer service must be to an agreed minimum standard.
**4.** They will maintain their status of promoting genuine local produce.
**5.** The food trail sign must be displayed in a prominent location where visitors can see it from the road.
**6.** Brochures promoting the group will be available at the farm and the team members will promote other producers that are on the trail.
**7.** Members must be involved in any events that are organized to promote the trail whether they be on- or off-farm.
**8.** Members will comply with surveys carried out by the group.
**9.** All members will comply with local legal regulations.
**10.** Pay the members fee every year when it is due.

The weakest link in consumers' eyes is often customer service. Everyone's perspective of what is excellent customer service is different. The group should provide a customer service workshop every year. One way to encourage members to come to training is to have a two-tier membership fee. If they attend customer service training it is one fee, if they do not attend training they will pay a higher fee.

## Remember

- 80% of companies believe they provide great customer service;
- 8% of their customers agree with them.

(Source: [7]Bain Customer Led Growth diagnostic questionnaire, n = 362; Satmetrix Net Promoter database, n = 375)

## References

[1] The Good Food Guide UK. Available at: www.thegoodfoodguide.co.uk/news/the-good-food-guide-2014-app (accessed).
[2] Potter, J., Guenther, J. and Zimmerman, B. (n.d.) 'Restaurant Research'. Available at: http://architecture.unl.edu/projects/bsfed/projects/restaurant_research.pdf (accessed 6 March 2014).
[3] Redzepi, R. (2014) The menu of the future. The World in 2014. *The Economist* January.
[4] The English Tourist Guide (1960) *How to Start a Small Restaurant or Tea Room*. Out of print.
[5] The Responsible Cafes programme: www.facebook.com/ResponsibleCafes (accessed 6 March 2014).
[6] National Geographic (2009) *Food Journeys of a Lifetime, 500 Extraordinary Places to Eat Around the Globe*. National Geographic, Washington, DC.
[7] James, A., Reichold, F., Hamilton, B. and Markey, R. (2005) 'How to achieve true customer led growth'. Bains and Company.

## Websites

Babylonstoren: www.babylonstoren.com/food (accessed 4 March 2014).
Beechworth Bakery: www.beechworthbakery.com.au (accessed 7 March 2014).
Chinatown: Binondo, the Philippines: www.tourism.gov.ph
   Brisbane, Australia: www.visitbrisbane.com.au
   Havana, Cuba: www.cubatravel.cu
   Jakarta, Indonesia: www.jakarta-tourism.go.id
   London, UK: www.chinatownlondon.org
   Manchester, UK: www.visitmanchester.com
   Manhattan, New York: www.explorechinatown.com
   San Francisco Chinatown, USA: www.sanfranciscochinatown.com
   Singapore: www.chinatown.org.sg
   Vancouver, Canada: www.vancouverchinatown.ca
Cookening: www.cookening.com (accessed 6 March 2014).
Eat With: www.eatwith.com (accessed 10 March 2014).
The Eden Project: www.edenproject.com (accessed 7 March 2014).

Gascoyne Food Trail: www.gascoynefood.com.au (accessed 5 march 2014).

*Growth Delivered* Newsletter September 2013. Available at: http://acgrowthdelivered.com (accessed 4 September 2013).

*Michelin Guide to Restaurants and Hotels.* Published by Michelin: www.michelintravel.com

Sat Bains Restaurant: www.restaurantsatbains.com (accessed 6 March 2014).

Richardson Farms: www.richardsonfarms.net (accessed 5 March 2014).

Genuinely Southern Forests: www.southernforestsfood.com (accessed 7 March 2014).

# IV Marketing and the Future

If there is one field of business management that is changing more than any other field we would say it is marketing. Gone are the days when you simply designed an advertisement, sent it to the local paper and your marketing for the year was completed. In today's crowded market it is difficult to get the message across.

According to research carried out by Yankelovich and reported in the *New York Times* on 15 January 2007 in an article by Louise Story entitled 'Anywhere the Eye can see it's like seeing an Ad', it is estimated that 30 years ago the average consumer was exposed to 2000 advertisements a day. In 2007 that had risen to 5000 and some estimates indicate that in 2015 that will be 30,000 messages. Your message is just one of these; it is a difficult job standing out from the crowd and getting your marketing message read, understood and acted on in the marketing clutter.

In the market of today a business needs a traditional marketing strategy that includes paper advertising and a 'clicks' marketing strategy that includes Facebook. There are more marketing tools available now than there have ever been and different consumers prefer different tools.

The following chapters look at ideas to develop a marketing strategy. Marketing has never been so affordable, but it has also never been so confusing. The challenge to catch the consumer's eye is a bigger challenge than it has ever been.

# 9  Marketing

> Why is marketing the most important thing in your business? Because
> marketing is concerned with attracting and keeping customers. Ever tried
> to run a business without customers?
>
> *Marketing on the Edge*, NAFMA[1]

## Introduction

The key to success is getting the message that the business exists across
effectively to the target consumers. Marketing is the tool used to achieve this.
The challenge is defining what the message is that should be promoted to
consumers.

Every successful business has a USP, a unique selling proposition.[2] Before
venturing into marketing a business the operator needs to identify what it is
that needs to be communicated, what the USP of the business is, and how it
can be explained in the marketing strategy to the target audience in a way
that captures their attention. A USP is rarely based on location as all locations
have USPs. It could be based on:

- The crop grown. It may be an unusual fruit or vegetable that nobody else
  grows in the region. In our local area we have the only grower of green
  tea in the state; that is a USP;
- The architecture of the farm buildings. It may be the farm has an Art
  Deco design that is unique to the area or region;
- A personality within the team who is a celebrity;
- The way a business adds value to the produce may be different from
  everyone else who deals in the product;
- The mix of food tourism activities in the region may make the region unique.

Marketing is critically important and covers many different forms. In simple terms marketing uses four basic media choices and as a marketer the key is to select the right mix from across all the choices.

**1.** Ink: print form can be used to promote a business via newspaper, magazines, direct marketing, billboards and other ink-based formats.
**2.** Broadcast: this includes television, cinema, video, digital television and events. It revolves around the film media to get the message across.
**3.** Voice: radio is the most common way of using the voice, but street noise and other techniques can be considered.
**4.** Net: Internet, Facebook, Twitter, web ads and net links. This is a rapidly expanding media choice.

Before selecting any of the many choices, the first question to consider is how rapidly does the message need to spread. For example, television, newspapers and radio are aimed at a rapid response today, whilst magazines and cinema advertising have a 'slow burn' option and the response may take weeks to get a call to action.

Consider placement quality in the media you select rather than quantity. The aim is to get maximum impact. Prime placement positions include the last TV commercial on a television break, advertising in high profile programmes for your target market and the inside covers of target magazines provide the most impact.

Before making a major investment in marketing, it is important to experiment and test various media you are going to use before making a large commitment and investment.

You also need to identify who is the real target consumer. This goes beyond gender, age, income etc. Marketers often use the acronym SPADE[2] to focus attention on the real target consumer.

- **S**tarter: the person who initiates an enquiry;
- **P**urchaser: the person who pays for the item;
- **A**dvisor: the person who influences the decision;
- **D**ecider: the real authority in the decision-making process; and
- **E**nd-user: the consumer of the product.

Consider a food tourist. A relative may read an article, the advisor, pass it on to a married couple, the purchaser, the wife or husband makes the final decision, the decider, and they take the children, the end-user, to a farm that has a petting zoo.

Marketing today is more complex because consumers are using a wide range of different tools to receive the message. When developing a marketing strategy, remember there are three types of consumers.

**1.** Traditional consumers: these are often older tourists who rely on traditional marketing tools such as leaflets, newspaper advertising and articles.
**2.** Digital consumers: these travellers will rely on a mix of traditional and online marketing messages. They may expect a leaflet and then look at your Facebook page.

**3.** Connected consumers: these tend to be younger, often called Generation Y, and they will expect all the marketing to be communicated to them via a range of mobile devices and will never look at traditional marketing techniques.

The research carried out by Brian Solis[3] shows how the modern consumer obtains information. When it comes to travel the potential visitors research 10.2 sources on average and when it comes to restaurants they will use 5.2 different sources on average. As a marketer you need to get your message into as many of those sources as possible.

Of the consumers in the study, 56% used offline social contact as an influence in obtaining the right information, compared with 24% who relied on the printed message.

## Developing a Tourism Product

Prior to developing a marketing strategy it is important to get the basics right.

As Erica Croce and Giovanni Perri mention in their book *Food and Wine Tourism*[4] a region has to get a number of developments in place before it can develop a tourism package. These are primarily:

- Natural, cultural and regional resources: the tourist has to have a reason to come to your area;
- Accommodation: this could come in a range of different styles of facilities;
- Services: today's consumer expects Wi-Fi and mobile telephone coverage;
- Information on the region and the tourism attractions in the region that are easily available;
- A hospitality culture in the region. Locals need to be open to tourists;
- The region is safe, secure and has high food and hygiene standards; and
- The area has a sense of civic and environmental responsibility.

In our work as consultants we are often asked why farmers should become involved in the tourism industry. We have found that many farmers look on tourists as a problem rather than an opportunity.

The advantages to the farmer include getting the consumer to discover what the product does, an opportunity to add value to the product. We have a sweet chestnut orchard and there are numerous ways to add value to sweet chestnuts, yet the majority of consumers have no idea what to do with sweet chestnuts; this is our opportunity to add value. It allows farmers to promote the region, educate the consumer and increase their income as well as develop a database for future sales.

The results include increased local employment and increased sales, but before that can be started a marketing plan needs to be put in place.

Food tourism is increasing in popularity and governments around the world realize that tourism is one of the main sources of income for an economy. It means the industry can engage with government as a partner to grow the sector. The key word is partner; if you expect the government via its tourism department to do all the work then you will be waiting a long time. The support and initiative has to come from the sector.

Let us give you two examples from Ireland.

### Product heroism between the industry and tourism

June is strawberry month around Ireland and local consumer awareness is an opportunity to create a hero product marketing campaign. The campaign was developed by Bord da Mia, the food development promotional arm of government. In cooperation with the industry they developed an 18-page insert in the *Irish Independent* newspaper to celebrate National Strawberry Week.[5] The insert was headed with *'Yum! It's Strawberry Time!'*. In our views the success of this promotion was around how the insert took a hero product and added value for the consumer.

**Fig. 9.1.** 'Yum' strawberry promotion in Northern Ireland, UK.

Articles were developed around the following themes:

- Meet the growers;
- Know the varieties;
- Recipes by local chefs Clodagh McKenna and Catherine Fulvo;
- How to grow your own strawberries;
- Strawberry window boxes;
- The health benefits of strawberries;
- Children's competitions;
- Strawberry face masks;
- Fruit facts; and
- The history of the strawberry in Ireland.

Many regions around the world have an iconic product that can be developed into a hero product to help the local tourism and economy.

Across the border in Northern Ireland the Northern Ireland Tourist Board has taken a different approach. They have produced a booklet for growers and producers titled *'Our food. So good. Growing your food tourism potential.'* The motto of this campaign is 'Grown here, not flown here.'

With tourists spending £132 million on food and drink in the province the investment in helping producers is seen as creating a new potential opportunity for the region. Northern Irish research indicates visitors would prefer to spend their money on fresh, local and seasonal produce. The booklet provides ten top tips for growers and restaurants to develop food tourism. The ten top tips are:

**1.** Local is the buzz word. Visitors want food with an identity and the industry needs to promote local.
**2.** Celebrate the story of the producer and be proud of the story.
**3.** Tell the story of the place and be genuine and authentic.
**4.** Menu messaging, the menu is a marketing tool. Connect the consumer with the producer on the menu.
**5.** Celebrate local food traditions and recipes. Promote the uniqueness of the region.
**6.** Re-evaluate value. Value does not mean cheap. Offer small add-ons to enhance the perceived value.
**7.** Meet consumer expectations and then exceed them. Make sure your whole team have the right attitude.
**8.** Go the extra mile. Visitors are looking for 'memories'. Involve their children and cater for them.
**9.** Work together. We are all involved in tourism.
**10.** Be consistent. Set the standard and stick to it.

## Your Marketing Strategy

When business is good and tourists are coming, it pays to market and advertise the business. When tourists are not coming, the business has to advertise.

Before looking at this in some depth, let us define marketing and advertising, as they are often confused:

- Marketing is the action or business of promoting and selling products or services, including market research and advertising;
- Advertising is the activity of producing advertisements for commercial products or services.

Advertising is one of the tools of marketing and is the mouthpiece of the business; it is the essential tool to get the brand message across to consumers. As a culinary business a multitude of different marketing and advertising techniques need to be used and the challenge is monitoring these so that the business receives the best return on its expenditure.

There are a number of keys to success, but one of them has to be the marketing strategy. You need to let your target market know your region and your business exists.

The key to selecting the right marketing and advertising media is:

**1.** Consider who is your target audience. Factors to be considered include geographic location, age group, gender, socio-economic group, occupations.
**2.** Focus on individual customer profiles and not all target consumers with one campaign.
**3.** Select the appropriate advertising media for each target group.
**4.** Do the research and decide which medium suits the business.
**5.** Keep to the advertising standards.
**6.** Keep within your working budget.

Most countries have advertising standards and an authority that monitors such standards. Regulations on advertising vary from country to country, but the following guidelines should be adhered to:

- Advertising should be legal, decent and truthful;
- Advertising should be prepared with a sense of responsibility to the consumer and society; and
- Advertising should conform to the principles of fair competition.

The most common question we are asked is how much you should invest in marketing. As a guideline we would recommend that you invest around 2–4% of your projected yearly turnover in marketing and advertising. If you are starting a business from scratch it could be higher, but once the business is established this is a good benchmark figure to work with.

### Free marketing – use it to your advantage

A comment we often receive from business owners is that they cannot afford marketing. There have always been free marketing opportunities in food tourism and in the future model there will continue to be free marketing opportunities. In fact there will be more free opportunities than are currently available. The key is to use those opportunities. Free marketing reduces expenses, increases your voice and brand reputation in the market and shows the consumer that you are up to date with trends, concerns and events that are taking place in the local market place.

The key is to make sure that the free marketing is reflected in what the visitor sees on their visit. Ideally one person should be responsible for the implementation, but they need to make sure the whole team is aware of what is being promoted and are engaged in the marketing campaign with customers.

## Free marketing opportunities

### Food TV
Cooking and food preparation has always been a popular lifestyle programme, but we now have the arrival of digital TV and dedicated food channels. Food preparation and cooking techniques are promoted on these programmes and there is an ideal opportunity to link in promotions in your farm to what dedicated consumers are watching on TV.

If your food tourism business is doing something interesting, local food TV shows will want to know about it.

There is also the opportunity to have you own food TV programme through the digital framework. This model will not suit all farmers and tourist operators. If you are the largest farm shop in your catchment area it should be considered part of your future marketing strategy.

### Food radio
Radio has reinvented itself and more and more people look to the radio as a form of entertainment. Food question times, for example, could be linked into promotions on the farm. If a question comes up about what is in season, for example, use this as a marketing opportunity in-house.

### Food magazines/newspapers
Food magazines often promote a recipe of the month. Why not use a magazine to promote the same recipe in your store. Laminate the magazine article and use it as a point of purchase sign next to the product.

### Local community events
Get actively involved with local community events. A float at a local parade can also create a lot of fun for the team and generates a goodwill message in town.

## Do the research

Before venturing into marketing it is important that research is carried out to discover who the consumer is and what they want.

Market research using consultancy companies that specialize in this area can be expensive. It may be the right decision to use such a business, but we would advise two other techniques to find out what potential guests want:

- Produce tasting sessions. Taking produce to the farmers' market and getting customers to taste the produce allows producers to engage with consumers. An engaged consumer will be prepared to talk about a marketing plan and help develop the strategy. It allows the business to get to understand and know potential customers;
- Focus groups. We are advocates of focus groups as it allows a business to really start to understand the potential customer. In our experience the ideal focus group is between 15 and 20 consumers who gather in a semi-formal situation and brainstorm the ideas being presented. Be prepared to provide refreshments, but we believe that guests should not be paid; you may wish to provide them with a gift token to spend on your product or provide a produce hamper, but do not pay them. Paid guests may not give you the answers you really want.

There is very little information on how industry members market their business. The best model is to look at the independent garden centres. In the USA in 2013, the Readex Research[6] report identified that businesses were using the following methods:

- 71% of garden centres used websites;
- 68% social media sites;
- 63% relied on word of mouth;
- 53% e-mails;
- 34% radio;
- 31% workshops in-house;
- 28% hosting events;
- 27% direct mail;
- 18% TV commercials;
- 7% other.

As can be seen, there is a wide range of marketing and advertising tools being used to get the message across.

## Interruption versus Permission Marketing

There are two styles of marketing: interruption and permission marketing. Interruption marketing is where you have to interrupt what the consumer is doing to get your message across; an example of this is a TV commercial that interrupts the viewing of a TV programme. Permission marketing is where the consumer gives the business permission to market to them; social media marketing is a great example of this. A business needs a combination of both techniques to ensure they get the message across.

The challenge is how much money and time to allocate to each type of marketing. Our advice is that 60% of the marketing budget should be focused on interruption marketing and 40% on permission marketing, but we accept that there is a shift and over time the percentages will alter and a business will need to invest more and more money into permission-marketing techniques.

When looking at the marketing budget, most of the money spent on interruption marketing goes on tangible items such as advertising space; when it comes to permission marketing most of the money is spent on time, the tangible aspects are often free. For example, with regard to a comment posted on a blog the cost is occurred in the writing and not the posting.

## Where do you start?

### Plan your marketing strategy

Marketing your business when visitors are likely to visit your region sounds obvious, but sometimes it is not obvious. Successful operators market their business before the visitors come to the region. If your major food tourism season is, for example, May, then make sure the marketing campaign is well established in April so that your enterprise becomes 'Top of Mind' before your season commences. Leaving it to May means other businesses have taken up that opportunity and the visitor will not have time to visit your establishment.

There may also be opportunities to market the business in more unusual ways, as follows.

### Celebrate the day

One of the keys to successful marketing is to be in tune with events in the world and planning proactively. This really came home to us when Prince George was born in July 2013 to the Duke and Duchess of Cambridge in the UK. At the time John was working with a garden centre and mentioned to the garden centre team that everybody had a 'Birth Tree' and that garden centres should build a promotion using the elm, Prince George's birth tree.

An apprentice at the business took it on himself to create a display of elm trees in the business. The normal turnover of elm trees in the business is three times a year, if they are lucky. John agreed with the apprentice that the display had a life of around a week and then would need to be dismantled. The display only lasted 4 days before the product had sold out. Marketing is about being proactive and making decisions 'on the run' based on what is catching the public attention.

The key lesson is that, in an ideal world, you need a 'festival' every week to attract consumers. Luckily working with seasonal products allows a business to develop and change the story every week.

Why celebrate?

- It creates a reason for the consumer to come every week to experience a new 'festival';
- It increases the overall stock turn of the enterprise;
- The average sale increases per customer;

- Word of mouth/click marketing is increased; and
- It motivates the team to keep the enterprise looking fresh in the eyes of the consumer.

When a celebration day occurs, celebrate it; there are numerous events every year that you can connect with, these include:

- Chinese New Year;
- Valentine's Day;
- April Fool's day;
- Vegetarian Week, May;
- Apple day, October in northern hemisphere;
- Red Aussie Apple Day, June.

Or you could create your own celebration; we have come across the following:

- Liquorice week;
- Chilli festival;
- Herb Festival;
- Rhubarb week;
- Cheese week.

Note: most countries have a directory of events, which can be found through Google searches on the Internet.

## Market Your Region

Not literally market the region, but rather than promote your business as the key reason to travel to an area, promote the surrounding region. The Manjimup region of south Western Australia is known as the Southern Forests Food Region and a group of culinary businesses promote the region, as a result of which all members benefit.

Italy and France are well known for their food and travellers go to those countries for a food experience rather than to a specific business.

One of the best examples we know is what Vancouver Island is doing in British Columbia in Canada. Marketing is made up of traditional marketing techniques and social media marketing techniques and this region is exceptionally good at the traditional marketing techniques.

This is what they are doing:

- Billboards promoting local food at key locations around the island;
- A *FarmFresh* magazine that is available via Tourist Information Offices (www.islandfarmfresh.com). This gives a profile of the grower and map on how to find them;
- A Flavour Route around the Saanich Peninsula, where most of the growers are located.

The key is, if a group of growers get together, they can really start to make a difference and create a local media presence.

**Fig. 9.2.** Lemon promotion in Limone on Lake Garda, Italy.

The first priority should be to get potential visitors to your region and then secondly to your business.

# Market to Your Community

### Talk to your local community as a partner – a key to success

Tourism is changing and community-based tourism with the right vision is a growth area.

Being local in business means being part of and engaged with the community. But, the challenge is local business engaging with each other to develop the opportunities.

We are often told by local businesses 'Everyone knows I am local'. This comment was said to John by a retailer recently, luckily the business owner followed that up with 'well those that come in my door know. The rest have no idea.' Business owners often assume too much.

According to research in the UK by the Today's Group (www.todays.co.uk), 80% of local businesses say they are involved in local initiatives and 15% of consumers say they are prepared to pay more for product purchased at a local store if the business is professional in their offer to the consumer and engaged in the community.

Community involvement is one of the most effective marketing tools a local business can develop to fight outside competition.

The key to success is to be proactive in getting involved with the community. You will need to make a decision on how much of the marketing budget time and money will be allocated to community marketing.

Most businesses will get involved in one of six ways:

- Volunteer space in store for local community promotion;
- Provide talks to the local chamber of commerce group;
- Give talks to community groups;
- Adopt a local project as their own;
- Allow the sales team members to get involved in a predetermined project for a set number of hours as part of their job;
- Gift product that is not selling to local events as a marketing tool.

Over the last couple of years we were involved in setting up a local community garden. It was interesting to see local involvement in action at close quarters and observe how retailers were prepared to get involved.

## Partnership not sponsorship

One of the first lessons to be learned is that progressive businesses want to be partners in the local community and not be sponsors. We ensured we developed partnerships to enable local businesses to feel they were partners on a journey. The partnership was divided up into bronze, silver, gold and platinum partners in the project.

We then contacted businesses who we felt would benefit the most from a partner arrangement. We highlighted the benefits and approached each business personally.

It was interesting how different retailers reacted and we are sure there is a lesson for all businesses based on our experience.

We approached one retailer in our town who read through all our literature and then came back to us and explained he would like to get involved, but retailing was tough and he did not feel he could help our cause. That was the end of the conversation.

As a result we then approached another retailer who was in the same retail sector. They again looked at our proposal and requested a meeting. Their spokesperson asked if they could use the community garden as a training area for their own team and would we provide barbecue nights for their team throughout the year. They asked if they could have a plot in the garden as an area where they could train their team and also engage with the consumer. This was apart from the partnership conversation we had with them.

That retailer could see the benefits of a true partnership at a local level to grow sales and engage his team with local consumers.

Partnerships are about engaging with the local community, sponsorships are about donating to the community. As a food tourism operator a business will get a better return on the investment by becoming a partner, plus the team members will have a lot more fun.

Marketing starts in the local community and with local partnerships. Culinary tourists want to engage with the local community and this is an opportunity for local networking.

## Build a good relationship with the press

The best advertising is always free, either by word of mouth or by free articles that have been placed in the press. As part of the marketing strategy we advise building a good relationship with the local press.

Invite the press out to the business and show them around, get to know the lead writer in the area and build a relationship with that person.

There are various strategies to build a relationship with the press:

- Find out what interests them. Help identify new leads for the local newspaper as this will help you build a relationship with them. They are always interested in:
    - Team matters: where one of the team has obtained a certificate, excelled in a sport or done something different;
    - New product development if the business is the first in the region to develop a new process then you have a story they may be interested in;
    - Winning awards: award winning is a great story for newspapers and can get excellent media coverage for the business;
    - Write the food or farm column for the newspaper, provide handy hints for the consumer and obtain regular exposure for your business in the newspaper;
    - Prizes: if the newspaper engages in competitions, offer prizes as long as the business name is mentioned;
- Be prepared for the unexpected. Always have a camera or smartphone nearby as you never know when there is a photo opportunity the newspaper could be interested in. The press love pictures of the unexpected;
- Write the story for the newspaper. They will probably modify it, but save them the time and the article is more likely to be published. Newspapers work on a tight deadline and aim to help them rather than give them more work;
- Always provide your name, telephone number and e-mail address when contacting the press;
- Write the article double spaced so that it can be edited easily.

## Developing Marketing Tools

As we have already discussed a business cannot rely on one system to get a marketing message across; some consumers prefer one channel of communications whilst others prefer another. The key is to spread the message across a number of different channels.

The most popular techniques are as follows.

# Interruption Marketing

This is the more traditional style of marketing and one many readers will be more familiar and comfortable with. There are many styles of interruption marketing; we will focus on the more common techniques you can use.

## Roadside marketing

The best place to start a marketing a venture is on the roadside. Regulations will vary with local governments and what you can and cannot do and you will need to seek local guidance.

There are six basic categories of roadside advertising.

**1.** Brown signs. These are signs provided by the local government to promote a business as a tourist attraction. They are called brown signs because this is the standard backing colour used on these signs around the world.

**2.** Large free-standing signs. These are often called billboard signs and are very familiar along the freeways of some American states. Different local authorities have different views on these signs. Some look on them as a marketing opportunity for business whilst others look on them as eye pollution and have banned them from the road system.

**3.** Signs on bus shelters, seats, city trash cans and illuminated signs under street names. These are strictly controlled by local councils, but allow you to repeat your message in high profile public spaces.

**4.** Small local business signs placed in public space and easily visible to passers-by. These signs are often temporary and although permission should be sought, these signs, being of a temporary nature are often placed in position just before an event.

**5.** Signs on private property that is not owned by the business. These signs will need permission from the local government authority and the owner of the property. These are ideal to promote your business on the roads leading to your enterprise as 'tasters' and guiders to the visitor.

**6.** Signs on your property to promote the business to the visitor.

## Magazine advertising and articles

Permission marketing is where an article is written either by yourself or on your behalf about your business and your tourism strategy. Interruption marketing is advertising and your placement of an advert in a target magazine.

Our opinion is that placing an advert without an article is nowhere as effective as having an article and an advert. The advert becomes the reinforcement and the call to action once consumers have read the article.

The key is to make life easy for the editor of the magazine. In most magazines the key is to write the article and provide good quality pictures for the editor. There is never a guarantee the article will be published unless it has been commissioned by the magazine, but keep feeding articles to an editor. We have found this to be effective and eventually the editor will take the bait (or tell you to stop sending articles).

Before you start sending articles do your homework:

- What 'food' and 'tourist' magazines are available to your catchment reader area?
- What is the circulation of the magazine?
- Contact the editor and find out how they look on your business and if they are interested in working with you;
- Will they publish articles without your advertising or are they expecting you to advertise as well?
- When is the magazine published?
- How long in advance do they need article by if they are to publish?
- How would they like articles and pictures to be presented to them?
- Is there an online version of the magazine?
- Can you use a QR code or phone app to accompany the article and can you link it to your business?

Magazines are still widely read and should be an important part of your marketing campaign. Our favourite magazines are the Edible Communities Publications magazines (www.ediblecommunities.com), who link their magazines to Facebook, Twitter and edible radio.

At the time of writing this book the company was producing 63 regional magazines on local food for communities in the USA and Canada. Each magazine focuses on a local community, both in articles and advertising. These well-produced and well-read magazines are an ideal marketing tool for food tourism venues within a location.

Another magazine that is well read in Australia is *Gourmet Traveller* (www.gourmettraveller.com.au), a glossy magazine that takes a global view of food tourism. This magazine has articles on food journeys from around the world and is ideal for the business that is looking for a wider market exposure.

## Food directories

Culinary tourists will often go to tourist offices as a source of information and one of the best ways to get the message across is to offer them a food directory. One of the first local food directories was written in 1997 as the *Forest Food Directory*[7] by Matt Dunwell and Kate de Selincourt to direct tourists around the local food producers in the Forest of Dean in Gloucestershire, UK.

The aim of a food directory is to help tourists easily find the relevant locations in the region. It may need to be developed as a phone app as well as
a hard-copy directory.

When compiling a food directory the following guidelines need to be
considered:

- The directory is an opportunity to involve other organizations such as
  the chamber of commerce, the local farmers' market, local restaurants
  and information centres;
- Set a timetable and keep to it. It will mean that you will have to follow up
  businesses that have failed to meet deadlines, but keep to a timetable;
- It is important to provide business that should be in the directory
  with a simple form to fill in, so that the information is provided in the
  format in which you require it to ensure the reader obtains consistent
  information;
- Many business owners will need a visit to build confidence and to have
  the directory explained to them;
- Aim to have the same space allocation for each member in the directory
  so that they all feel they are taking an equal exposure;
- Sell advertising space to fund the directory, as the tourist will expect it
  for free;
- Make sure the key providers of information have the directory. This includes libraries, petrol stations, information offices and cafés.

## 'How to' leaflets

'How to' leaflets could be inserted in a number of sections of this book, but
apart from being a form of education, they are also a marketing tool and
hence we have decided to discuss them in this section of the book.

One of the biggest downfalls in marketing is assuming the consumer
understands. This was illustrated to us in the northern part of the USA.
A farm retailer had a special on mangoes, yet these wonderful fruit were
not selling. When we analysed why they were not selling, we found that
his local consumers did not know how to peel the fruit and therefore
were resistant to purchasing them. What may be common sense to you
can be rare sense to someone else. Traditionally, 'how to' leaflets have
been the standard format for getting information across to consumers.
In today's world that information can also be communicated via a phone
app, QR or Microsoft code and YouTube; we advise using all these tools
to get information to consumers.

The rules in designing a 'How to' leaflet for consumers are as follows:

- Keep the leaflet simple, the consumer is not a technical person and therefore use the language they would use. Pictures are more helpful than
  words. Use short sentences and bullet points wherever possible;
- Use words such as 'You' or 'Yours' rather than 'I' or 'We' when writing a
  'how to' leaflet as it relates to the consumer better;

- Answer the question a customer would ask, for example 'How to peel a Mango' or 'How to make a Radish Salad';
- Provide extra information in information boxes that are separate to the main text. This could include 'Did You Know' or unusual facts;
- Include a shopping list as this will encourage further shopping; this is not pressure selling, this is providing solutions for the consumer;
- Make sure the leaflet is legible. Ensure the reader can read it easily. The most easily read typeface is serif-based;
- Introduce colour into the leaflet, this ensures the leaflet stands out;
- Position leaflets in stands rather that scattered across a table. Place in a well-positioned location on the premises. Where possible place leaflets next to the produce being discussed in the leaflet;
- Train the team to hand the leaflets out; they are a marketing tool and should be used as such by the team.

### Taste masters

Tourism Australia promotes the 'Best Jobs in the World'[8] as part of their marketing strategy. Each state enters their idea for their own marketing campaign. Western Australia entered with 'Taste Master'. They selected a UK foodie and blogger, Rich Keam, out of 90,000 entries to spend 6 months travelling the state, tasting local foods and then writing a blog to report on his experience (http://tastewesternaustralia.com). The budget was US$100,000 to cover his expenses and travel costs and local food tourism venues were encouraged to invite him to visit and blog about his experiences.

This is a wonderful example of marketing by thinking outside the box and to develop ideas that will spread via social media.

### Newspapers

Newspapers are still a valuable marketing tool. Reading the local newspaper is still an activity that many tourists participate in. Whereas magazines have a relatively long life when it comes to reading, newspapers are old news the next day. Use newspapers to promote events that will occur this week; they are a 'now media'. Remember that the newspaper may have a large circulation, but calculate on around 2% of readers reading any advert you place in the paper.

*Plan print advertising in magazines and newspapers*
Consumers are exposed to thousands of advertisements every day of their lives and the aim is to make the advertisement you have written stand out from all the others. This is not an easy task. However, by following a few simple guidelines you can get the message across to relevant readers.

*Plan an effective layout*

A good layout embraces four essential factors: sequence, focus, simplicity and eye appeal. Begin with these key components in mind and on completion of the design check that the layout reflects these essential elements.

*Get the sequence correct*

To make sense the advert needs to be in logical order when read. In advertising, sequence is important when preparing an advert. Aim to make the content capable of creating what advertisers call AIDCA:[2]

- Attention: the advert grabs the reader's attention;
- Interest: it gets the reader's interest;
- Desire: it arouses the reader's interest to delve further;
- Conviction: the reader makes a decision;
- Action: the reader knows the call to action.

Always consider what the most important part of the message is that you want the reader to concentrate on. This can be achieved by different type face, colour, pointed finger or arrows.

*The KISS principle*

Successful advertisements rely on the KISS principle: 'Keep It Simple Sells'. Remember space in an advert sells, too many adverts are too cluttered and therefore confuse readers.

## Television

The development of digital TV has now made TV a potential marketing tool for many more businesses. This is especially true for rural businesses as they can often get cheaper time slots than city-based businesses. Plus cooking and food programmes are very much in vogue and the Food Channel is available in many countries.

Getting on television is very much the same as getting into a magazine; get to know the key players and market your business to those players. Do not be afraid to invest in a 'dummy' programme of your facility and send it to the programme editor. Even if they reject it you can still use it as a marketing tool on your webpage.

## Radio

Local radio is a wonderful way to become accustomed to dealing with the media and it is an effective marketing tool. Compared with many other ways of marketing in non-central business district areas, it is a cost effective way of advertising and will often reach more people than any other media.

Before doing a radio interview or advert, talk to the radio company and find out who their target market is. Often the demographics change by the hour and the radio marketing representative should be able to explain the demographic details. Radio listeners are loyal to a station and/or programme so the chances are that the message will be repeated to the same person and this will increase market penetration. When using radio, remember this is an instant media; radio is not the place to talk about a long-term marketing campaign, unless you are being interviewed about your culinary initiative. The target listener wants to know about an event or offer that is *now*.

Radio is one of the best media to allow listeners to work on their imagination; they can put a story together in their mind, the radio announcement is the story telling. An effective radio commercial paints a story in the listeners mind.

Radio is built around a voice, background sound and music; these are the only tools that are available to make the story. The picture in the listeners' imagination can be painted by using more than one announcer, creating a dramatic situation, using mood music, humour and/or building a memorable jingle. The business name should be mentioned about five times in the 30-second time slot. The time is short, but the opportunities are exciting.

Local radio will often agree to come to an arrangement and it may be possible to reduce the initial cost. In addition, they need the adverts and if they are short of adverts they may make an arrangement for extra placements for free. You may even sponsor a section of a programme or the news to get extra exposure.

Radio stations have 'day parts' and break the day into units.

The expensive units are 'rush hour' in the morning and the evening, which is often called 'drive time'. These are the most expensive parts of the day, which is when they have the most listeners, the challenge is whether or not these are the listeners you are looking for. Radio advertising is about quality not quantity.

## Coupons

Coupons are a very successful marketing tool, especially in the USA where they have been used in retailing for many years. September is National Coupon Month. In the USA, 92% of consumers use coupons and only 7.7% never use coupons.[9]

According to research by Banwari Mittal,[10] he identified four classes of consumer coupon use. These are cost/benefit perceptions, shopping-related person preferences, non-demographic general consumer characteristics, and demographics.

The first coupon was established in 1887 when Coca-Cola offered a coupon to get a free glass of coke. In 2010 the first mobile coupon was launched on smartphones by Target. Most coupons are based on a price-reduction incentive when redeemed at the outlet. Coupons really took off in the 1980s when manufacturers discovered how powerful coupons were at pulling customers into supermarkets to purchase products.

Coupons can be used by culinary tour operators in a similar way to the way they are used in general retailing and business. The consumer is familiar with using coupons and they are a major marketing tool.

Coupons come in different channels, they are:

**1.** Online coupons: delivered to the consumer via Twitter, Facebook, webpage etc. The consumer receives them on their smartphone and brings their phone to the establishment to redeem the coupon.

**2.** FSI: Free Standing Inserts. These are booklets of coupons often found in American newspapers at the weekend.

**3.** ROP: newspaper Run Of Press. These are coupons that are placed in the newspaper, often in the advertisement, and the consumer cuts them out.

**4.** Direct mail coupons: come to the consumer directly in the mail from the provider via their database.

**5.** Merchandise distributed coupons: these are ideal for food tourism. The consumer purchases a product and the agent then offers the consumer a coupon to use on their next visit. These can also be used where a group of food tourism ventures network and offer a voucher to the next venue on a food trail.

## Contests

The food industry is an ideal sector to engage the consumer using contests. Contests can be developed with a local school, tourists, via Facebook or the Internet.

The great thing about contests is that they engage consumers and can be entertaining. They can also help you obtain further marketing exposure for your business.

The wonderful thing about the product we are involved in is that every produce has a story that can be developed into a marketing opportunity using a contest that will get people talking.

Contest ideas could include:

- Why are carrots orange? (Answer: due to a breeding programme developed by the Dutch celebrating the orange that is reflected in their national flag.) This could be followed up with carrot recipes to everyone who enters;
- What is the most hated children's fruit or vegetable in the UK? (Answer: the avocado[11] – it is celery for adults in the UK.)[12] Follow up with recipes on avocado that children would enjoy.
- What fruit is claimed to help reduce jetlag? (Answer: cherries, as they are rich in melatonin.) Again this could be followed up with cherry recipes.[13]

The list for contests is endless and your consumers will love to get engaged.

## The Taste Awards

There are numerous Taste Awards around the world, but one of the best models is the Great Taste Awards in the UK (www.greattasteawards.co.uk) held by the Guild of Fine Foods as this covers a whole range of foods.

The Great Taste Awards are the British Oscars of the food industry and a benchmark for speciality food and drink. The awards are judged by over 400 judges and take 50 days of judging. Winners have a huge marketing advantage and the culinary tourist will search them and their product out. This type of award can really grow the culinary food sector. Regions that do not have such an award should be encouraged to develop similar promotions.

In Australia there is an example of a more specific awards programme with the Australian Grand Dairy Awards,[14] which are held each year.

## Food Thinkers

**Fig. 9.3.** The hero team in the publicity brochure of Ludlow Food Hall, UK.

Traditionally the hero in the industry was the celebrity chef, but the industry as well as consumer perceptions have moved on. 'Food Thinkers' include celebrity chefs, farmers, food critics and a host of other different people who can engage with the community to develop food tourism. Identify who are the 'characters' and food thinkers in your community who can work within the region to develop the culinary tourist offer.

## Distribution Points for Information

Once you have gathered together marketing information on your business, that information needs to be located where tourists are most likely to search for it. Key locations include the following.

### Tourist information offices

Tourist information centres are ideal connection points between food tourism venues and tourists. Many tourists use tourist information offices as their first 'port of call' when they arrive in a new region.

Tourist information centres are located at many international airports, hotels and national landmarks around the world.

Most tourist regions also have a tourist information office in local towns in the region, and it is critical that a tourism-centred business ensures these offices are aware of their business, how it operates, when it is open and what facilities it provides. A culinary business needs to be 'top of mind' when team members in the information office are talking to visitors about where to spend their leisure time. If a network package between a group of food tourism ventures is on offer there is more chance that the package will be promoted rather than a single location.

### Libraries

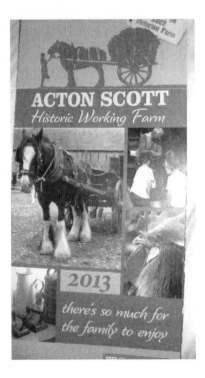

**Fig. 9.4.** The brochure for Acton Scott Historic Working Farm in the UK.

Traditionally libraries were a place to borrow books. Today, with changes in consumer habits and new technology libraries have had to change their focus to remain relevant in today's society.

The local library is now another source of promoting local businesses. Some visitors use libraries as a first contact point in a region and your publicity material should be close at hand.

Approach your library at certain times of the year and enquire about whether you can work with them to build a display in the library to promote the culinary events in the region. This may also be linked in with the local school and books related to your activity in the library. In our experience libraries are keen to work with local businesses to develop relationships and to generally build awareness in the community of the activities taking place.

### Accommodation

The ideal location for any publicity on the business is next to a guest's bed. Many bed and breakfasts and hotels will have folders containing flyers that promote local attractions; these folders are often placed in guests' rooms. This is an ideal location, as the tourist has the inclination and the time to browse the folder while relaxing in their room.

It may only be one couple at a time who look at the brochure, but they are most likely to be the target consumer and the ones most likely looking for the tourist facility.

### Secondary distribution locations

Getting marketing information to food tourists is the challenge, and if you can reach them in unexpected ways they are more likely to absorb the message. If petrol or gas station attendants would hold conversations with tourists they could suggest a visit to a specific tourist location and then hand them a leaflet, the traveller is more likely to visit that location. Why? It was an unexpected caring gesture that will be remembered by the traveller. The challenge is to get such parties to engage in marketing their community tourist venues. If you could provide them with an incentive, based on success, the chances of success are improved. This could include having a sun downer for local business people from the chamber of commerce. They may not be the key target group, but they have friends and acquaintances who could promote the business and as a result the message keeps spreading.

## Permission Marketing

We live in a world of 'clicks'. The computer, smartphone and IPad are now major means of communication. Once a consumer gives you permission to market to them, then 'clicks' marketing will become a major marketing tool in your business.

Before we look at permission marketing as an online marketing tool we should also focus on the other important permission marketing tools, word-of-mouth marketing being the most important marketing tool for any business.

## Word of mouth marketing

The best marketing tool you can have is word of mouth. Consumers who have experienced what you have offered will tell their family, friends and colleagues about the experience.

Word of mouth marketing revolves around people. Your team is engaged in marketing. If they engage with consumers then the chances are your team will be talked about. If they process the visitors then they will probably not be talked about in a favourable way.

Food tourism is about visitor experiences. Visitor experiences have three key elements: what the consumer tastes, sees and experiences via human contact.

We used to call this customer service, but customer service is now something in the past. Research indicates that customers believe 'service' deteriorates every year. Consumers have become jaded with customer service and this is one reason online shopping has increased over recent years.

Most customer service is about processing customers, something that should never happen on a culinary experience.

Leading businesses around the world now talk about ROE or return on engagement, it is not about serving customers anymore, it is about engaging with them.

The ambassadors for the business are important in the marketing of the business and should be trained in being 'day-makers'. Day-makers do not process customers, they set out to make the customers' day; it is a thinking process and one that makes a huge difference to a business.

The aim of any successful business is that the visitor leaves the premises in a happier state than when they entered the premises based on the engagement they have had with the business ambassadors. Walt Disney built an empire on this thinking process and the same principle is equally important in food tourism. The keys to success are:

**1.** Recruitment. Recruit people who are passionate about engaging with people and food tourism. These people exist, but are not easy to find.
**2.** Set standards. Make sure every ambassador who works for your organization knows the minimum standards on how to deliver the day-maker experience you are aiming for.
**3.** Train the team. Do not assume that everyone understands how you want your guests to be treated. Every team member needs to be trained in what you expect them to do as 'hosts' within your business, 'consultants' within your business and as 'sellers' within your business. They need to be trained in how to engage with customers and how to use 'open' conversation rather than 'closed' conversation when dealing with guests.
**4.** Empowerment policy. You will not be present and able to be monitoring every consumer engagement. Businesses need to set out an empowerment

policy so that all team members know what they can and cannot do if a problem is raised by a guest. This is critically important if you are involved in selling produce. Some consumers will complain and you do not want the team member saying 'I will have to ask the boss.' You want them to resolve the issue with the customer straight away and own the problem with the customer. This can only be achieved once an empowerment policy is in place and the team have confidence in it.

**5.** Mystery shop audit. The key is to maintain a minimum standard of consumer engagement in the business. The management needs to ensure this standard is maintained. It is common practice in retailing to employ a professional mystery shopper to check on standards at least once every 6 months. It is important that this shopper remains unknown to everyone on the team, including the owner, to ensure that a fair assessment of the business takes place. The mystery shopper should engage with as many of the team as possible and follow up with a report. This report should be made available to all team members. Team members who excel in the report should be praised in public in front of the rest of the team, whilst those who are below standard should have the opportunity to discuss this with management in private.

We have seen many businesses who developed wonderful marketing campaigns, but forgot that the team is involved in marketing as well. Word of mouth marketing of a business is one of the most important methods, but often the most neglected. Business should put aside money for training; as a guide, many businesses place 1% of the labour budget aside for team training. Training should be ongoing as it will make a major difference to a business's bottom line.

## Newsletters

Some customers prefer to have an online newsletter, whilst others will prefer a hard-copy newsletter. The challenge for a business is whether it can justify sending newsletters out using the postage system as it may not be cost effective.

Build a database of customers of your business; you then have the opportunity to write a newsletter to send to your target customers.

Building relationships with customers who have visited your establishment is an important way of building loyalty. The newsletter is a well proven way of helping in this process. It is not a sales letter or a direct selling tool, it is a means of building a relationship. It should provide news about the company, your team and consumer activities as well as produce and events.

The keys to developing a successful newsletter are:

- Decide on a regular schedule and keep to it. Newsletters work most effectively if the consumer receives them every 90 days. Any more frequently and they will often be treated as junk, less frequently and the consumer thinks that the business has lost touch with them;
- Keep it short. Customers are generally busy people and do not have the time to read long newsletters. Limit the newsletter to a maximum of four

pages or at a maximum a 7-minute read; you may want to keep it to two sides of one page. If the decision is on a four-page newsletter structure it as follows:

- Page 1: this is the 'grab' page and it should grab the attention of the reader and encourage them to read further. Place new seasonal items, innovations and ideal topics on this page;
- Page 2: this is the page for the news stories, a photograph of the business owner and an editorial;
- Page 3: key stories go on this page and ideally ones from customers, for example their favourite recipes;
- Page 4: the 'relaxation' page where short stories can be placed as well as upcoming events and community news. At the bottom of this page always promote the business as a final reminder.
- Always be on the lookout for newsworthy items. There are four elements to look for:
  - Human interest: people like reading about people;
  - Timeliness: news on something about to happen;
  - Uniqueness: something the reader does not know about;
  - Novelty: the unusual.
- Be selective. Do not cram too much information into the newsletter, a few well written items is better than a whole pile of information;
- Use colour to highlight and liven up the newsletter;
- Seek reader feedback. Most people will not bother, but give them the opportunity to give feedback if they desire.

Many business say they would love to produce a newsletter, but do not have the time. This is a task that can easily be designated between the team to ensure the job gets done. Develop a template for the newsletter and then keep to that template. The owner should be the editor, not the writer.

## Social Media Marketing Tools to Help Grow Your Business

[Note: Edwin Meijer, Managing Director of Garden Connect, Holland co-authored this section of the book.][15]

Social media marketing is moving rapidly, probably more rapidly that most of us are aware. For example, the Mobile Marketing Association of Asia caused quite a stir on social media websites when they announced 4.2 billion people own a toothbrush, yet 4.8 billion own a smartphone.[16]

As authors we are fully aware that this area of communications and marketing is changing so rapidly that this section will already be out of date as you read. Having said that there are some basic social media marketing tools that you need to implement in your business.

Culinary tourists take photographs and "selfies" as they travel and thus promote food businesses. Do not discourage this activity. On a typical day in 2013,

350 million photos were uploaded to Facebook, 350 million to Snapchat and 55 million to Instagram. At the same time, 1000 hours of video was uploaded every minute and 6 billion hours of video is watched every month. Taking photos is now a major marketing tool.[17] Visitors that take photos share their photos with their friends and do your marketing for you.

The challenge for many food tourist operators is how do they manage social media. Polyface Farms in Swoope, Virginia has a blog that attracts 60,000 readers; it is called the 'Hen House' blog. Each day a different member of the team of seven writes something on the blog. These seven individuals create a variety of messages and make this a manageable task for the farm.

Social media marketing is essential to a food tourism venture. The essential marketing tools required are the following.

## Website

The first and most important thing to start with as a marketing tool is a website. Whatever you are communicating online, the website should look superb and it should reflect the business and its values. A few key questions are enough to check if the website is performing to the level that it should:

- Can consumers recognize whose website it is even if they do not see the logo?
- Is the website updated multiple times per week with relevant information?
- Does the website inspire consumers and provide practical tips that are valuable to consumers?
- Is the website an online 'showroom' for your food tourism venture with relevant product information and products?

If one of the above questions is answered with a 'no', then the business is missing chances to drive more customers to the company via the web.

In November 2013, 41% of Americans visited a food and cooking website, up 2 million from the previous month. That represented 86 million visitors who spent 25 minutes on average on the webpage.

We often see outdated information on websites or pages with a lot of texts. Based on the above research, all food tourism operators need to focus on developing the best webpage to promote their business that they can.

A food tourism destination website should inspire potential visitors with beautiful products, scenery and offerings.

The webpage is the most important shop window and most consumers look at a food tourism shop window before venturing to the destination.

Use photos of fresh produce and the venue: successful culinary businesses put a lot of effort into making their business look superb on-site. Take photos or a YouTube walk around the facility and put them on the website to achieve the same result online! Do not do it once a year, update photos every month or at

The top food and cooking websites by unique US audience in November 2013.[18]

| Brand/website | Unique audience | Average time spent (HH:MM:SS) |
|---|---|---|
| All food and cooking sites | 86,350,000 | 0:25:30 |
| Scripps Networks food websites | 22,433,000 | 0:10:37 |
| Allrecipes | 17,397,000 | 0:06:38 |
| About.com food | 9,249,000 | 0:02:56 |
| Kraft Foods | 8,110,000 | 0:05:38 |
| Betty Crocker | 7,554,000 | 0:05:19 |
| Pizza Hut | 6,198,000 | 0:09:22 |
| Starbucks coffee | 6,164,000 | 0:08:26 |
| Pillsbury | 5,268,000 | 0:05:45 |
| MyRecipes.com network | 5,167,000 | 0:07:10 |
| Cooks.com | 5,005,000 | 0:03:51 |

least every season. Use a smartphone to take them, the quality is good enough. Consumers want to see something fresh every time they go to the webpage.

Today's time-poor consumers are looking up information online before they decide where to visit or where to purchase from. The business should display what is on offer to them online. Do not put every single product on a website, but at least include a range of products per product group to tempt consumers to visit the attraction. If consumers are unable to find what they are looking for on a website, they will go elsewhere.

Last but not least: the website is a key knowledge hub. Provide cooking tips, news items, tutorials and more information to existing and potential tourist visitors. It will help them while they are researching on the Internet to prepare purchases and tours but it will also help them to make better use of the products once they buy at your business. If you sell them a vegetable and you educate them how to prepare and cook that vegetable so that it will last longer and taste better, it is certainly more likely they will come back sooner or later!

### Know the facts

- 84% of UK adults are online at least once a week;
- It is called the World Wide Web, but 97% of traffic is local.

## Online shopping

As a retailer or tourist operator you might think running a web shop is too complicated, but think again. A web shop is an essential part of food tourism in the future – it will be a major traffic generator for your business in the coming years! Culinary tourism operations should not be afraid of selling online; look on it as an improved mail order catalogue. Businesses used to sell from mail order catalogues 30 years ago and can do that again online using modern technology.

Nowadays, consumers go online before they decide where to visit. The majority of culinary tourists still prefer to visit or buy from businesses that inspire them rather than ordering everything online. A business therefore needs to integrate a web shop along with a physical culinary store.

Some essential tips:

- Do not try to compete with Amazon and other major online businesses. If you think you can move boxes from warehouses to consumers as they do – forget about it. You will not win that game unless your budget is nearly unlimited;
- Focus on your local tourist catchment area and on your existing visitors. If you decide to ship produce to visitors, keep it local to help you keep control of delivery;
- The web shop is an online showroom. Customers orient online but often buy offline, so encourage them to visit your facility. At every product description you can add a line such as 'Visit our attractions if you want to see, touch, smell and feel the experience';
- Don't focus on price; focus on being a day-maker. Add testimonials from your existing clients to your web shop and add practical tips. This helps customers recognize that you are not just another web shop, but a knowledge hub for consumers and have customer advocates.

Click and collect is an excellent way to drive more traffic to a business. You can set up a web shop and collect orders from the web, but you do not have the hassle of deliveries. Surveys confirm that click and collect is getting more and more popular and at present is the most profitable delivery model. Consumers do not have to walk through the entire facility and are assured of the availability of the products they ordered. You can add a free coffee coupon to encourage them to come back soon to make a longer visit.

### Know the facts

- It is estimated 10% of products will be sold online during the next few years;
- The challenge is the delivery system, not the online page.

## Facebook

Facebook was found in 2004 by Eduardo Saverin (business aspects), Dustin Moskovitz (programmer), Andrew McCollum (graphic artist), Chris Hughes and Mark Zuckerberg who took over the business and grew it within a decade to the most important social network of the world. It should not surprise you that a lot of your potential and existing guests are using Facebook. And as a business you should be where your customers are and a food tourism business should have an active Facebook page with a good, effective Facebook strategy. Just playing with Facebook will not grow a business; once a business has over 1000 likes on Facebook it becomes a major marketing tool for the business.

Social media is a bit different than most other marketing outings because the key is the participants have to interact and engage with people, so it is not a once-a-week task in the business agenda. The good thing is that business owners and team members that spend time communicating with customers can and do grow sales and visitor counts.

Second, the person involved in marketing should be enthusiastic about Facebook and social media in general, but do not over-estimate the number of messages people want to read from a business. Are you interested in, say, seven updates per day from your local hairdresser? Probably not and your customer will not appreciate too many posts. So just post once or twice a day and a bit more during special events and bank holidays, but do not over-do it.

How can a business drive traffic to a culinary destination via Facebook? Here are some examples that can be copied by every reader of this book:

- Use coupons that are only available to your Facebook friends. This will increase the number of followers and you can encourage your friends to come to your store to use the coupon(s);
- Do a flash sale. Just reduce one popular product in price for 2 or 3 hours for (say) 70% and announce it once on Facebook only. You will be surprised how many people rush in to your centre to get that deal! One of our clients did this with great results and major up-selling occurred in store.
- A pre-season opening, depending on your climate zone, is always appreciated by loyal customers. Invite your Facebook friends to visit your season sale the evening before it officially opens and give them a 10% discount on everything. A client of ours did this and out of 2000 Facebook friends he got over 400 visitors. With just one post!
- Every member of your team should take at least one photo during his or her work per week of something attractive, new or inspiring. You can use these photos to show your customers what is happening at your facility. The majority of your team will love it, you get your products directly on Facebook with photos and it is free.

These are just four random tips and you can use them today or tomorrow! They all drive traffic to your business and that is where a lot of businesses miss an opportunity: they are using Facebook but they do not have a clue how to drive traffic to their facility.

### Know the facts

- UK social networking growth is strongest among middle-age and senior Internet users;
- Two-thirds of the followers on Facebook are women – your most important group to target!

## Twitter

We like Twitter, but why would we would recommend you use Twitter? It is text based while your business is colourful and inspiring – anything but textual. However, a lot of your customers are using Twitter or are reading tweets without having an account so you should not ignore this network. A culinary business should have a Twitter account as part of the market toolkit.

Twitter is as easy as Facebook, do not make the mistake to link them together. Tweets are different than Facebook posts and being lazy never resulted in a lot of new customers, and it will not work with Twitter either.

Tweets are short messages of 140 characters or less, so here are some quick tips in a random order:

- Set up an account with the business name but add the name of the person posting in the description;
- Interact: the 'social' part of 'social media' means participants have to talk and listen. Most companies know how to talk but they do not listen – and therefore they do not interact!
- Be helpful. People ask a lot of question about cooking and produce on Twitter. Answer those questions. You are the knowledge hub, which the supermarket is not;
- Ask your followers questions, they are your customers;
- You do not have to follow back everyone. As a golden rule you should have more followers than accounts you are following yourself;
- Post photos, you can do it from your smartphone within a few seconds;
- Place an inspiring picture on your Twitter page. Remove the common blue background, inspire visitors from the first second;
- Do not tweet offers only, no one is interested in a digital advertisement of your business. You can do it once in a while but social media is like a family reunion: people talk about everything and nothing and no one is interested in your promotions all the time;
- Let customers know what is going on in your business: new produce being harvested, new farm activities available, a great added value your team created: it is all interesting!

These are just nine tips you can use to get started with Twitter. Many of the food tourism ventures are not using Twitter or other social media in case people complain about their business. Those people will probably complain about you anyway and the benefit of being on social media is that you know exactly who is complaining and you can respond immediately to resolve the complaint.

For most consumers a complaint is not a problem, the real problem occurs when you fail to solve it in a satisfying way. We also found that consumers who complained continuously about the service of a client who was not willing to look at a solution were corrected by other customers of the business. It does not get more social than that.

*Know the facts*

- One or two tweets per day gives 40% higher engagement.

## YouTube

We all enjoy watching movies and now businesses can have their own TV channel on YouTube.

It is easy to combine YouTube into other social media programs as well as have the movie clips running in a business facility on a television screen.

Imagine you are a typical consumer, you go into the business with a question, the team member explains how to solve your problem and you go home trying to remember everything you were told to do in the right sequence of events.

The chances are quite high that you will get it wrong.

Now, imagine going to the business, the team member still explains the solution, but also recommends a YouTube clip that you can watch when you get home that reinforces what you have just been told. Most people would be impressed and recommend this business to their friends.

YouTube can be used in so many ways in your business. Here are our top ten ways of using YouTube:

- A virtual tour of the business that can go on your webpage; this will say more than 1000 words and 100 photos and can generate traffic: people want to see your beautiful facility!
- Show what is in season and new produce that has been harvested. Again: inspiration is key, so do not be shy;
- Introduce your team to your consumers; personalize their visitor experience;
- 'How-to' videos are a great way to explain how to harvest, prepare and cook and how customers should use produce;
- Problem-solving videos are useful, so you can explain how to solve common problems associated with cooking;
- Share local recipes to inspire both your customers and your own staff;
- Ask your customers to submit a video of their recipes and meals or how they use the products bought at your business;
- An online cooking school in which you teach a new subject every week is a great tool to stimulate usage of your products. It is like a workshop but you can use it far more often;
- Networking with other (local) retailers to show what you can offer together;
- The seasons are changing and so is your business, so there are plenty of opportunities to create new videos over and over!

If you are enthusiastic but wondering how to make a video, then use your smartphone with a camera, make the video and upload it to YouTube directly from your phone. Success is guaranteed!

*Know the facts*

- 23% of people watch online video every day.

## Pinterest

Pinterest seems to be made for food tourism: it is colourful, inspiring, the majority of the users are women (who are your most important customers) and it is all based on photos. The main benefit of using photos rather than text (like on Facebook and Twitter) is your visitors do not have to think too much: they can be inspired without reading. And as you know, Internet users prefer to skip long texts. Do not underestimate this; surveys show that offers on a Pinterest board get more attention because of this than offers on Twitter!

So what is Pinterest and how should you use it? Pinterest is called after digital pinboards. You can collect photos and images and post them to boards. As a business you know how easy it is to get a decent number of photo collections that can be used on Pinterest but also on your website or Facebook page.

Christmas is an excellent moment to inspire your customers. Post photos of your Christmas food offer on your Pinterest page so you give visitors a showcase of things you have in stock.

Another real benefit of Pinterest is that you can inspire your customers without decreasing your margins. When you post a great photo of a combination of products, easy to set up at home and available within the store on a hotspot, you can easily see sales going up. The price becomes less important since you actually showed your customer what to do with the (combination of) products.

Most consumers use Pinterest to discover new brands and to find new products, with new products coming in almost every week.

*Know the facts*

- Pinterest users tend to spend more at your store than Facebook or Twitter users;
- Over 80% of the users are female.

## Google

If there is one company that changed the world of business we should point to Google. The search engine changed the way you work within a decade, but it also offers many opportunities to your business.

What you should do to drive more traffic to your business via Google is the following:

- Google is literally reading your website. So if you are the best stop for consumers who are looking for fruit trees, you should have information (multiple pages) about fruit trees on your website. If you do not have the right words on your website, you will never get good rankings;

- Update your Google Maps profile. This is the information shown within the results if you look up your own business. You can add a photo, text, opening times and much more all for free. Search for 'Places for business' to do this;
- Use Google Analytics. This is a very valuable tool to see what is going on with your website, how many people visit your pages, what keywords they use, etc. Even if you do not have any experience you should sign-up for Google Analytics to build a history of your statistics. It will help you to make decisions next week or next year – and as it is free, there is no reason to skip this step;
- Only advertise with Google Adwords if you have a web shop. Some retailers advertise their business via Google Adwords but it is not cost effective most of the time and it is hard to measure the number of people visiting your business after clicking on ads. Adwords is great if you have a web shop, though;
- Think how your customer would think to find out what keywords you should have on your website. Customers often use less complicated keywords and terms than you would. If you are able to get this done you are almost halfway!
- Setup your Google+ account. It is not as big as Facebook yet, but Google+ is pushing its own social network more and more so it probably is only a matter of time until it is adapted by the masses.

Understanding Google can be a major driver of traffic to your business. It might also be much more cost effective than publishing ads in a newspaper. Why? The key difference between all your ads and marketing and getting ranked well in Google is the fact that consumers are looking for a solution in Google – and your website is the answer. Having an advertisement in a newspaper only distracts from the actual news items. For the real marketers: you go from push to pull marketing!

*Be inspired!*
Have a look at:

- www.google.com/think
- www.googleshopping.blogspot.com

*Know the facts*

- 58% of purchase decisions begin on search engines;
- Researching products and services is the second most popular online activity in the UK with three out of four Internet users doing so.

## Text marketing

Text marketing is, together with e-mail newsletters, another communication method that may not be top of mind for most business people. Most serious phone users are not on WhatsApp, KIK or Viber, but they are very happy to read (and write) text messages.

Building a database with phone numbers is even more tricky than an e-mail database since the impact of a text is a lot higher. To set up a proper database you might want to develop special promotions. One retailer gives a discount on a weekly basis to customers who have a phone number ending with, say, number 9. They have to register to get the discount. Be creative and find your own way forward on this one.

To be successful in your text marketing campaigns you should obey the following rules:

- Be focused and spot on. Like Twitter, you only have a limited number of characters so you have to be very clear. People also might get annoyed if you send them confusing texts that are not saying anything at all. So be very, very straightforward!
- Your offers are not 'amazing' so avoid words like that, since it will look like spam. Be enthusiastic but do not be too enthusiastic;
- As a business it will not be a positive thing to use smileys :-)
- It should be valid or available today – not tomorrow. Text marketing is, like Twitter, excellent for a here-and-now promotion;
- Make the reader feel special, use words like 'you' to appeal to the recipient and try to offer something else than in your local newspaper;
- Timing is essential, since no one wants to receive a text at 7.30 in the morning, while 7.30 in the evening is too late;
- Make clear who is sending the text. This might be obvious, but we would not mention it if every business was doing it!
- Do not do it too often, it is quite a direct way of communication!

Text marketing is a great way to interact with your customers and there are many providers that can be used to send out bulk messages. It might be an idea to add all your customers to this list but, as with e-mail, you have to get an opt-in from your customer before you can contact them.

## E-mail marketing

Many consultants are putting forward the argument that e-mail is dead or at least dying. It is undeniable that people are using social media more frequently to communicate with relatives but e-mail is still a valuable marketing tool. Have an up-to-date e-mail list; it gives you a kick start if you want to communicate new products, promotions or events you are organizing in your business.

The first thing you need to do is build an e-mail database. If you have a customer loyalty scheme that would be the most obvious start, but if you do not you can still build a decent database. It is important to encourage your staff and let them participate in this. Set an objective for the first 2 weeks and encourage them to sign customers up at the till. You can use Microsoft

Excel print outs for these or any other straightforward forms. Do not put the goal for the first 2 weeks too high: having 100 customers on your e-mail list within 2 weeks is fine for a small business. After the first 100, go for the 250, and build from there.

Most people want to know 'What's in it for me?' So you need to make clear what the benefits are of signing up. A small incentive will help, like a herb or a $2.50/£2.50 coupon. You can also do a monthly prize draw with a product or gift voucher from your business. If you just ask them to sign up so you can send them your latest offers you should not be surprised that most people will not be interested in your newsletter!

After adding your list to your e-mail marketing tool, you can start sending out your first newsletter. We sometimes receive newsletters with a title like this:

XYZ Business special offers January

Why would we want to read this newsletter? Is it inspiring? Is it inviting? No, it is only commercial. Do not do this! Be a bit more creative.

You need to make the recipients curious about your newsletter. You should also include links from your newsletter to your website and do not add too much text to it. Keep it plain, straightforward and have multiple messages in your newsletter.

## Smartphone and apps

Team members in your business who have never seen a person using a smartphone while travelling probably do not exist anymore. Over 1.8 billion people around the world are using their smartphone to share ideas, to ask relatives for advice, to compare prices or get directions when they are travelling. The smartphone is the one and only device customers go home for if they forgot it and, together with their money and keys, the only thing you can be sure they have in their pocket while they visit your attraction, farm or centre.

So how do you turn this device into your most successful marketing tool? There are plenty of things you can do.

Be aware most people use their smartphone to go online and socialize via Facebook, Twitter and Pinterest. Using social media keeps your brand in their mind even while they are on the run. The second thing you should do is having a responsive website. Consumers tend to search Google for 'Business in XYZ' if they are on the road. Have a website which resizes automatically if visitors open it via a smartphone, a so-called responsive website.

You can also develop your own app for iPhone and Android, which is not too expensive anymore. You can add your loyalty card to this app or you can send out coupons for specific discounts. Having your own app helps to keep your brand visible and it gives you a unique opportunity to interact with your customers. Share news items, culinary tips and promotions with your customers and send them push messages if you have very select offers.

Most visitors are 'talking' via their smartphone about purchases and visits to culinary venues before they arrive, while they are there and after they have left. Be sure your brand is visible during every one of those stages. And are you spotting customers comparing prices or what is now called 'Showrooming'? Do not worry! They often forget to think about the costs for shipping. It is an excellent opportunity – and a challenge – for you to make the sale. Customers who are comparing prices are ready to make the purchase, so use that moment if you spot it! And remember, it is not all about the price, even today.

### Know the facts

- Two in three mothers that own an iPhone or Android smartphone use them as part of their shopping process;
- 71% of UK mobile phone users would be interested in receiving mobile coupons while shopping in store.

### Phone apps

The fastest growing marketing tool any of us has experienced has been the smartphone. If you take Australia as an example, 2 years ago 37% of the population had a smartphone. In 2013 that had risen to 64.4% of the population.

These phones are not used just to make phone calls, in fact this is one of the lesser used functions: 70% are used to watch videos, 49% of people use them to read the news and 33% use them to download phone apps.

Phone apps are one of the new marketing tools you can develop for your business. Paddock to Plate in Western Australia are developing a number of farm walks around the state using phone apps.

### Imagine your loyalty programmes on a phone app

Kurt Fromherz from Connecticut[19] identified that loyalty clubs are still an essential marketing tool, but consumers do not want their wallets and purses filled with different loyalty cards for different retailers and restaurants. At the same time, phone apps are one of the fastest developing retail marketing tools. This an opportunity to combine a loyalty scheme with a phone app.

Imagine as a consumer you go to your favourite restaurant or farm market, but before going, or even as you enter, you download the restaurant or farm market's own phone app.

You have your meal or purchase your produce and get the bill, plus you show your phone app to the company team member who keys in a four digit pin. You then collect points for visiting the establishment based on how much you have spent.

As a consumer you can check on your points whenever you like, plus see what rewards and offers are available from the business.

Once you have enough points to redeem for a meal or future purchase, you let the team member know when you get to the pay point that you wish to use your points. The business has a relationship with you and can link the conversation into Facebook.

The business has complete control over the loyalty programme and can engage with individual customers. We love the simplicity of this system and it takes customer loyalty management to the next level.

*Useful Reference*
Phone Apps: UK Food Spotting[20]

## Where to Start

The success of a business and combined ventures revolves around the marketing: you may have the best food tourism offer in the world, but if nobody knows about it then it will never be successful.

The challenge is putting the marketing jigsaw together so that it works for your venture.

The rules are simple: do not over-invest, have a marketing budget and keep to that budget. Spread the budget over the season that works for your venture, remember you have to invest ahead of the event. If, for example, September is your main food tourism month then you will need to invest in marketing in August to receive a return in September.

The simple ideas can often also be the most effective.

## References

[1] Marketing on the Edge: A Marketing Guide for Progressive Farmers. Author: Farm Management Canada. Available at: www.fmc-gac.com/publications/marketing-edge-marketing-guide-progressive-farmers#sthash.iaoe9FGU.dpuf (accessed 20 February 2014).
[2] Stanley, J. (2003) *Just About Everything a Retail Manager Needs To Know*. Lizard Publishing, Australia.
[3] Solis, B. (2013) *What's the Future of Business? Changing the way business create experiences*. John Wiley & Sons, Hoboken, New Jersey.
[4] Croce, E. and Perri, G. (2010) *Food and Wine Tourism*. [A tourism text from Italy on food tourism.] CAB International, Wallingford, UK.
[5] Yum It's Strawberry time, *Irish Independent Newspaper*, 11 June 2013, Bord Da Mia.
[6] State of the Industry 2013: not your parents garden center. Readex Report as published in *Garden Center Magazine*. Available at: www.gardencentermag.com/garden1013-state-of-industry-report.aspx
[7] Dunwell, M. and de Selincourt, K. (1998) *Forest Food Directory: a guide to local food production in the Forest of Dean*. Vision 21.
[8] The Best Jobs in The World. Rich Keam. Available at: www.tourism.wa.gov.au/marketing/Marketing_activities/Documents/How%20to%20connect%20with%20the%20Taste%20Master%20v3.pdf (accessed 8 March 2014).
[9] Meloy, M.G., McLaughlin, E. and Kramer, S. (1988) Consumer Segmentation Analysis of Grocery

Coupon Users. Department of Agricultural Economics, Cornell University. Available at: http://dyson.cornell.edu/research/researchpdf/rb/1988/Cornell-Dyson-rb8817.pdf (accessed 20 February 2014).

[10] Mittal, Banwari (1994) An Integrated Framework for Relating Diverse Consumer Characteristics to Supermarket Coupon Redemption. *Journal of Marketing Research* 31, 4 November, 533–544. Available at: http://personal.psu.edu/users/j/x/jxb14/JMR/JMR1994-4-533.pdf (accessed 20 February 2014).

[11] Avocado tops children's food "hate list". *Daily Mail*. Available at: www.dailymail.co.uk/health/article-114315/Avocado-tops-childrens-food-hate-list.html (accessed 20 March 2014).

[12] Top 10 most-hated vegetables: Celery VERY unpopular among Brits. *Express* 10 March 2010. Available at: www.express.co.uk/news/weird/166105/Top-10-most-hated-vegetables-Celery-VERY-unpopular-among-Brits (accessed 20 March 2014).

[13] Cherry Research. Available at: www.choosecherries.com/for-media (accessed 20 March 2014).

[14] Australian Grand Dairy Awards. Available at: www.dairyaustralia.com.au/Dairy-food-and-recipes/2014-Australian-Grand-Dairy-Awards.aspx (accessed 20 March 2014).

[15] Meijer, Edwin. Garden Connect. Available at: www.youtube.com/watch?v=liKEZJw_c_w (accessed 20 March 2014).

[16] Byer, Max. 12 Mobile Marketing Statistics for Small and Large Businesses. Available at: www.business2community.com/mobile-apps/12-mobile-marketing-statistics-for-small-and-large-businesses-0196574#!r3Zid (accessed 20 March 2014).

[17] Trend Report 2014. Available at: http://trendwatching.com/premium (accessed 20 March 2014).

[18] Nielsen Research (2014) Recipe for Success: 86 Million Americans Visited Food and Cooking Websites. Available at: www.nielsen.com/us/en/newswire/2014/recipe-for-success-86-million-americans-visited-food-and-cooking-websites.html (accessed 13 February 2014).

[19] Fromherz, Kurt: Available at: http://sunrisemarketing.com/author/kurt-fromherz (accessed 16 March 2014).

[20] Phone Apps. UK Foodspotting. Available at: https://play.google.com/store/apps/details?id= com.foodspotting (accessed 12 March 2014).

## Websites

Edible Communities Publications: www.ediblecommunities.com
Farm Fresh Magazine 2013. Available at: www.islandfarmfresh.com (accessed 6 March 2014).
Gourmet Traveller: www.gourmettraveller.com.au
Great Taste Awards: http://greattasteawards.co.uk (accessed 20 March 2014).
Today's Group: www.todays.co.uk
Western Australia Taste Master, Rich Keam's blog. Available at: http://tastewesternaustralia.com (accessed 20 March 2014).

# 10 The Future of Food Tourism

A mind that is stretched by a new experience can never go back to its old dimensions.

Oliver Wendell Holmes Jr

## The Golden Opportunity

Food tourism is a growth industry; this does not mean that you can set up a food trail and be successful. Today's tourist is not like the tourist of the past. Our parents would go out on a Sunday drive, often not knowing where they were going; they wanted to explore. Today's tourist wants a destination, they may make stops on the way, but they need a reason, a destination and that means the destination has to stand out from the crowd.

Many consumers look at farmers' markets as one of the key destinations. Research carried out in January and February 2014 in Australia by Colmar Brunton Omnibus on behalf of the Australian Farmers Markets Association[1] shows that 14% of shoppers now use farmers' markets to purchase vegetables and 4% purchase directly from the farmer.

Many businesses around the world are concerned about their viability, in the new world order, food tourist ventures around the first world are ideally situated to take full advantage of the 'trust shift' taking place in society. The consumer wants to support local businesses who have ideas and solutions and who appeal to their 'values'. This means food tourism business operators have to be proactive and build a strong relationship with target consumers. This is an advantage that regional, national and international businesses will find increasingly difficult to implement and it gives the local businesses an extra opportunity.

Consumer trust in food has become a key issue for food choice. For example, the production process of food is not always transparent for consumers. To provide more transparency and to enhance consumer trust, different initiatives communicating traceability to consumers exist. Visualized traceability systems, such as the initiative 'Bio mit Gesicht' (www.bio-mit-gesicht. de) in Germany allow consumers to gather information about the farmer who has produced the food as well as information about his farm and family, will become more common place.

Halk (1993)[2,3] examined mistrust by consumers in food and found that consumers do not trust or mistrust a piece of food itself, they trust or mistrust the actors who are responsible for the production, processing, marketing and control of the food. Again this is one area where food tourism has an opportunity to remove doubt.

A number of previous studies on the consumption of organic food identified trust as one of the most crucial aspects when consumers decide whether or not to buy organic products (e.g. Naspetti and Zanoli, 2009[4]).

Different possibilities for consumers to investigate the origin of their food have already been developed to assist consumers to research the origins of their food. One example is 'Nature and More' (www.natureandmore. com). Nature and More customers enter the number stamped on the product on the homepage and can obtain information on the product's origin and how sustainable that product is.

The aim of these initiatives is to create transparency for consumers. Increased transparency might enhance consumer trust in food, especially organic products, and it is critical in building food tourism in the future.

Trust in food origin and in organic food can be conceptualized as a multidimensional concept embracing the consumers' willingness to rely on other actors such as farmers, retailers, certification bodies, or labels ('**trusting intention**') on the one hand, and consumer beliefs in the trustworthiness of these actors ('**trusting beliefs**') on the other.

Food and water will also be two critical issues as we move into an area where we are going to see an increase in the global population and the effects of climate change.

Food tourism is becoming and will continue as a major tourist activity and we will see more governments and tourist organizations take more interest in developing this sector.

The big change we are about to experience is a sector that is moving from being a 'cottage' industry into a serious major tourist activity and that means larger businesses will want a slice of the action.

The legislation that revolves around the local food tourist sector will become more strict and we will see the development of accreditation.

## Food Tourism Accreditation

To reach their full potential, food tourism ventures will need to up-skill their standards to meet the needs of today's more demanding consumers. State, regional and national tourism councils will need to introduce and implement accreditation schemes along the lines of retail tourism accreditation. In Western Australia the aim of the Tourism Western Australia Council[5] is to have 1500 accredited tourism businesses by 2020.

These businesses will be:

- quality accredited;
- listed on media releases;
- bookable online;
- have an effective marketing and workforce plan;
- all staff trained to Cert 3 level; and
- all managers trained to Cert 4 level.

The TWA approach is a five-step approach:

Step 1 Accreditation
Step 2 Distribution
Step 3 Advice via workshops
Step 4 Training
Step 5 Awards

According to a report on tourism in June 2013 produced by WA Tourism,[6] Australia attracted 22.1 million visitors in the previous 12 months, 9.1% of whom visited Western Australia. The total spend by tourists was AUS$7.5 billion an increase of 3.3% over the year before. Most tourists look for part of their tourism experience to be around engagement with local food.

One of the main challenges for independent food tourism operators will be getting their message across when large businesses will be spending large amounts of money convincing consumers they are also local businesses with food and community factors in their business strategies.

We believe we will see a divergence in the market place.

Large corporate business will continue to expand and try to edge their way into food tourism.

Retailing and tourism will become difficult to distinguish as separate activities; consumers will both buy online and look for a tourism experience, often from the same provider.

Regional growers and added value suppliers in the food tourism sector will be encouraged to join forces and develop regional marketing strategies. This means that some small enterprises will lose some of their individual marketing prowess, but the overall campaigns will grow tourism in specific regions.

There will be a shift in tourism; local tourism will grow with weekend-away activities based around food increasing in popularity, whilst food tourism in western countries will see more visitors from Asian countries venturing out into country areas looking for a new adventure.

For businesses involved in the sector, one of the biggest challenges will be the same challenge facing every other person in business: getting to grips with communications with potential, existing and past consumers.

What is the future for food tourism businesses? According to Brian Solis[7] the real challenge is changing the way we create experiences for tourists in the future. In the future culinary tourists will be more empowered due to the technology at their disposal. This means that positive and negative experiences will be communicated at great speed and be immediate. Tourism operators will have to listen better, learn quicker and adapt faster.

The key question that all food tourism operators will need to ask is 'What is the experience you want the tourist to have?' Once that has been answered then a strategy can be put in place. The thinking process in developing that strategy should include:

- How do you convince the prospective culinary tourist – what is the marketing plan?
- What is the actual hook that will get them to come to visit your establishment?
- What products can you sell to the culinary tourist that will add value to the experience and help build loyalty?
- What plans can you put together to enchant the tourist to come back to your establishment on another visit?

Although the questions are straightforward the answers and implementation in the future are more difficult.

As we discussed earlier in this book there will be three types of culinary tourists:

**1.** Traditional communicating tourists: these are the tourists that will be influenced by traditional marketing, they will rely on word of mouth and rarely use the online marketing techniques; they will become less in number, but will still be a group of significance.
**2.** Digital communicating tourists: these tourists live mostly online when communicating and sourcing information, but will cross-reference with traditional marketing avenues.
**3.** Connected tourists: this will be the generation that will be maturing in the next few years and are connected all the time. They rely on mobile devices and expect all marketing communications to come to them on a portable mobile device.

In presentations we often have talked about the 'Moment of Truth' and how important this is when dealing with tourists. Most of us were first exposed to this concept by Jan Carlzon, the CEO of Scandinavian Airlines and author of the excellent book *Moments of Truth*.[8] In that book Jan highlighted how important the consumer experience is and how the little points of difference made a difference; for example, his airline was the first airline that placed olives with a gin and tonic.

That rule of on-site moments of truth applied throughout the 1980s and 1990s but will not work with tourism businesses going forward.

The moments of truth can now be segmented in new ways. The first step is now called the Zero Moment of Truth, ZMOT, which occurs when potential tourists search for your business or location, what is called their social discovery. This needs to make them want to pursue the journey further.

They then travel to your business and experience the first moment of truth on-site. This should be when they experience a more impressive moment of truth than they expected. These are the physical moments of truth.

They then continue on their engagement with the business and experience the second moment of truth. This is another physical moment of truth and represents their total physical impression of the experience.

Finally, they return to their home and experience the Ultimate Moment of Truth when they share their experience online with their friends and the global community. The whole moment of truth cycle will then start again.

According to Google/Shopper Sciences 'The Zero Moment of Truth' Macro study in April 2011 and reported in Brain Solis' book *What's the Future of Business?*,[7] the ZMOT were as follows:

- 50% mentioned the experience to friends;
- 21% mentioned the experience to co-workers;
- 10% wrote about it on Facebook;
- 6% put a comment on a webpage;
- 4% mentioned the visit on a blog; and
- 4% posted a tweet on the visit.

Clearly these percentages will change in the future, but indicate how important it will be in the future to have a wide range of communication tools at a business's disposal to ensure all touch points of communications are achieved.

A survey in 2012[9] identified that 92% of the public rely on people they know for recommendations; this indicates that trust will be a key driver in the future. Compare this to only 46% of readers trusting an advertisement in a newspaper. The same survey looked at how peer recommendation drives consumers:

- 70% of recommendations were via Facebook friends;
- 61% by phone call or face to face; and
- 59% via recommended online articles.

All these are indicators that suggest that the successful food tourism operator of the future will need to be social media-savvy if they are to grow their business.

On a practical front food trails will continue to be developed and will be the fastest growing sector of food tourism. This will result in more networking between regional food tourism businesses, which will be to the benefit of the region. The result will be stronger regional brands and these brands will be used both as tourism and retail brands. Hence our belief that retailing and tourism will start to blend in both the producer's and retailer's mind. This is already happening with some food brands and will accelerate as more growers see the opportunity.

## The Future Will Include the Past

One of the drivers of food tourism is 'nostalgia' and a desire by tourists to rediscover the past. One area of food tourism that will increase in importance is prehistoric and traditional cooking and food preparation, i.e. what our ancestors ate, how they prepared that food, cooked it and ate it. Tourism operators will be able to pick an era and create a food experience based on that era. This will include cooking using hot stones, clay-baked food and other cooking techniques.

Food tourism in the future will be about the past, but using modern marketing techniques.

# References

[1] Australian Farmers Markets Association. Colmar Brunton Omnibus Press release 13 March 2014, contact Denise Hamblin (denis.hamblin@colmarburton.com).

[2] Halk, K. (1993) Bestimmungsgründe des Konsumentenmißtrauens gegenüber Lebensmitteln. Ergebnisse von empirischen Untersuchungen an ausgewählten Verbrauchergruppen. *Studien zur Agrarwirtschaft* (30), Ifo-Inst. für Wirtschaftsforschung, Munich. Cited in: Kriege-Steffen *et al.* (2010).[3]

[3] Astrid Kriege-Steffen, Hermann Boland, Julia Lohscheidt, Flurina Schneider and Matthias Stolze (2010) Transparent Food and Consumer Trust. Available at: http//centmapress.ilb.uni-bonn.de/ojs/index.php/proceedings/article/viewFile/67/65 (accessed 14 March 2014).

[4] Naspetti, S. and Zanoli, R. (2009) Organic Food Quality and Safety Perception Throughout Europe. *Journal of Food Products Marketing* 15(3). Available at: www.tandfonline.com/doi/abs/10.1080/10454440902908019#.Us-kEp6SyFU (accessed 14 March 2014).

[5] Tourism Western Australia Accreditation. Available at: www.tourismcouncilwa.com.au/accreditation (accessed 13 March 2014).

[6] WA Tourism Report 2013. Available at: www.tourism.wa.gov.au/Publications%20Library/Executive%20Services/Tourism%20WA%20Annual%20Report%202012%20-%202013.pdf (accessed 14 March 2014).

[7] Solis, B. (2013) *What's the Future of Business? Changing the way business create experiences*. John Wiley & Sons, Hoboken, New Jersey.

[8] Carlzon, J. (1989) *Moments of Truth*. Harper Collins, USA.

[9] The Power of Peer Influence. Available at: http://corp.crowdtap.com.s3-website-us-east-1.amazonaws.com/whitepapers/Crowdtap-Power-of-Peer-Influence.pdf (accessed 14 March 2014).

## Websites

Bio mit Gesicht: www.bio-mit-gesicht.de (accessed 12 March 2014).
Nature & More: www.natureandmore.com (accessed 13 March 2014).

# Appendix 1: Culinary, Retail and Tourism Terms

| | |
|---|---|
| **FARMA** | National Farmers' Retail and Markets Association, UK |
| **FIT** | Fully independent travellers |
| **FS** | Free-standing insert |
| **IGCA** | International Garden Centre Association |
| **IGCAT** | International Institute of Gastronomy, Culture, Arts and Tourism |
| **KV** | Known-value item in a shop |
| **NAFDMA** | North American Farm Direct Marketing Association |
| **Non KV** | Non-known-value item in a shop |
| **PDO** | Protected Designation of Origin |
| **PGI** | Protected Geographical Indication |
| **PYO** | Pick Your Own |
| **ROE** | Return on engagement |
| **ROP** | Run of press |
| **UMOT** | Ultimate moment of truth |
| **U Pick** | You Pick or Pick Your Own |
| **WFTA** | World Food Travel Association |
| **WWOOF** | Willing Workers On Organic Farms |
| **ZMOT** | Zero moment of truth |

# Appendix 2: 51 Ways to Promote Your Culinary Business to the Local Community

Why 51? Readers are more inclined to read and engage with odd numbers than even numbers. An odd number implies more research and effort has gone into the thinking process.

1. Sponsor the entertainment at the farmers' market.
2. Promote the fact you are a local business in your first impressions to the consumer.
3. Tell consumers why they should buy local.
4. Promote the fact that your team are local people.
5. Give all your team business cards.
6. Network with other businesses to provide solutions for the customer.
7. Network to plan events such as weddings for local consumers.
8. Do demonstrations at one of the markets.
9. Have a sundowner for the local chamber of commerce and tell people what you do.
10. Work closely with the local school and help when you can at events.
11. Support local charities.
12. Present ideas on the local radio station.
13. Provide stories for the local paper.
14. Enter awards and use them in marketing.
15. Have a local loyalty card.
16. Be active on Facebook with a business page.
17. Make sure the team wear name badges to build local trust.
18. Make sure you are registered on Google Local.
19. Ask local 'heroes' for referrals and use them in PR.
20. Give a talk to groups of people in your network.
21. Write an article on your expertise and distribute it to relevant bodies.
22. Get a phone app and promote it via the chamber of commerce.
23. Place magnetic signs promoting your business on your vehicle.

24. Network with the library to do demonstrations and displays.
25. Make sure you have the right 'keywords' on the first page of your webpage.
26. Enter the Christmas shop window display competition, especially if there are some empty shop windows in your local town.
27. Make sure your team are day-makers not sales people.
28. Network with the local coffee shops to promote your business.
29. Exchange coupons and do joint mailings with non-competing local businesses who serve the same clientele.
30. Consider some type of giveaway – refer a friend, get a free service, or whatever might be appropriate for your business.
31. Become a walking advert for your business, be able to tell people what you do in your business in a short sentence.
32. Get involved in local online coupon offers.
33. Link in promotions in store to one of the events held in your local community each year.
34. Promote your business in the local business directory.
35. Develop a newsletter for your advocates.
36. Build window displays using the familiar with the unfamiliar so you get noticed.
37. Promote something new each month … it works for Zara.
38. Promote your services to other businesses around your business.
39. Provide personalized product to local residents.
40. Read the book *Growing Local Value* by Laury Hammel and Gun Denhart and implement their ideas.
41. Focus on marketing to specific segments of the community, not just everyone.
42. Make sure your team never start a conversation with the customer using a 'closed' question.
43. Be emotional in your signage in store and relate to local events.
44. Be proactive and involved with local marketing activities.
45. Delight customers with Delight = Expectation + 1: the most effective marketing tool.
46. Develop a daily image checklist to ensure your business looks like it is ready for business.
47. Be prepared to do things outside your comfort zone.
48. Attend as many workshops as you can as the world is changing and you need to keep learning what is new.
49. Just Do It – not trying something is sure to create failure.
50. Write down your ideas as you think of them or as you see them.
51. Advertise your business on the chamber of commerce phone app if they have one.

## Reference

Hammel, L. and Denhart, G. (2007) *Growing Local Value. How to Build Business Partnerships that Strengthen Your Community.* Berrett-Koehler Publishers, San Francisco, California.

# Further Reading

Alderson, L. (1990) *The Chance to Survive*. Christopher Helm Publishing, London.

Australian Farmers' Markets Association (2006) *Guide to Farmers Markets: Australia and New Zealand*. AFMA, Potts Point, New South Wales.

Baker, M. (1989) *Folklore and Customs of Rural England*. David & Charles, Newton Abbot, UK.

Canadian Farm Business Management Council (2002) *Marketing on the Edge – A Marketing Guide for Progressive Farmers*. NAFDMA and Agriculture and Agri-Food Canada.

Corum, V., Rosenzweig, M. and Gibson, E. (2001) *The New Farmers Market, Farm fresh Ideas for Producers, Managers and Communities*. New World Publishing, Auburn, California.

Croce, E. and Perri, G. (2010) *Food and Wine Tourism*. [A tourism text from Italy on food tourism.] CAB International, Wallingford, UK.

Eckert, J. and Kline, D. (2005) *Fresh Grown Publicity – an easy guide to getting news coverage*. Eckert AgriMarketing, St Louis, Missouri.

Edlin, H.L. (1974) *Woodland Crafts in Britain*. David & Charles, Newton Abbot, UK.

Hall, C.M., Sharples, L., Mitchell, R., Marcionis, N. and Canborne, B. (2003) *Food Tourism Around the World*. Taylor & Francis Ltd, Abingdon, UK.

Harding, M. and Ogryzlo, L. (2011) *Ontario Table featuring the best food from around the region*. Epulum Books, ISBN 978-0-9810031-0-8.

Johnstone, H. and Dodd, C. (1999) *Aphrodisiac Foods, eat your way to ecstasy*. Carlton Books Limited, London.

Kitchen, L. (2006) *Growers Market, cooking with seasonal produce*. Murdoch Books, Sydney, Australia.

Louv, R. (2008) *Last Child in the Woods*. Algonquin Books, Chapel Hill, North Carolina.

National Geographic (2009) *Food Journeys of a Lifetime, 500 Extraordinary Places to Eat Around the Globe*. National Geographic, Washington, DC.

Pegler, M.M. (2001) *Gourmet and Specialty Shops*. Visual Reference Publications, New York.

Peyton, J. (2005) *Fabulous Food Shops*, 5th edn. John Wiley & Sons, West Sussex, UK.

Pinkerton, T. and Hopkins, R. (2009) *Local Food, How to Make it happen in Your Community*. Transition Guides, Silver Spring, Maryland.

Porter, V. (1987) *Practical Rare Breeds*. Pelham Books, London.

Rhodes, T., Schwartz, J. and Hoskins, J. (2009) *Ohio Consumer Opinions of Roadside Markets and Farmers Markets*. Ohio State University Report to the Rehabilitation Program, May 1994. Transition Books, Silver Spring, Maryland.

Russell, A. and associates (1998) *Marketing on a Shoestring Budget.* Canadian Farm Business Management Council, Ontario Agricultural Training Institute, Canada.

Salatin, J. (2006) *You Can Farm, The Entrepreneur's Guide to Start and Succeed in a Farm Enterprise.* Polyface Inc, Swoope, Virginia.

Salatin, J. (2013) *Fields of Farmers.* Chelsea Green Publishing, Vermont.

Shave, J. (2012) *Forage: A Culinary Journey through Western Australia.* Upside Nepal, Dalkeith, Western Australia.

Sheffer, N. and Sheraton, M. (1997) *Food Markets of the World.* Harry N Abrams Inc, New York.

Solis, B. (2013) *What's the Future of Business? Changing the way business create experiences.* John Wiley & Sons, Hoboken, New Jersey.

Stanley, J. (2002) *The Complete Guide to Garden Center Management.* Chicago Review Press, Chicago, Illinois.

Vaughan, D. and Peterson, E. (2011) *Amazing Festivals, 100's of Hometown Celebrations.* Publications International, Lincolnwood, Illinois.

Wood, J. (2001) *Prehistoric Cooking.* The History Press, Stroud, UK.

## Magazines

*Australian Gourmet Traveller.* A monthly consumer magazine: www.gourmettraveller.com.au

*Edible* magazines. Edible Communities Publications: www.ediblecommunities.com

# Index